Know Your Mind

'An engaging and lucid summary of the best psychological research and clinical practice. It will be enormously valuable to very many readers.'
Professor Aaron T. Beck, University of Pennsylvania

'If only all reference books were as entertaining and enlightening! *Know Your Mind* is reliable and authoritative, but never dry or dull. It's a book we've long needed.'
Professor Allison Harvey, University of California–Berkeley

'*Know Your Mind* is unique in that it offers practical advice on how best to prevent psychological problems from arising as well as how to deal with problems when they do occur. Most people have more than one difficulty and this book enables multiple problems to be understood and addressed. It is a fantastic contribution to the self-help literature.'
Professor Roz Shafran, University of Reading

'*Know Your Mind* is a fantastic resource for all readers and not least parents, providing as it does sensible and constructive advice on how best to handle a wide range of problems in children, from anxiety and depression to bedwetting, tantrums, and sleep problems. Keep it next to your family medical encyclopaedia!'
Dr Sam Cartwright-Hatton, University of Manchester

'This authoritative, accessible and comprehensive book provides readers with a clear insight into the nature of a wide range of everyday problems from insomnia and stress to depression and anxiety. It offers clear, up-to-date and helpful guidelines on how we can help ourselves with these distressing conditions.'
Professor Paul Gilbert, University of Derby and author of Overcoming Depression

'*Know Your Mind* puts a welcome emphasis on mental wellness, setting out the steps we can all take to prevent psychological problems from developing. But it doesn't stop there, because the authors provide all the information and advice most of us will ever need on the full range of those problems.'
Professor Kate Davidson, University of Glasgow

Know Your Mind

Everyday Emotional and
Psychological Problems and
How to Overcome Them

Dr Daniel Freeman & Jason Freeman

idea

Library Learning Information

To renew this item call:

020 7364 4332

or visit

www.ideastore.co.uk

TOWER HAMLETS

Created and managed by Tower Hamlets Council

RODALE

This edition first published 2009 by Rodale
an imprint of Pan Macmillan Ltd
Pan Macmillan, 20 New Wharf Road, London N1 9RR
Basingstoke and Oxford
Associated companies throughout the world
www.panmacmillan.com

ISBN 978-1-9057-4430-5

1 3 5 7 9 8 6 4 2

A CIP catalogue record for this book is available from the British Library.

Printed and bound in the UK by CPI Mackays, Chatham ME5 8TD

This book is intended as a reference volume only, not as a medical manual. The information given here is designed to help you make informed decisions about your health. It is not intended as a substitute for any treatment that you may have been prescribed by your doctor. If you suspect you have a medical problem, we urge you to seek competent medical help.

Mention of specific companies, organizations or authorities in this book does not imply endorsement of the publisher, nor does mention of specific companies, organizations or authorities in the book imply that they endorse the book.

Addresses, websites and telephone numbers given in this book were correct at the time of going to press.

Visit **www.panmacmillan.com** to read more about all our books and to buy them. You will also find features, author interviews and news of any author events, and you can sign up for e-newsletters so that you're always first to hear about our new releases.

Contents

Acknowledgements   vi

Part I

Introduction   3

Part II

Addictions   26
  Alcohol   26
  Drugs   33
  Gambling   38
  Smoking   43

Anger and Irritation   55

Anxiety   65
  Fears and Phobias   65
  Panic   72
  Obsessions and
    Compulsions   79
  Shyness and Social
    Anxiety   88
  Trauma and Post-
    Traumatic Stress
    Disorder   97
  Worry   106
  Body Image Worries   112
  Health Anxiety   119

Bereavement and Grief   126

Problems in Children
and Young People   137
  Depression, Fears and
    Anxiety   137
  Bedwetting   153
  Sleep Problems   157

  Hyperactivity,
  Impulsiveness and
    Inattention   164
  Tantrums in Preschool
    Children   173
  Difficult Behaviour in
    Teenagers   181
  Child Abuse   183

Depression   186

Eating problems   199

Hallucinations   226

Memory Problems   232

Mood Swings   244

Pain   252

Paranoia   260

Relationship Problems   269

Self-injury   288

Sexual Problems   296

Sleep Problems   334
  Insomnia   339
  Nightmares   345
  Other Sleep Problems   349

Stress   353

Tiredness   361

Part III

Resources   369
Useful Organizations   372
Index   374

Acknowledgements

It is more than three years since we began to kick around ideas for the project that has become *Know Your Mind*. But getting from those sketchy, explorative conversations in 2006 (conducted, like so many of our working discussions, during lulls in play while watching Watford FC) to the book you now hold in your hands couldn't have happened without the help, support and encouragement of numerous individuals.

We are very fortunate to be represented by Zoë King at the Darley Anderson Agency – an ever-dependable source of astute advice and spirit-raising enthusiasm, and we have benefited enormously from her guidance. We owe a huge debt of gratitude to Liz Gough at Rodale for her belief in the project, her invaluable contribution to the shaping of the book and for making the publishing process so painless. We are grateful to Anne Newman for her meticulous copy-editing of the typescript. And we thank Katrina Power at Midas Public Relations, and Katie James and the team at Rodale, for their fantastic efforts publicizing and marketing *Know Your Mind*.

Dr Ailsa Russell and Dr Helen Startup at the Institute of Psychiatry carefully scrutinized every entry and offered helpful suggestions as to how the text could be improved. We are also grateful to the authors of the self-assessment questionnaires for permission to include their work in *Know Your Mind*. Craig Brierley at the Wellcome Trust and Camilla Palmer and colleagues in the media office of King's College London, have helped us to communicate our work to the wider world over recent years with great effectiveness and energy.

Daniel would like to thank the Wellcome Trust, an independent charity that supports research to improve human and animal health, which funds his research programme. He would also like to thank all the therapists, researchers and clients that he has learned from over the last 15 years at the Institute of Psychiatry, King's College London and the South London and Maudsley NHS Foundation Trust.

Jason would like to thank Eleanor for, well, more or less everything and Ethan, Evelyn and Jude, who finally get to see what their dad and uncle have been working on for so long.

Part I

Introduction

Over the following three hundred or so pages, you'll find information on more than 50 of the most common psychological and emotional problems – how to recognize them, how they're caused and, crucially, what to do about them.

Know Your Mind is, therefore, a kind of super-self-help book, offering in one volume the very best psychological thinking and therapeutic advice. But though the bulk of *Know Your Mind* focuses on 'problems', this is only one part of the story. Just as important are the steps you can take to minimize the chances of being affected by these issues.

So, in this Introduction we show you how to stay in the best possible psychological and emotional health. Before that, however, we explain how we came to write *Know Your Mind*, the theoretical background we draw on and what to do if more help is needed.

HELPING YOU TO HELP YOURSELF

If you've ever browsed the self-help section of a large bookshop, you'll know just how bewildering an experience it can be. The choice is simply overwhelming. And if you do happen to recognize a title on the groaning shelves, how can you be sure that the advice you'll be getting is reliable?

Know Your Mind is designed to rescue readers from this predicament. Rather than having to plough through thousands of self-help books of often unknown quality, you will find here a comprehensive distillation of the very best information and advice. This book is thus the culmination of countless hours reading self-help books!

But more importantly *Know Your Mind* is also the product of many years of clinical practice and psychological research, together with analysis of the latest psychological and scientific literature, clinical trials and officially recommended treatment guidelines. Each of the entries has also been reviewed by clinical psychologists.

The information in *Know Your Mind* is scientifically tried and tested, but not – we hope – dry or difficult. Indeed, one of our main objectives has been to present this material in as entertaining and accessible a style as possible. That said, the questionnaires are exactly the same as those used by clinicians; if you find some of them a bit tough to get through, do keep going as you'll be getting the most accurate self-assessment possible.

The personal accounts featured in this book are not direct quotations from real-life contributors. They are illustrations of problems based, in each case, upon diagnostic criteria and examples.

Where you see the names of other conditions in bold throughout the text, this indicates that they are also listed in the book.

In most cases, *Know Your Mind* is likely to provide all the information you'll need to overcome whatever psychological or emotional problem is troubling you. But what should you do if you feel you need more help? And how, for that matter, can you tell whether or not you should seek personal professional advice?

There's no easy answer to this second question. Basically it comes down to:

- how distressing you're finding the problem *and*
- how much it's disrupting your life.

But however well you think you're coping, if you want to explore further treatment options, you should do so.

Start by seeing your family doctor. Just chatting things over with your GP can be a huge help. If you think psychological therapy (also called 'psychotherapy' or 'talking therapy') might be useful, your doctor should be able to guide you through the options and make a referral. Medication is also an option in some cases.

Incidentally, the UK's National Institute for Health and Clinical Excellence (NICE) produces guidelines on how best to treat psychological (as well as physical) problems. They're aimed primarily at health professionals, but there's no reason why you shouldn't consult them too. NICE also publishes summaries of the guidelines for the general public. You can find the guidelines and summaries at www.nice.org.uk.

The therapeutic advice in *Know Your Mind* draws on numerous theoretical approaches – if it's been scientifically proven to work, it's in here. That said, our main influence is a type of psychological therapy called Cognitive Behaviour Therapy (CBT).

CBT was first developed in the 1960s by Professor Aaron T. Beck as a treatment for depression. Since then, it's been used very successfully to help people with many other psychological problems. CBT is based on the insight that if we can understand and change the way we think and the beliefs we hold about ourselves and the world around us, we'll also be able to change the way we feel and behave.

CBT has been subjected to repeated, rigorous clinical assessment. Though it doesn't work for everyone, it's generally so effective that it's now the official treatment of choice for a very wide range of emotional and psychological problems.

If you do see a therapist (either specializing in CBT or in other approaches), it's crucial that they have been properly trained. This may seem obvious, but in the UK the terms 'counsellor', 'therapist', and 'psychologist' can be used by people with hugely varying levels of experience and training. Your best bet is to check with one of the professional organizations that keep registers of accredited therapists. In the UK, these are the British Association for Behavioural and Cognitive Psychotherapies and the British Psychological Society. You'll find their contact details under Useful Organizations on p. 372.

Last but certainly not least, if there's one message we hope you'll take from this book it is that emotional and psychological problems are normal. Far from being a sign that you're weak or inadequate, or that you're going crazy, they're as much a part of life as any physical problem.

Most people don't feel ashamed when they come down with the flu, or when their back is causing them pain. They don't believe that these ailments are a reflection of their worth as a human being. They tell people how they're feeling (sometimes ad nauseam!) and try to sort out the problem, whether by taking over-the-counter medication, seeing their doctor or reading up on the issue in question.

Although the tide is slowly turning, most people are still not nearly so comfortable when it comes to being open about their psychological and emotional health: almost everyone goes through periods of feeling very stressed, anxious or down; sometimes finding it difficult to sleep or to get a grip on drinking or eating; struggling with relationships and how best to raise children. Yet they're much less likely to share these sorts of problems with friends and family or to seek professional help.

Know Your Mind aims to dispel the awkwardness and stigma surrounding these issues. Remember: whatever you're going through, you can be certain that someone you know has had exactly the same problem at some stage in their life.

Your emotional and psychological well-being is just as important as your physical health (indeed, as we'll see in the next part of this Introduction, the two are often very closely connected). In recognition of this fact, we hope that *Know Your Mind* will sit proudly next to the medical encyclopaedia on your bookshelf, helping you through life's ups and downs just as its neighbour helps you through the coughs and colds.

STAYING WELL: HOW TO BOOST YOUR EMOTIONAL AND PSYCHOLOGICAL WELL-BEING

My life has no purpose, no direction, no aim, no meaning, and yet I'm happy. I can't figure it out. What am I doing right?
Charles M. Schulz, creator of the *Peanuts* comic strip

When it comes to our emotional and psychological health, there's an awful lot at stake. For individuals, even relatively mild problems can disrupt life and bring distress. For society as a whole, the consequences – purely in financial terms – are devastating. Indeed, the UK government estimates the annual cost of mental ill health at £77 billion for England alone.

But it's not all doom and gloom. As with your physical health, there is a lot you can do to look after your psychological well-being, both to prevent problems from occurring and to help you bounce back as quickly as possible if they do.

To do this, you need to work on five main areas of your life:

- Thoughts
- Relationships
- Diet
- Activity and exercise
- Sleep

We'll look at each of these areas over the next few pages. But before we get started, it's worth saying that we're not suggesting you become a paragon of psychological virtue. It's probably not realistic, and it may even be counterproductive (as implied by the words of Charles M. Schulz, above). None the less, we hope you'll find it useful to be aware of the factors that can help you stay happy and healthy. Aim to introduce one positive change in each of these five aspects of your life – thoughts, relationships, diet, activity and exercise and sleep – and see where it takes you.

'5 a day' for mental health

The importance of taking proactive steps to maintain and improve our psychological health was recognized by the UK government's 2008 Foresight report into Mental Capital and Wellbeing. The report, which drew on advice from more than 400 experts, recommended a '5 a day' programme for mental health:

Connect: developing relationships with family, friends, colleagues and neighbours will enrich your life and bring you support.

Be active: sports, hobbies such as gardening or dancing or just a daily stroll will make you feel good and maintain mobility and fitness.

Be curious: noting the beauty of everyday moments as well as the unusual, and reflecting on them helps you to appreciate what matters to you.

Learn: fixing a bike, learning an instrument, cooking – the challenge and satisfaction brings fun and confidence.

Give: helping friends and strangers links your happiness to a wider community and is very rewarding.

Self-assessment: how happy are you?

Measuring happiness is notoriously difficult – not least because there's so much disagreement about what happiness actually is. But if you want to take your happiness temperature, the following short questionnaire is a good place to start.

1. In most ways my life is close to my ideal.

Strongly disagree	Disagree	Slightly disagree	Neither agree nor disagree	Slightly agree	Agree	Strongly agree
1	2	3	4	5	6	7

2. The conditions of my life are excellent.

Strongly disagree	Disagree	Slightly disagree	Neither agree nor disagree	Slightly agree	Agree	Strongly agree
1	2	3	4	5	6	7

3. I am satisfied with my life.

Strongly disagree	Disagree	Slightly disagree	Neither agree nor disagree	Slightly agree	Agree	Strongly agree
1	2	3	4	5	6	7

4. So far I have got the important things I want in life.

Strongly disagree	Disagree	Slightly disagree	Neither agree nor disagree	Slightly agree	Agree	Strongly agree
1	2	3	4	5	6	7

5. If I could live my life over again, I would change almost nothing.

Strongly disagree	Disagree	Slightly disagree	Neither agree nor disagree	Slightly agree	Agree	Strongly agree
1	2	3	4	5	6	7

Diener, E., Emmons, R. A., Larsen, R. J., & Griffin, S. (1985). The Satisfaction with Life Scale. Journal of Personality Assessment, 49, 71–5.

Now add up your total score for the five questions. Here's what the figures may indicate about how content you are with your life:

31–35	Extremely satisfied
26–30	Satisfied
21–25	Slightly satisfied
20	Neutral
15–19	Slightly dissatisfied
10–14	Dissatisfied
5–9	Extremely dissatisfied

1. Thoughts

Over the last few decades, psychologists have demonstrated just how powerfully our thoughts – half-formed, random and haphazard though most of them are – can influence our feelings and behaviour.

This is a really important insight, because from it follows the idea that, if you can change your thinking for the better you can also help yourself to feel and behave more positively. (It's this principle that forms the bedrock of Cognitive Behaviour Therapy, as we've mentioned above.)

A two-pronged strategy is best. First, you must learn to cope with negative thoughts; and second, you need to increase the number of positive thoughts you have.

Coping with negative thoughts

Let's start with the following basic guidelines for handling negative thoughts:

A world of happiness

Which are the happiest and least happy nations on the planet?

Professor Ruut Veenhoven and his team at Erasmus University in Rotterdam have analysed a mass of data gathered between 1945 and 2007 to produce the World Database of Happiness. Here's who came out top:

Denmark

Switzerland

Austria

Iceland

Finland

And here are the five unhappiest countries (with number 1 being the least happy):

Tanzania

Zimbabwe

Moldova

Ukraine

Armenia

Britain is ranked joint 22nd with Honduras, Australia is equal 6th, Ireland and Canada are among the nations tied in 9th, the USA is 17th, France 39th and Japan is equal 45th.

To a certain extent, a nation's happiness is related to its wealth – rich nations tend to be happy and very poor countries are generally very unhappy. But once a country reaches a certain level of wealth, that correlation breaks down. Japan, for example, is ranked 45th in terms of happiness, but according to a 2006 study by the World Institute for Development Economics Research its citizens are the richest on the planet (with a net worth, on average, of $180,837 per person). The super-happy Danish, on the other hand, average $70,751 per person. And Britain, whose people have assets worth an average of $126,832, is tied in the happiness stakes with Honduras, whose citizens own $2356. (In case you were wondering, the net worth of the average Tanzanian is $681.)

Veenhoven, R., World Database of Happiness, Distributional Findings in Nations, Erasmus University, Rotterdam.

Don't treat them as though they were facts. Most thoughts are anything but reasoned and logical. Generally they're just a snap reaction to what you see or feel. Imagine for instance that a colleague passes you in the corridor without saying hello. If you're feeling a bit low, you might worry that they're deliberately ignoring you. But this reaction probably reveals far more about your own emotions than it does about your colleague's.

Think of the evidence for and against the thought. What grounds do you have for believing that your colleague has ignored you? What evidence is there to the contrary?

Think of alternative explanations. There are almost always several potential reasons for any event – perhaps your colleague is worried about an important meeting or has had a row with their partner; maybe they've simply forgotten their glasses. You just have to take the time to think through these possibilities.

Test out your explanations. There's no better way to find out whether your assumptions are correct. If you're really worried that you've offended your colleague in some way, invite them to join you for lunch. You'll soon discover whether there are any grounds for your worries.

Keep an open mind. Most of us want certainty most of the time, but we have to accept that there are some things we'll never know for sure. You can't be 100 per cent certain about what was going on in your colleague's head (though you can make a reasoned judgement). Think through the probabilities and then let the matter go.

If you're really worried about something, focus your energies on *solving* the problem:

- Define the issue as specifically as you can.
- Think of all the possible solutions to the problem. What's worked for you in the past? What would you advise someone else with the same problem to do?
- Weigh up the pros and cons of each possible solution.
- Choose the solution you think is best and decide how you're going to carry it out. Try to guess what problems you might face with it and how you're going to deal with them.

- Try out the solution you've chosen and then have a think about how well it's worked. If things haven't gone to plan, try the next solution.

For more on coping with worry, see pp. 109–12.

One increasingly popular technique for dealing with unwanted thoughts is to cultivate a 'mindful' approach: when you find yourself thinking a negative thought, don't fight it or try to pretend it hasn't occurred. Notice it – and then let it go. Don't spend time thinking about it. Try to be detached, as if you're watching something happen to someone else long ago. Watch the thought come to you, remind yourself that it doesn't matter, then let it fade into the distance. Focus on what you're doing, not what you're thinking.

Increasing positive thoughts

Mindfulness can also help us with the second part of our task: increasing the number of positive thoughts we have. Mindfulness is a synthesis of modern Western psychological thinking and ancient Buddhist beliefs and practices, particularly meditation. There's evidence to suggest that it reduces the risk of depression and helps combat stress. It's also generating some excitement as a possible method of increasing individual happiness.

Mindfulness involves learning to live in the moment, developing your awareness of what it feels like to be alive in this present instant and understanding that your thoughts and feelings are temporary, transient and not necessarily a reflection of reality. Mindfulness is best practised by means of regular meditation sessions, but you can get a taste right now: for the next few minutes, stop what you're doing and concentrate instead on the rise and fall of your breathing, the colour of the sky above you, the feel of your body as it rests. You'll experience a feeling of calmness as your thoughts and worries are, for a few minutes at least, replaced by a simple, relaxed awareness of the present moment.

Mindfulness – like yoga, other forms of meditation or even muscle relaxation exercises – can be a really effective way of developing greater calm and contentment. If you'd like to read up on it, we heartily recommend:

Happiness (Atlantic, 2007) by Matthieu Ricard; *The Mindful Way through Depression* (Guilford Press, 2007) by Mark Williams, John Teasdale, Zindel Segal and Jon Kabat-Zinn; *Wherever You Go, There You Are* (Piatkus, 2004) by Jon Kabat-Zinn

For advice on relaxation techniques, and in particular how to combat stress, have a look at *The Wellness Book* (Simon & Schuster, 1993) by Herbert Benson and Eileen Stuart.

Increasing your positive thoughts – and thereby your well-being and happiness – is also the focus of one of the most influential recent schools of psychological research. Led by Martin Seligman, Positive Psychology aims to understand what we can do to make ourselves happier (unlike most modern psychological thinking, which focuses on treating various types of unhappiness).

Positive Psychology, of course, isn't the first to consider these questions – philosophers, writers and other thinkers have mulled over the question of happiness for thousands of years – but it does offer an intriguing new perspective; not least in its analysis of the huge benefits to be gained from increased happiness (including better relationships, better physical health and greater levels of achievement in work and other areas of life), as well as in its reminder that much of what we traditionally think will bring happiness (money, youth or fame, for example) actually has no effect at all.

Is it possible to raise substantially and permanently your levels of happiness? The consensus seems to be that it is – albeit within the parameters set out by your genes. But then, of course, the question becomes how do you do it?

For Martin Seligman, happiness lies in:

- developing positive feelings about your past, the present moment and the future
- building strong relationships and engaging in enjoyable, varied and absorbing activities, whether work or leisure
- identifying your core values and strengths and using them to serve something that you see as bigger than yourself (perhaps a religion or a community project, your family or the nation as a whole).

What could you do to develop your life in each of these areas?

Seligman suggests a number of helpful tips and techniques, among them that you:

- identify your top five strengths and think of ways to use them more often in your daily life

- write down each evening three good things that happened to you that day
- write down every night for two weeks five things in your life you are grateful for
- think of someone who has helped you in your life but whom you've never thanked; write them a letter, call them up or, better yet, pay them a visit and express your gratitude
- try, at least once every day, to react in a positive and enthusiastic way to someone else
- set aside a day to do exactly what you want; plan your day of luxury and pleasure in advance so that you can maximize every moment of it.

Try these strategies too:

- Spend time visualizing a positive outcome for a situation you're worried about (this is a technique used by many sports people).
- Write a list of your positive qualities and talk it through with someone you trust. For a week, make a note of every piece of evidence in support of these positive qualities. It'll help you to shift your attention away from your failings (or, more likely, your imagined failings) and on to your strengths.

For more on Positive Psychology, check out:
Authentic Happiness (Nicolas Brealey, 2003) by Martin Seligman
Positive Psychology in a Nutshell (PWBC, 2008) by Ilona Boniwell

Martin Seligman also runs a website that's well worth a visit:
ⓘ www.authentichappiness.sas.upenn.edu.

2. Relationships

Let us be grateful to people who make us happy: they are the charming gardeners who make our souls blossom.
Marcel Proust

Many millions of words have been written on the nature of happiness, and much scientific (and not-so-scientific) research has been carried out on

The perils of pessimism

Let's begin with the bad news: thinking pessimistically can seriously damage your health.

In a landmark study, psychologists Christopher Peterson, George Vaillant and Martin Seligman followed the fortunes over 35 years of 99 Harvard students whose pessimism had been assessed in 1946 (when they were in their 20s). The researchers found that the students who'd been most pessimistic as young adults were significantly more likely to experience physical ill health between the ages of 45 and 60.

Toshihiko Maruta and colleagues came to a similar conclusion when in 1994 they followed up several hundred patients who'd been admitted to hospital in the mid-1960s. As part of the admission process, each patient's level of optimism and pessimism had been measured. Thirty years later, it was the most pessimistic patients who were more likely to have died – and the optimistic ones who were most likely to be alive.

No one knows why pessimism is linked to physical ill health, but the good news is that we can train ourselves to think more optimistically. To do this, we need to recognize and then change our thought processes.

When a pessimist experiences a negative event, they tend to think:

- everything in my life is going to get worse
- things won't improve
- it's my fault.

An optimist, on the other hand, will conclude that:

- it's not going to affect my life
- it's temporary
- it's not my fault.

When you spot a pessimistic thought, challenge it. Ask yourself what evidence there is to support it – and to disprove it. What alternative explanations can you come up with? What would you advise a friend in a similar situation? And if there really is a problem, ask yourself whether it's really as bad as you might initially have thought. You'll save yourself a lot of worry; and you may also be helping to safeguard your health.

the subject. Theories about how best to increase our happiness abound. But on one issue there is almost total agreement: the stronger our relationships, the happier we are likely to be.

Clearly, not everyone can be a bubbly extrovert with dozens of friends and a wild social life. Nor does everyone have a close and loving relationship with their family. And some people either never find the right life partner, or prefer to remain single.

None the less, we can all improve the relationships we do have. One very effective way is simply to make time for the other people in your life. Don't let friends, family or partners be squeezed out by work or other commitments. Try keeping a record of the time you spend with those close to you and then schedule in more.

What's the secret of a happy romantic relationship? Well, almost without exception, it's within our control:

- Shared decision-making
- Trust
- Intimacy – physical, emotional and psychological
- Sexual attraction
- Time and energy working at the relationship
- Agreement about who does which household chores
- Emotional support for each other
- Positive actions, whether that's giving your partner a hug, bringing them a cup of tea in bed or being ready to listen when they need to talk
- Clear communication
- Tolerance, flexibility and patience
- Negotiation skills

To find out more about how to strengthen your relationship with your partner, check out the entry on pp. 269–87. You may also find it helpful to have a look at these books:

Love is Never Enough (Harper, 1989) by Professor Aaron T. Beck; *Overcoming Relationship Problems* (Robinson, 2005) by Michael Crowe; *Stop Arguing, Start Talking* (Vermilion, 2001) by Susan Quilliam; *Reconcilable Differences* (Guilford, 2002) by Andrew Christensen and Neil Jacobson; *Everyone Can Win* (Simon & Schuster, 2006) by Helena Cornelius and Shoshana Faire.

One skill that will help in all your interactions with other people is

The power of expressive writing

One tried-and-tested technique to boost your sense of well-being is to spend 20 minutes each day writing about your deepest thoughts and feelings. Psychologists call this expressive writing, and it's been associated with a host of benefits, from greater happiness to an enhanced immune system.

Now there's research to suggest that expressive writing can also strengthen relationships. For a 10-day period, psychologists tracked all the instant messages sent between 86 young couples. The researchers also selected one person from each of the couples and assigned them to one of two groups (which we'll call A and B). For three days in the middle of the 10-day period, group A was asked to spend 20 minutes writing about their deepest feelings regarding their relationship, while group B jotted down their thoughts on whatever they liked.

The researchers discovered that couples in which one member had been in group A were subsequently much more likely to use emotionally expressive language in their instant messages. They were also more likely to still be together three months after the study.

Interestingly, it wasn't only positive emotions (for example, 'love') that featured prominently in group A's instant messages, but – for the men, at least – negative ones too. This indicates that what may be really valuable about this form of expressive writing isn't so much the opportunity it provides to affirm our happiest feelings, but rather the space it gives us to think deeply about the partnership in all its aspects. And that in turn suggests that expressive writing may help strengthen all kinds of relationships, not just romantic ones.

assertiveness. This is a word that's often bandied about, but what exactly does it mean? Essentially, assertiveness involves being able to express your opinions and desires honestly, confidently and directly without being rude or aggressive.

Most of us could benefit from a little assertiveness training. After all, who doesn't sometimes find it difficult to ask for what they want, to disagree with a colleague or friend or simply to say 'No' when they're asked to do something?

The first step towards asserting yourself is to know what you'd like to happen (or to stop happening). Once you're clear about that, you need to tell the person concerned how you feel and then what you want.

Be honest about how you feel, but don't get carried away. Focus on the issue in hand. If your manager's behaviour is making you unhappy, give them specific instances and not a broad lament.

When it comes to expressing what you want, again be really specific. For example, if you'd like your partner to do their share of the housework, suggest that they do particular tasks (for example, cooking three times a week) rather than making a general plea for more action.

Try to keep the conversation as calm and friendly as possible. No one responds well when they feel they're being got at. And remember, assertive is not aggressive.

Saying 'No' can be particularly difficult for many people. But you can make it easier by buying yourself time. When someone asks you to do something, say you'll think about it. Then, when you're ready to give your response, be sympathetic and constructive but not apologetic. You have the right to say 'No' and you don't need to explain your reasons.

Assertiveness is like any other skill: it gets easier the more you practise. So don't get disheartened if you're not suddenly super-confident: stick with it. Rehearse in your mind (or on paper) how you'd like to handle a conversation, watch how other people deal with discussions and disagreements and use your new assertiveness techniques as often as you can.

For more on assertiveness skills, we recommend:
The Assertiveness Pocketbook (Management Pocketbooks, 1997) by Max Eggert; *Assert Yourself* (Thorsons, 2001) by Gail Lindenfield.

Difficult Conversations (Penguin, 2000) by Douglas Stone, Bruce Patton and Sheila Heen is also well worth checking out.

3. Diet

. . . .

'I see, I see,' said Pooh, nodding his head. 'Talking about large somethings,' he went on dreamily, 'I generally have a small something about now – about this time in the morning,' and he looked wistfully at the cupboard in the corner of Owl's parlour; 'just a mouthful of condensed milk or what-not, with perhaps a lick of honey …'
  A. A. Milne, *Winnie The Pooh*

. . . .

Food and drink are two of the great pleasures of life – and for that reason if none other they deserve a mention here. As the old saying goes: a little of what you fancy does you good.

Of course, the words 'a little' are key here (unless what you fancy happens to be, say, a mixed salad). Occasional indulgences can raise your mood, but a generally healthy diet will have a much more profound and longer-lasting effect on both your physical and psychological well-being.

We all know that eating sensibly is one of the most important steps we can take (along with regular exercise) to keep ourselves in good physical shape. But what many people don't realize is that there's plenty of evidence to suggest that physical and psychological health are inter-linked. So, by looking after your body, you'll also be looking after your mind.

One fascinating study, for example, followed more than 10,000 people in the UK between 2002 and 2004. The researchers found that those who made major improvements in their diet (even without increasing the amount of exercise they took) reported feeling much happier, calmer and more peaceful, and far less nervous and unhappy.

So, what exactly is a healthy diet? Well, despite the impression you might get from the hundreds of books on the topic, healthy nutrition is actually pretty straightforward. In fact, it can be summed up in just nine key guidelines:

1. Base your meals around starchy foods

Starchy foods like bread, cereals, rice, pasta and potatoes should make up about a third of your daily diet. They're a great source of energy and are rich in fibre, calcium, iron and B vitamins. Try to include one portion with every meal. Go for wholewheat or wholegrain varieties if you can – they contain more fibre and other nutrients.

2. Eat lots of fruit and vegetables

Try to eat at least five portions of fruit and vegetables a day. Include a glass of juice and a piece of fruit in your breakfast, and you'll be almost halfway there before you've reached lunchtime. Go for fruit if you feel peckish, and include at least one portion of vegetables in every meal (although potatoes don't count). If you're not sure how much a portion is, check out www.5aday. nhs.uk/WhatCounts/PortionSizes.aspx.

3. Eat more fish

Fish contains lots of protein, minerals, and vitamins – and oily fish are rich in the omega 3 fatty acids that can help keep our heart healthy. So, aim to eat fish at least twice a week – and make sure that one of those is an oily fish like salmon, mackerel, trout, herring, fresh tuna, sardines, pilchards or eels.

(Note: women who are breastfeeding, pregnant, trying for a baby or who may want to have a child in the future should be cautious about the amount of oily fish they eat. For more information, visit www.eatwell.gov.uk/healthydiet/nutritionessentials/fishandshellfish.)

4. Cut down on saturated fat

Everyone needs some fat in their diet, but you need to be wary of saturated fat, which can increase the amount of cholesterol in your blood and increase the risk of heart disease. Unsaturated fat on the other hand actually lowers cholesterol.

Foods high in saturated fat include meat pies, sausages, cured meats, hard cheese, butter and lard, pastry, cakes and biscuits, cream, soured cream and crème fraîche. Good sources of unsaturated fat are vegetable oils (including sunflower, rapeseed and olive oil), oily fish, avocados, nuts and seeds.

Check labels when you're buying food. If an item has more than 20g fat per 100g it's a high-fat food; between 3 and 20g fat per 100g indicates a medium-fat food. Try to go for a low-fat option if you can: below 3g of fat per 100g. Some labels give the saturated fat content too. More than 5g per 100g is a high-saturated-fat food and between 1.5 and 5g per 100g indicates a medium level of saturated fats. Again, opt for the low-saturated-fat food wherever possible – less than 1.5g per 100g.

5. Eat less sugar

Sugary foods and drinks cause tooth decay and are high in calories. Most of us know that eating too much sugar is bad for us, but we carry on doing it anyway! Food labels can be a real eye opener, with sugar often showing up as a major ingredient in foods you might not think of as being particularly sugary. Watch out for foods that contain more than 5g of sugar per 100g.

6. Reduce your salt intake to no more than 6 grams a day

Eating too much salt increases your chances of having a stroke or developing heart disease. Adults and children over 11 should have no more than 6g a day; younger children should have even less.

Although we are now more aware of the dangers of salt, and may have stopped adding it to our food, in fact 75 per cent of the salt we eat is already in the food we buy, such as bread, breakfast cereals, soups, sauces and ready meals. Maybe that's why 85 per cent of men in the UK and 69 per cent of women are eating too much salt each day. So always check labels before you buy and go for low-salt options – less than 0.3g of salt per 100g.

7. Drink plenty of water
You should aim to drink around 1.2 litres of water (6–8 glasses) every day to prevent dehydration. And you'll need more than this when it's hot or when you've been active. Water's best, but other drinks count too – such as fruit juice or tea (though you shouldn't make tea your main drink of the day). Be careful to avoid sugary drinks.

8. Watch your alcohol intake
Alcohol isn't usually a problem provided you don't drink too much. Men shouldn't generally drink more than 3–4 units a day; for women the limit is 2–3 units. More than this on a regular basis can lead to health problems. Alcohol is also high in calories – cutting back is a great way to lose weight.

(Note: there are about 2 units of alcohol in a pint of ordinary strength beer or cider, and 3 units in a pint of strong beer or cider. A 175ml glass of wine contains about 2 units and a pub measure of spirits 1 unit. Alcopops usually contain around 1.5 units. Drinks manufacturers now often include this information on cans and bottle labels.)

9. Don't skip breakfast
People often skip breakfast when they're trying to lose weight, thinking what better way to reduce their calories than by cutting out a meal?

In fact, missing breakfast just means that you're hungry midway through the morning, and more likely to fill the gap with tasty snacks like biscuits, pastries and chocolate – hence consuming far more calories than you would have done with a healthy breakfast. Eat regular meals, including a nutritious breakfast – wholewheat cereal and fruit, for instance – and stave off the snack attack!

4. Activity and exercise

. . . .

Indolence is a delightful but distressing state; we must be doing something.
Mahatma Gandhi

. . . .

We are all for laziness. Sometimes nothing can lift the spirits like an afternoon spent dozing on the sofa, or frittered away in front of some instantly forgettable but immensely enjoyable TV detective yarn.

Everyone needs downtime. But to keep yourself really psychologically healthy, all the evidence suggests that relaxation needs to be balanced by a wide range of other activities.

Variety is the key here. In an ideal world, your week should include:

- rewarding and enjoyable work
- social activities
- hobbies
- physical exercise
- learning new skills
- relaxation.

This may seem a hopelessly optimistic proposal. How, you may be wondering, are you supposed to find time for all that? And things may seem particularly discouraging if you have a job that seems neither rewarding nor enjoyable.

The answer is to go for gradual changes. Start by keeping a record of your week – everything you do on an hour-by-hour basis. Then add one of the positive activities listed above, even if it's just for half an hour a week. Once you've built that into your schedule, you can try making other changes.

If you're struggling with work, ask yourself whether there are any elements you do find fulfilling and talk with your manager to see whether these can be developed. Try to identify the kind of job that would best suit you and make a plan for how to get it.

We all need a mix of activities, but two in particular are worth highlighting. The first is physical exercise. As we've mentioned, mind and body seem to be intimately linked; if you can boost the health of one, you'll also improve the health of the other.

Exactly how this works is a topic for another – very lengthy – book. But the changes in the brain that physical exercise causes – specifically the release of pleasurable endorphins – are a well-documented effect. If you stick at it, exercise really will make you happier.

Aim for at least 30 minutes of exercise five times a week. Ideally, your exercise should at least make your heartbeat and breathing a little faster than normal. You'll feel warm and may well work up a sweat. Aerobic activities like swimming, jogging and tennis are particularly good but, whatever you go for, make sure it's something you enjoy. Best of all is if you can build the exercise into your daily routine – that way you'll get your exercise without really noticing it. So, instead of driving to work, for example, walk or cycle instead. Or try getting off the bus a couple of stops early and walk the rest of the way.

The second activity we want to highlight is something called 'flow'. Actually, it's not a specific activity, but rather a description of what happens when you're busy doing something especially absorbing.

The term 'flow' was coined by the psychologist Mihaly Csikzentmihalyi, who argued that it's an essential part of a truly happy life – an insight that's shared by the proponents of Positive Psychology (see above). When you're experiencing flow, all your mental resources are focused on the task in hand. You're no longer aware of what's going on around you. You lose track of time. Your worries, the sensations of your body, your entire self-consciousness – all of them disappear as you become one with your activity.

To produce this feeling of flow, a task generally has to be right at the limit of your skills and knowledge: if it's too easy, you become bored; if it's too difficult, you get frustrated. Classic examples of flow-inducing activities are playing a musical instrument or sport; painting, writing or some other creative endeavour; or working on puzzles or other logical problems. Think what produces flow for you – and aim to do more of it.

5. Sleep

How do you usually feel after a poor night's sleep? Tired? Irritable? Generally out of sorts? What about after you've had your eight hours? Much happier, we'd imagine.

Most of us know that sleep can have a dramatic effect on our mood and sense of well-being. Even so, the stresses and strains of contemporary life mean that more and more people aren't getting the sleep they need.

Try to make sleep a priority. How much you need is very much a personal thing, though most adults function best on at least seven or eight hours per night. Just as important as quantity, however, is the quality of your sleep. Eight hours in bed at night doesn't necessarily mean eight hours deep and restorative rest.

If you're having trouble sleeping, there are some simple steps you can take to get back on track:

Exercise every day
There's no better way to ensure a good night's sleep than being physically tired.

Avoid caffeine, alcohol and nicotine in the evening
Caffeine and nicotine are stimulants, and alcohol – though it may help you fall asleep – will interfere with your normal sleep cycle.

Develop a relaxing evening routine
Whether it's with a warm bath or a relaxing book, you need to wind down around half an hour before bed.

Have a bedtime snack
Go for something relatively plain, like a banana, a glass of milk or a slice of wholemeal toast.

Make your sleeping environment a good one
You won't sleep well if your bed is uncomfortable, your room is too hot or cold or if it's too noisy or light.

Just putting these basics into place should make a big difference to how well you sleep. For more information on these and other ways of tackling sleep problems, have a look at the entry on pp. 334–52.

As we've seen, you can do a lot to strengthen your psychological and emotional health. It really is possible to improve your levels of happiness and all-round well-being. None the less, life being what it is, problems will inevitably crop up from time to time. It's these problems – and most importantly, what you can do to overcome them – that the remainder of *Know Your Mind* is devoted to exploring.

Part II

Addictions

It is not I who becomes addicted, it is my body.
Jean Cocteau

In this section you'll find information about the most common types of addiction – to alcohol, drugs, gambling and smoking. But whatever the habit, the techniques for dealing with it are the same. So once you've read the specific entry that interests you, turn to pages 48–54 for advice on overcoming addictions.

ALCOHOL

Wine is a turncoat; first a friend and then an enemy.
Henry Fielding

Human beings have been drinking alcohol for tens of thousands of years. And it's no wonder: for many of us, alcohol is a great way to relax, helping us to forget our worries and making socializing much easier.

Alcohol has this effect on us because it's a depressant, which doesn't mean that it makes us feel miserable (though it can certainly do this as well), but rather that it slows and dampens down our physiological reactions. And the first things to be affected in this way are the parts of the brain that make us cautious and on edge.

Drink enough, of course, and before long other parts of the brain won't be working normally either. So speech becomes slurred, we sway and stagger when we walk, and, if we keep on boozing, we may even pass out.

But alcohol can also have much more serious and long-term effects. Medical problems associated with heavy drinking include brain damage, gastrointestinal problems, cancer, cirrhosis of the liver, hepatitis, high blood pressure, reduced immunity to coughs, colds and other infections, impaired sexual performance in men and damage to unborn children in the case of pregnant women. There is also a much higher chance of having an accident when drunk and drinking too much can take 10 to 15 years off a person's life.

Then there are the social consequences, which are often devastating. In the UK, alcohol is a factor in 20 per cent of psychiatric admissions, 60 per cent of suicide attempts, 40 per cent of domestic violence incidents and 15 per cent of fatal traffic accidents. More than half of all murderers and/or their victims are believed to be drunk at the time of killing. Twelve million working days are lost to alcohol each year and the total annual cost of alcohol misuse in the UK is around £6 billion.

Problem drinking comes in a variety of forms. You may only drink occasionally, but if that occasion is a binge that leaves you at risk of injury, or if you decide to drink and drive, the consequences can be catastrophic (this has been called 'dumb drinking' by some professionals). An 'overdrinker', on the other hand, is someone who regularly exceeds safe alcohol limits (though quite possibly without any apparent adverse effects). In the UK, men are advised to regularly drink no more than 3–4 units of alcohol a day (or 21 units per week), and women no more than 2–3 units per day (or 14 units per week) – a unit being half a pint of ordinary strength beer or cider, a small glass (120 ml/4 fl oz) of wine and a pub measure of spirits. (Women are generally more susceptible to the effects of alcohol because of their physical make-up.)

More severe problems are known by doctors as 'alcohol abuse' and 'alcohol dependence'.

Alcohol abuse is defined by the regular occurrence of one or more of the following:

- an inability to meet commitments at work or at home because of alcohol (for example, missing work because of a hangover, neglecting a partner and/or kids to go drinking)
- drinking in dangerous situations (for example, while driving or operating machinery)

The morning after...

If a man has taken strong wine, his head is affected and he forgets his words and his speech becomes confused, his mind wanders and his eyes have a set expression; to cure him, take licorice, beans, oleander ... to be compounded with oil and wine before the approach of the goddess Gula (or sunset), and in the morning before sunrise and before anyone has kissed him, let him take it, and he will recover.

Ancient Mesopotamian hangover remedy

- legal proceedings as a result of drinking (for example, being arrested for drunkenness)
- relationship problems caused by alcohol (for example, arguing with a partner).

Alcohol dependence used to be called alcoholism and is defined by three or more of the following occurring together:

- increased tolerance for alcohol (needing to drink more to get drunk)
- physical and psychological problems when alcohol intake is reduced (withdrawal)
- drinking more or for longer than intended
- repeatedly trying, but failing, to cut down or give up
- spending lots of time planning the next drink, drinking or recovering
- prioritizing alcohol over other parts of life
- continuing to drink despite knowing that it's causing harm.

Drinking more than the safe limit does not mean that alcohol dependence is inevitable. It is not known for sure why some people develop severe problems with alcohol while others don't (though a range of risk factors, including our genes, have been identified). But many people do progress from drinking socially to drinking at times of stress, and then to feeling an increased need for more.

However, alcohol is only ever a temporary solution to life's stresses and strains. Not only does the sensation of relaxation and well-being soon wear off, alcohol can actually increase feelings of depression and anxiety. And regardless of all these definitions of problem drinking, there is a simple bottom line: however much you're drinking, if you or those close to you think you may have a problem, it might be time to consider cutting back or stopping altogether.

Problems with alcohol: some personal accounts

I love drinking, but I have finally admitted that it does not love me. I never drank on my own. In fact, I often went several days without thinking about alcohol. But I'm pretty shy and I relied on a drink to help me when I was socializing. Unfortunately, I'd often get carried away. If I was having a great time, I wanted to go on having a great time – so I carried on drinking. I had to miss work at least once a month because of horrendous hangovers. And I used to get aggressive when I was very drunk – picking fights with total strangers.

I don't drink at all now. A couple of beers make me a more fun person, I think, but I don't trust myself to stop there. The person I become after that isn't someone I want to be. I still find social situations hard, but I'm so proud of myself for stopping.
Paul, aged 35

When my husband moved out, I was devastated. A glass of wine was the only thing that made me feel I could cope. Pretty soon things were out of control. I'd have a vodka in the morning; I'd pester colleagues to come to the pub at lunchtime; and I spent my evenings drinking. If I wasn't drinking, I felt physically awful. All I could think about was how I was going to sneak my next drink. I'd booze all weekend on my own – wouldn't see a soul. Then I'd have to miss work on Monday because of the state I was in. I had blackouts – whole evenings disappeared. I

> think I'd be dead now if it wasn't for the fact that my sister came round one evening and found me passed out on the floor. When I left hospital we talked for hours and hours. For me, it was the beginning of the road back. I take it a day at a time, but I haven't had a drink now for over eighteen months.
> **Nancy, aged 40**

How common are alcohol problems?

Many societies, and especially those in the West, seem to revolve around alcohol – an observation that is borne out by the figures for drink-related problems.

A 2006 survey of UK drinking habits, for example, found that 23 per cent of men and 14 per cent of women drink more than the recommended

---

Alcohol and the brain

That life can seem a whole lot better after a glass of our favourite tipple isn't news to drinkers. But a recent study by researchers in the Netherlands has given a fascinating insight into why this should be the case.

A team led by the psychiatrist Ingmar Franken gave one group of volunteers drinks containing low to moderate amounts of alcohol and a second group a non-alcoholic drink. The researchers then showed the volunteers a selection of pictures, some unpleasant, some pleasant and some neutral. While the volunteers were looking at the images, their brain activity was recorded.

What the researchers found was remarkable, because when the unpleasant pictures were put in front of the volunteers who had been given alcohol, their brain activity was significantly less than that in those who had not had an alcoholic drink. Alcohol reduced the impact of the negative images.

At a fundamental neurological level then, alcohol changes your view of the world. The problems that seem so pressing when you're sober literally do not make the same impression on your brain when you've had a drink. But you probably knew that already!

---

weekly limit; 50 per cent of men and 35 per cent of women had exceeded the daily limit on at least one day in the week before the survey; and around 20 per cent of men and 8 per cent of women are likely to suffer from alcohol abuse or dependence at some point in their lives, with around 5 per cent being dependent at any one time.

In the US, around 125 million people aged 12 or older drink alcohol – that is 50 per cent of the population. Fifty-seven million Americans are 'binge drinkers', defined as five or more drinks on at least one occasion in the thirty days prior to the survey. Around 15 million Americans are thought to be dependent on alcohol.

In Australia, the proportion of people drinking at risky levels has increased from 8.2 per cent in 1995 to 10.8 per cent in 2001 and 13.4 per cent in 2004–5.

Self-assessment

Judging whether or not you have a problem with alcohol can be hard. Ours is a culture, after all, which regards drinking – even to excess – as normal. If you're concerned about your alcohol consumption, have a go at the following questionnaire.

Please select the box that best describes your answer to each question.

	0	1	2	3	4
1. How often do you have a drink containing alcohol?	Never	Monthly or less	2–4 times a month	2–3 times a week	4 or more times a week
2. How many drinks containing alcohol do you have on a typical day when you are drinking?	1 or 2	3 or 4	5 or 6	7 to 9	10 or more
3. How often do you have six or more drinks on one occasion?	Never	Less than monthly	Monthly	Weekly	Daily or almost daily

	0	1	2	3	4
4. How often during the last year have you found that you were not able to stop drinking once you had started?	Never	Less than monthly	Monthly	Weekly	Daily or almost daily
5. How often during the last year have you failed to do what was expected of you because of drinking?	Never	Less than monthly	Monthly	Weekly	Daily or almost daily
6. How often during the last year have you needed a first drink in the morning to get yourself going after a heavy drinking session?	Never	Less than monthly	Monthly	Weekly	Daily or almost daily
7. How often during the last year have you had a feeling of guilt or remorse after drinking?	Never	Less than monthly	Monthly	Weekly	Daily or almost daily
8. How often during the last year have you been unable to remember what happened the night before because of your drinking?	Never	Less than monthly	Monthly	Weekly	Daily or almost daily
9. Have you or someone else been injured because of your drinking?	No		Yes, but not in the last year		Yes, during the last year

© World Health Organization (2001)

Now add up your total score. Anything above 8 indicates a potential drinking problem. That problem is likely to be moderate if you scored between 8 and 15, serious if your score was 16–19 and very severe if you totalled more than 20.

DRUGS

Let's start with a brief look at the main types of illegal drug.

Most widely used is marijuana (also known as cannabis or hashish, or by a range of street names such as dope, skunk, grass, weed and pot). This is a type of 'hallucinogen', the name given to a drug that distorts the way in which we perceive the world around us. Other hallucinogens include LSD (often known as acid) and certain types of mushroom.

'Opioids' give users a feeling of extreme relaxation, even euphoria. The best-known opioid is heroin, which goes by a plethora of street names including smack, brown, skag, gear and thunder.

'Stimulants', on the other hand, make users extremely energetic, talkative and sociable. Major illegal stimulants include cocaine (known as Charlie, coke or blow), amphetamines (also called whiz, speed, meth and crystal meth, ice or crank), and Ecstasy (E, XTC, hug drug). Ecstasy is the most high-profile of the so-called 'designer' drugs, which also include MDEA (Eve), BDMPEA (Nexus), PCP (angel dust) ketamine and GHB (liquid Ecstasy).

Abuse of prescription drugs is now a major problem, especially painkillers like oxycodone (better known under the brand name OxyContin), propoxyphene (Darvon), and hydrocone (Vicodin). Anti-anxiety drugs are also often used illegally, notably barbiturates like pentobarbital (Nembutal) and benzodiazepines such as diazepam (Valium), lorazepam (Ativan), and alprazolam (Xanax). And there is an illicit market for stimulants like Dexedrine and Ritalin (prescribed legitimately by doctors for problems such as obesity, narcolepsy and Attention-Deficit Hyperactivity Disorder or ADHD).

'I've never had a problem with drugs,' joked Rolling Stones guitarist Keith Richards; 'I've had problems with the police.' And indeed, it is possible to take virtually any of the drugs listed above occasionally without doing any lasting harm. Millions of people do just that, for the same reason that many consume legal substances like alcohol and tobacco: they make people feel better (at least in the short term) about themselves and the world around them.

But, just like alcohol and tobacco, there is a real risk that the use of illegal drugs can develop into a pattern of abuse or dependence. And there is no sure way for anyone to know in advance whether they will be able to keep their drug use on a strictly recreational level.

Drug abuse is defined by doctors as one or more of the following happening regularly:

- an inability to meet commitments at work or at home because of drugs (for example, missing work because of the after effects of drugs or neglecting a partner and/or kids to go looking for drugs)
- being under the influence of drugs in dangerous situations (for example, while driving or operating machinery)
- experiencing legal problems because of drugs (for example, being arrested for behaviour while high)
- relationship problems caused by drugs (for example, arguing with a partner).

Drug dependence is defined by three or more of the following occurring together:

- increased tolerance for the drug, so that more is needed to get high
- physical and psychological problems when drug intake is reduced (withdrawal)
- taking more drugs, or taking them over a longer period, than intended
- repeatedly trying, but failing, to cut down or give up
- spending lots of time planning how to get drugs, taking them or recovering from taking them
- prioritizing drugs over other parts of life
- continuing to take drugs despite knowing they are causing harm.

It is possible to become dependent on any of the drugs listed above. But although all of these substances are addictive, some are more so than others. It is difficult to be precise about such a complex issue, but a panel of expert professionals concluded in 1990 that the most addictive illegal drugs were crack cocaine and methamphetamines (a type of amphetamine). Barbiturates and benzodiazepines were ranked next most addictive, closely followed by heroin, amphetamine and then cocaine. Marijuana, Ecstasy, and LSD were seen as least addictive. (Interestingly, the experts saw nicotine as more addictive than any of the illegal drugs, and alcohol as marginally more addictive than heroin.)

How common is drug use?

Drug use is extremely widespread. According to a government survey carried out in 2003–4, around 3.3 million people in England and Wales are thought to have used marijuana in the previous year. Over the same period,

Problems with drugs: some personal accounts

I have been smoking weed on and off since I was seventeen. I use it to relax. These days I hardly ever get really wasted. I'll just have a smoke when I get home from work. I don't consider myself a drug addict. Dope isn't like crack or heroin. I have a full-time job, lots of friend and no health problems. But I want to quit, or at least cut down. My wife is five months pregnant, and neither of us wants smoke in the house on account of the baby. Plus, I think dope and childcare won't mix well. I'm going to need to be awake and alert, not nodding off on the sofa after a joint. Maybe I'm just getting old and boring, but it feels like the time is right for a change.
Jake, aged 27

I started taking cocaine five years ago, but I never bought the stuff. I'd just do a line with friends occasionally. I loved how cocaine made me feel: confident and upbeat and sociable – and all without a hangover. About a year ago I had a promotion. I had more money but also a lot more stress. Through work, I met some guys who were seriously into coke and soon I was getting through 2–3 grams a week. It was the first thing I thought about when I woke up in the morning. I built my day around when and where I'd snort my next line. I'd never noticed any real side effects in the past, but now I felt tense and irritable a lot of the time, and my concentration was shot. Cocaine was no fun any more. Not only that, but it was dominating my life. I knew I had to stop. Telling my GP was one of the toughest things I've ever done, but I don't like to think where I'd be now if I hadn't. She put me in touch with a drugs counsellor and I've been clean for the past six months.
Tom, aged 35

three-quarters of a million people took cocaine; 600,000 Ecstasy; and 480,000 amphetamines. Twelve per cent of adults had used an illicit drug in the previous twelve months, and 7.5 per cent in the previous month.

In the US, the 2006 National Survey on Drug Use and Health estimated that 20.4 million Americans, or 8.3 per cent of the population aged 12 or older, are illegal drug users. Marijuana is the drug of choice for 14.8 million people, with 3.1 million using it on a daily or almost-daily basis over a 12-month period. Almost two and a half million Americans use cocaine; a million people take hallucinogens such as LSD or 'magic mushrooms'; and 528,000 take Ecstasy.

Around 3 per cent of the population of the UK and US are either dependent on drugs, or have what doctors would define as a drug abuse problem. Mostly, the drug in question is marijuana.

Age is a big factor in patterns of drug use. Young people are much more likely to take illegal drugs than older adults, and the 20–25 age group is most at risk of developing a drug dependency.

Marijuana and mental illness

How dangerous is marijuana to our mental health? This is a question that took on a new significance following the decision by the UK government in 2004 to downgrade the drug's legal status.

In fact, we have known for a very long time – since French psychiatrist Jacques-Joseph Moreau, did his research in 1845, to be precise – that using marijuana can lead to feelings of paranoia and other symptoms of 'psychosis' (the technical term for severe mental illness). And this is particularly true for young people taking the drug.

Why then are most people able to use marijuana without any such ill effects?

New light has recently been cast on this key question by a research team led by psychologist Avashalom Caspi. The team analysed a group of 1000 people all born in Dunedin, New Zealand, between April 1972 and March 1973. They found that 92 per cent of marijuana users did not go on to develop psychosis. But, crucially, the 8 per cent that did all had higher rates of a genetic vulnerability (specifically, a variant of the catechol-o-methyltransferase gene).

Now this is not to say that psychosis is simply the product of a rogue gene. There are lots of factors at play, including age, marijuana use and numerous other environmental issues. But the research of Caspi and colleagues does highlight for the first time the way our genetic make-up can interact with our drug use to produce mental illness.

Self-assessment

To help you judge whether or not you have a drug problem, think back to your experiences over the past 12 months and answer the following questions.

Circle Yes or No as appropriate.

1. Have you used drugs other than those required for medical reasons? Yes/No

2. Have you abused prescription drugs? Yes/No

3. Do you abuse more than one drug at a time? Yes/No

4. Can you get through the week without using drugs (other than those required for medical reasons)? Yes/No

5. Are you always able to stop using drugs when you want to? Yes/No

6. Do you abuse drugs on a continuous basis? Yes/No

7. Do you try to limit your drug use to certain situations? Yes/No

8. Have you had 'blackouts' or 'flashbacks' as a result of drug use? Yes/No

9. Do you ever feel bad about your drug abuse? Yes/No

10. Does your spouse (or parents) ever complain about your involvement with drugs? Yes/No

11. Do your friends or relatives know or suspect you abuse drugs? Yes/No

12. Has drug abuse ever created problems between you and your spouse? Yes/No

13. Has any family member ever sought help for problems related to your drug use? Yes/No

14. Have you ever lost friends because of your use of drugs? Yes/No

15. Have you ever neglected your family or missed work because of your use of drugs? Yes/No

16. Have you ever been in trouble at work because of drug abuse? Yes/No

17. Have you ever lost a job because of drug abuse? Yes/No

18. Have you got involved in fights when under the influence of drugs? Yes/No

19. Have you ever been arrested because of unusual behaviour while under the influence of drugs? Yes/No
20. Have you ever been arrested for driving while under the influence of drugs? Yes/No
21. Have you engaged in illegal activities to obtain drugs? Yes/No
22. Have you ever been arrested for possession of illegal drugs? Yes/No
23. Have you ever experienced withdrawal symptoms as a result of heavy drug intake? Yes/No

© Elsevier (1982)

Give yourself a point for every question to which you answer Yes, with the exception of questions 4 and 5: for those, you get a point if you answer No. If your total score is 6 or more, you may have a drug problem.

GAMBLING

Horse sense is the thing a horse has which keeps it from betting on people.
W. C. Fields

Human beings love a flutter. As long as 4000 years ago, ancient Egyptians were betting on (would you believe) four-sided dice fashioned out of knucklebones. According to anthropologists, gambling has been a feature of practically every human society throughout history. So when you buy your weekly lottery ticket, think of yourself as participating in an age-old ritual: it may be some small consolation if (when) your numbers don't come up...

For the vast majority of people, gambling is an exciting leisure activity that has no more of a hold on them than going to the cinema or enjoying a meal out with friends. (An indication of just how exciting is revealed by studies that show that our heart rate can increase by up to 50 beats per minute when we gamble.) Most people gamble for fun, not to win, and they don't bet more than they can afford to lose.

A small proportion of people, however, can find that their gambling has got out of control, and it can be as addictive and as damaging as any drug. In fact, at a basic, biological level, the effect of gambling can be much the same as that of alcohol, nicotine or any other drug, the buzz of winning (or nearly winning) being very much like the 'high' we get from drugs (the same mechanism is triggered in our brains). Also, we can suffer 'withdrawal' symptoms when we don't gamble for a while. It's when we chase that buzz that gambling problems can start.

Of course, gambling takes many forms – from lottery and raffle tickets to bingo, horse-racing, slot machines, casinos and Internet betting. Those most likely to lead to addiction involve one or more of the following:

- a short time between the bet and the result (e.g. slot machines)
- the chance to bet again very quickly (slot machines again)
- the opportunity to bet a large amount of money (e.g. horse-racing, casinos)
- ease of accessibility and/or anonymity (especially Internet gambling).

Gambling addiction (also known as 'compulsive' or 'pathological' gambling) is defined by doctors as involving at least five of the following:

- spending all or most of the time gambling or thinking about gambling
- needing to bet increasing amounts of money to get the same buzz
- failing repeatedly to give up or cut back on gambling
- being restless or irritable when trying to give up or cut back
- gambling in order to escape from problems and feelings
- gambling to try to get back money lost through betting ('chasing losses')
- lying to hide gambling
- committing crimes (such as stealing) to finance gambling
- losing or jeopardizing a relationship, job, or other opportunity because of gambling
- relying on others to lend money because of financial problems caused by gambling.

Becoming a compulsive gambler is a three-stage process. First comes the 'winning phase', during which a person is introduced to gambling, grows to like the excitement of it and – usually – enjoys a relatively big win, leading them to conclude that gambling is easy. The 'losing phase', on the other

Problems with gambling: a personal account

It started when a friend took me to the local casino. We played roulette and it seemed as though we couldn't stop winning. I fell in love with the whole scene. I think I was hooked there and then. When my friend couldn't make it one night, I went on my own. I won again and I thought – I'm pretty good at this; maybe I can do it for a living. Of course, my luck soon ran out. I owed money to pretty much everyone I knew. But I didn't stop gambling; I wanted to win back what I'd lost. When I wasn't gambling, I was thinking about gambling. My lowest point was very low. I couldn't sleep for worry, my friends and family wouldn't speak to me, and I was in debt to some pretty nasty guys. The penny finally dropped and I got in touch with Gamblers Anonymous.

Danny, aged 26

hand, demonstrates that it is not. The gambler's losses mount up, and they 'chase' them by betting larger amounts of money and more often. Gambling begins to have a major impact on life at home, on relationships and on work. Eventually they enter the 'desperation phase', in which their gambling is completely out of control.

The consequences of compulsive gambling are usually very serious, including poverty, damage to the gambler's physical and mental health, and huge strain on family relationships. Almost all problem gamblers report that their addiction has interfered with their work. As if that were not enough, research suggests that almost two-thirds of compulsive gamblers resort to crime to fund their addiction and up to 75 per cent suffer depression, with around 60 per cent experiencing suicidal thoughts. The damage to the partners and children of compulsive gamblers is just as severe, often resulting in lasting physical and mental health problems.

How common is compulsive gambling?

Gambling is a huge worldwide industry, with an annual turnover of around £90 billion in the UK and more than $100 billion in the US. Around 68 per cent of adults in the UK (that's about 32 million people) have had a bet within the last year. Indeed, the average British household spends more on gambling each year than it does on fresh fruit (it's a little better on the fresh vegetable front, where the same amount is spent as on betting). The most popular gambling activities in Britain in 2007 were the National Lottery (with 57 per cent of UK adults taking part), scratch cards (20 per cent), betting on horse races (17 per cent) and playing slot machines (14 per cent). Only 6 per cent of people used the Internet to gamble.

Around 0.6 per cent of the UK population is addicted to gambling (roughly 300,000 people). The highest rates are among people who participate in spread betting or use fixed odds betting terminals (gaming machines normally found in betting shops), and betting exchanges (a form of Internet gambling). In the US, around 3–5 per cent of adults – or 10 million – are compulsive gamblers.

Anyone can develop a gambling addiction, but the young – and young men in particular – are especially vulnerable.

Inside the mind of the compulsive gambler

Compulsive gambling is, for the most part, no fun at all. The list of problems it can cause runs all the way from poverty and family breakdown to prison and suicide. So why do compulsive gamblers keep on betting? There is no simple answer to this key question, but the way in which problem gamblers think does provide some fascinating insight into compulsive gambling.

It turns out that compulsive gamblers share a number of thought processes (psychologists call them cognitive distortions). They believe, for example, that they can actually influence the outcome of the game they're betting on – whether by clutching a 'lucky' object, performing a superstitious ritual or praying. They also tend to overestimate both their own skill at gambling and the role of skill (as opposed to sheer luck) in winning. The compulsive gambler believes, in other words, that they are in control.

Supporting this fantasy is a range of other typical thought patterns. For example: compulsive gamblers tend to remember their successes and forget their (probably far more numerous) failures; nearly winning is taken as a sign that hitting the jackpot is just around the corner; and a series of losses is seen as inevitably being followed by a series of wins, provided the gambler sticks at it for long enough.

It is easy to see how this way of thinking digs the compulsive gambler deeper and deeper into the mire.

Self-assessment

Here is a tried-and-tested way to gauge whether your gambling is getting out of hand. When you answer the questions below, focus on your experiences over the past twelve months.

	0	1	2	3
1. Have you bet more than you could really afford to lose?	Never	Sometimes	Most of the time	Almost always
2. Have you needed to gamble with larger amounts of money to get the same feeling of excitement?	Never	Sometimes	Most of the time	Almost always
3. When you gambled, did you go back another day to try to win back the money you lost?	Never	Sometimes	Most of the time	Almost always
4. Have you borrowed money or sold anything to get money to gamble?	Never	Sometimes	Most of the time	Almost always
5. Have you felt that you might have a problem with gambling?	Never	Sometimes	Most of the time	Almost always
6. Has gambling caused you any health problems, including stress or anxiety?	Never	Sometimes	Most of the time	Almost always
7. Have people criticized your betting or told you that you had a gambling problem, regardless of whether or not you thought it was true?	Never	Sometimes	Most of the time	Almost always
8. Has your gambling caused any financial problems for you or your household?	Never	Sometimes	Most of the time	Almost always

	0	1	2	3
9. Have you felt guilty about the way you gamble or what happens when you gamble?	Never	Sometimes	Most of the time	Almost always

© Canadian Centre on Substance Abuse (2001)

Now add up your total score. A score of between 3 and 7 suggests a moderate gambling problem. A score of 8 or more indicates a serious gambling problem.

SMOKING

Smoking is hateful to the nose, harmful to the brain and dangerous to the lungs.
King James I (1566–1625)

These days there can be precious few people who are not aware of the dangers of smoking (at least in the developed world). Fewer and fewer people in the West are smoking, and almost 70 per cent of those who are still puffing away say they want to give up.

The list of health problems associated with smoking is practically endless. When you realize that there are around 600 poisons in a typical cigarette, with tar being the most damaging of all, it's not surprising that smokers have a significantly higher risk of diseases including cancers of the mouth, throat, larynx, oesophagus, bladder, kidney, pancreas, stomach and, most notoriously, lungs; coronary heart disease; stroke; and all manner of breathing problems from chronic bronchitis to emphysema.

Half of all smokers die as a result of their habit. That is a lot of people: nearly 120,000 annually in the UK and around 440,000 in the US. Smoking accounts for one in five deaths.

But the dangers of nicotine are not confined to smokers. People who regularly breathe in other people's smoke – 'passive smokers' – have an increased risk of cancer, heart disease and breathing problems. For example, a study of women who lived with smokers, but who had never touched a cigarette themselves, found that they were 26 per cent more likely to develop lung cancer than people who were not exposed to tobacco smoke. Passive smoking is also a real problem for children, making them suscep-tible to infections like bronchitis and pneumonia. Children who live in households where both parents smoke have a 72 per cent risk of develop-ing these sorts of breathing-related illnesses. Passive smoking has also been strongly linked to asthma in children.

Then there are the hazards of smoking while pregnant. These include medical complications during the pregnancy, such as sickness, miscarriage and bleeding. The baby may be born prematurely, or have a low birth weight; it may be weaker and grow slowly. It is also likely to be at risk from breath-ing problems and asthma. Smoking during any part of pregnancy is not a great idea, but the first three months are particularly critical.

Given the risks of smoking – not to mention the cost, the smell and the less than appealing effects on skin, teeth and hair – it might seem surprising that anyone ever lights up. But like most drugs, smoking – and specifically nicotine – stimulates the part of our brain that responds to pleasure. Nicotine, at least in the short term, makes people feel good, so that every time they take a drag on a cigarette they get another almost instantaneous shot.

Unfortunately, nicotine (named after Jean Nicot, who first brought tobacco to the French court in the sixteenth century) is also highly addic-tive. In fact, some doctors argue that it is the most addictive drug, outstrip-ping heroin, cocaine and alcohol. Around 80–90 per cent of regular smokers are probably addicted to nicotine.

Nicotine dependence is characterized by one or more of the following:

- increased tolerance – smoking more and more, without feeling sick or dizzy, and the first cigarette of the day giving the biggest boost
- going without nicotine for even just 24 hours (withdrawal) produces a range of side effects including craving a smoke, depression, anger, restlessness, anxiety, dizziness and increased appetite
- choosing not to do things that mean we can't smoke – for example, spending the day at a non-smoking venue
- spending a lot of time smoking and/or thinking about smoking
- carrying on smoking even though we have health problems
- finding it very hard to not smoke.

Tough as it is to quit smoking – and though most smokers think they will never manage it, half do eventually succeed – the benefits make it well worth the effort. Ex-smokers save money, look and feel better and have a huge (and well-deserved) sense of achievement.

And then there are the health benefits, which kick in pretty much as soon as that last cigarette has been stubbed out: within 20 minutes, blood pressure and pulse return to normal; by 48 hours, all the nicotine has left the body and senses of smell and taste are vastly improved; between months 3 and 9, any breathing problems will start to disappear and lungs will begin to work more efficiently; after a year, the risk of a heart attack falls by 50 per cent; after 10 years, the chances of developing lung cancer are half that of a smoker; and 15 years after quitting, an ex-smoker is as likely to have a heart attack as someone who has never smoked.

The human body is a tremendously resilient system. All we have to do is give it a chance.

How common is smoking?

Thanks to massive government health campaigns, and a big hike in the cost of cigarettes, smoking is in decline in the developed world. Back in

Problems with smoking: a personal account

I began smoking when I was 12. It was what you did to be cool. But by the time I was 25, I was smoking 20–30 a day – I loved a ciggie with my morning coffee, and when I got home from work, and I especially loved having a smoke with a glass of wine when I was out with friends. I knew smoking could kill me, but I told myself I'd stop soon. When I did try giving up, I couldn't handle the cravings. Plus I put on weight. When I was 42 I got a really bad chest infection. I kept smoking, developed pneumonia, stopped smoking – and started again as soon as I was better. My husband pleaded with me. He thought I'd die if I carried on, and that shocked me.

I sat down and made a list of the things smoking gave me – and what it could cost me. That's when I truly understood that I had to stop.
Heather, aged 47

A tale of two worlds

Smoking may be on the decline in the developed world, but in developing countries it is a very different story.

According to the World Health Organization, there are more than 1 billion smokers worldwide, 70 per cent of whom live in the developing world. Smoking currently kills 5.4 million people a year (or one every six seconds). Unless strict anti-smoking measures are put in place around the globe, that figure is expected to rise to 8 million by 2030. And of those 8 million deaths, a massive 80 per cent will occur in developing nations.

The smoking epidemic has taken particular hold in China, where almost two-thirds of men smoked in 2003, compared to around 50 per cent in other developing nations and 35 per cent in developed countries. China consumes a third of the world's cigarettes and, unless things change dramatically, it will pay a terrifying price: over the next half a century 100 million Chinese people will die from smoking.

1974, for example, 45 per cent of people in the UK smoked, but by 2005, that figure had dropped to just 24 per cent (although rates were higher in Scotland and the north of England). In the US, around 20 per cent of adults smoke, and at 45 million people that's still a frightening figure, but it's much better than the 45 per cent of Americans who smoked in 1965.

In both the UK and US, smoking is especially common among young people, and particularly young women. There is also a clear link between smoking and educational and economic status. In the UK, for instance, 29 per cent of manual workers smoke, as compared with just 19 per cent of non-manual workers. And in the US, 41 per cent of people with a General Education Development qualification (a high-school level diploma) smoke, compared to 6.6 per cent of those with a college degree.

The rise of roll your own

Pipe smoking may have virtually disappeared in the UK (down to just one per cent of men in 2005), but hand-rolled cigarettes are undergoing a renaissance. In 1990, 18 per cent of male and 2 per cent of female smokers rolled their own; by 2005, those figures had swollen to 34 and 16 per cent respectively. And hand-rolling is also on the rise in the US and Canada.

The main reason for this is cost: as the price of manufactured cigarettes has rocketed, hand-rolling is a substantially cheaper option. But some smokers also believe it's a healthier one. However, in actual fact, since hand-rolled cigarettes often contain more tar and nicotine than manufactured brands, their addictiveness and risk to health is likely to be even greater.

Self-assessment

Are you caught in the clutches of a nicotine addiction? Take the test below to find out.

1. How soon after you wake up do you smoke your first cigarette?	After 60 minutes (0) 31–60 minutes (1) 6–30 minutes (2) Within 5 minutes (3)
2. Do you find it difficult to refrain from smoking in places where it is forbidden?	No (0) Yes (1)
3. Which cigarette would you most hate to give up?	The first in the morning (1) Any other (0)
4. How many cigarettes per day do you smoke?	10 or fewer (0) 11–20 (1) 21–30 (2) 31 or more (3)
5. Do you smoke more frequently during the first hours after awakening than during the rest of the day?	No (0) Yes (1)
6. Do you smoke even if you are so ill that you are in bed most of the day?	No (0) Yes (1)

© Fagerstrom (1991).

Now add up your score. If your total is 0–4 you have a low or very low level of nicotine dependence. A score of 5 indicates a medium level of dependence; 6–7 is high; and 8–10 suggests very high dependence.

How to Overcome Addictions

Whether the problem is with alcohol or gambling, smoking or illegal drugs, the method for overcoming the addiction is basically the same.

Tools for quitting

The next few pages will take you through a series of techniques, which you can put into practice on your own. If, however, an addiction has reached a severe level make sure you also speak to your GP. They will be able to advise on medication – which can be especially useful in helping you cope with withdrawal symptoms – and may also suggest a referral to a specialist substance abuse unit or a smoking clinic.

The motivation for change

Making any major change in life takes huge amounts of motivation and determination, and no more so than when you're trying to break an addiction. Psychologists have identified six stages that people normally go through in these situations:

- precontemplation (the person has not yet acknowledged a need to change)
- contemplation (they have admitted the problem but are not yet ready to make a change)
- preparation/determination (getting ready to change)
- action/willpower (changing behaviour)
- maintenance (sticking with new behaviour) and, in some cases,
- relapse (going back to old problematic habits).

Only you can judge what stage you're at and when you're ready to move on to the next one.

An effective way to boost your motivation is to weigh up the pros and cons of making the change in question, as against leaving things as they are. All you need is a piece of paper and a few minutes thinking time:

	Advantages	Disadvantages
Carrying on with behaviour		

	Advantages	Disadvantages
Reducing or stopping behaviour		
Conclusions		

When you do this exercise, try to imagine what friends and family would say – or the advice you would give to someone else who is in the same boat. Think how you would like your life to be in, say, a year's time. And don't forget the financial consequences of your addiction: what could you do with all the money you would save by quitting?

Monitor your behaviour

How much do you drink in a week? How much money have you lost on the horses so far this month?

You may suspect you have a problem, but it's often hard to know how big that problem is. So keep a written record of your addiction – how much you're doing it, when and where. Not only will this give you a clearer picture of your habit, you will also be able to see whether there are any patterns to your behaviour. For example, are there particular events or feelings that make you think about alcohol? What situations do you tend to smoke most in?

The more you understand your addiction, the better equipped you'll be to tackle it. And there is one more advantage of keeping a record of what you have been up to: you will see how things are improving.

Cut down or give up completely?

There is an old saying: 'If you don't know where you're going, you won't know when you get there.' One of the key questions you need to ask yourself as you set about overcoming your addiction is whether you want to give up completely (abstinence) or simply cut back to safe limits.

Abstinence is the objective of organizations like Alcoholics Anonymous, and it also tends to be the model preferred in the US. In Europe, on the other hand, moderation is a more common approach. Abstinence is best for certain substances – smoking, for example. But ultimately the decision is yours: go for whichever you think will work best for you.

If you decide to cut back, it is really important that you set yourself clear limits – for example how many units of alcohol you will drink a week, or how much money you will bet.

And remember that there are some situations in which you should never drink or take drugs, including: driving a vehicle or operating machinery, if you're taking certain medications or if you have a medical condition that can be triggered or made worse by alcohol or other substances.

Change your behaviour

Every addiction is structured around particular situations that make us want to indulge. These situations – or 'triggers' – can be anything from spending time with certain people or walking past a particular place (the pub for example) to thoughts, feelings and memories.

Keeping a record of your habit (see p. 49) is an excellent way to identify your triggers. But once you have done this, you'll need to work out how to combat them. What will you do instead of your problem behaviour? For example, if feeling lonely makes you smoke more, think about who you could talk to in these situations, or what you could do to take your mind off your feelings. If you use drugs when you're with certain friends, try to steer clear of them for a while. And if you drink to take your mind off unpleasant thoughts, you may want to find someone to talk them through with.

Alongside the triggers for your behaviour, try to work out the function of your habit. Is it to get high, for instance? Or to make you feel more outgoing and confident? Or to help you deal with difficult situations? And what else could you do to achieve the same results without all the downsides of your addiction?

Overcoming an addiction usually means changing behaviour that has built up over years. And that can create what seems like a very big hole in your life. So it is especially important that you find time in your week for doing things that you enjoy (but which are not connected with your addiction). You'll feel much happier about your situation – and there is no better way to take your mind off your habit than by having fun.

Change the way you think

'I can't face this evening unless I have a drink.' 'I've had a terrible day – I deserve a spliff.' 'There's nothing I can do about my smoking.' 'Gambling is the only thing I enjoy. If I don't have a bet, life's just miserable.'

Every addict is familiar with these sorts of thoughts (or 'addictive beliefs', as psychologists call them). They give permission to indulge and, as you might guess, it is crucial that you challenge them. The following five simple steps will help you to do this:

- Write down your addictive beliefs.
- Rate how strongly you believe them.
- Think of evidence for and against the beliefs.
- Weigh up the evidence. Talk it through with a friend if you can.
- And try testing your beliefs. For example, if you think you can't get through a social occasion without a drink, have a go: you may well be pleasantly surprised.

Now re-rate how strongly you believe the thoughts. Do they really provide a good enough reason to indulge?

Tackle cravings

Sooner or later, and whatever habit it is that you're trying to break, you will experience cravings – a desperate urge for whatever it is you have decided to give up.

Cravings can be caused by withdrawal symptoms, or sparked by the triggers mentioned on p. 50. Sometimes they hit you because you miss the pleasure you used to get from your habit, but whatever their cause, you need to be ready for them. Here are some tried-and-tested techniques:

- Distract yourself by chatting to someone or doing something physical.
- Talk yourself through the craving. Reassure yourself that you can beat it, that you won't give in.
- Try a substitute: if you're craving a beer, try a non-alcoholic drink instead. If you're desperate for a cigarette, chewing gum might help.
- Challenge your addictive beliefs (see p. 50).
- Try a relaxation exercise (see p. 359).
- Don't act on a craving for at least 20 minutes (you'll probably find that it's disappeared by then).
- Choose a particular image to call to mind when you experience a craving. For instance, some people think of a big 'Stop!' sign and then visualize themselves successfully resisting the craving.

Whichever strategy you decide on, think it through and practise it in advance. You may find it helps to write it down and carry it around with you, so that you can be prepared when the craving strikes.

Even if you find yourself beginning to act on a craving, all is not lost. You still have the chance to stop yourself. Having a beer, for example, might involve several stages: fetching a glass, going to the fridge, finding a bottle opener and so on – a chain of behaviours in which each link represents an opportunity for you to change your mind. Try to think through this chain of behaviours in advance and see whether there is anything you can do to improve your chances of breaking it (not keeping the beer in the fridge, for example, or limiting the amount you keep in the house at any one time).

Dealing with other people

Giving up is a whole lot easier if you have a network of friends, family, colleagues and a partner to support you. But many people's addictions are intimately linked to their social life. If your friends are drinkers or smokers, for instance, the chances are that you will be too. So when you're trying to break a habit, you may experience a certain level of pressure to indulge from those around you. You might need to use assertiveness skills (see p. 16), or even have to explain to certain people why you'll be spending less time with them, at least for a while.

Coping with slips

At the risk of stating the obvious, breaking an addiction is tough. Some days it can seem like a constant battle to stop yourself sliding back into bad habits. But you can successfully beat it, and a key part of this is being able to deal with the occasional slip – the drink you were not meant to have, or the line of cocaine you thought you had left far behind. Some people take these little stumbles as a sign that they will never be able to quit their habit – and pretty soon they're back to square one. But it does not have to be that way.

Be aware that the odd slip is pretty much inevitable, and don't let it distract you from your overall objective. In other words, get right back on (or off?) that horse!

Other treatments

Support groups

Organizations like Alcoholics Anonymous (AA), Narcotics Anonymous and Nicotine Anonymous all use a 12-step treatment programme designed to achieve total abstinence. There is no point in aiming for moderation, according to this school of thought, because addiction is an incurable physical, psychological and spiritual illness.

AA and its related organizations work primarily through group meetings.

The objective is to get participants to accept that they can't control their drinking and to entrust themselves to a 'greater power' (be it God, AA or something entirely personal). Many thousands of people have beaten their addiction with the help of these groups. At the very least, they offer a ready-made support network of people who understand what you're going through.

Medication

Medication is only used for the most serious alcohol and drug problems. Drinkers might be prescribed Antabuse, which makes them physically ill when they drink alcohol. Drug users are sometimes treated with substitute drugs – the best known of which is methadone, often given to heroin addicts.

But medication plays a much bigger role in helping people give up smoking. It's the nicotine in cigarettes that makes them addictive, and nicotine replacement therapy (NRT) is designed to help smokers cope with the withdrawal symptoms that occur when they give up cigarettes. NRT – available in a variety of forms including patches, gum, tablets, inhalers, and nasal sprays – gives ex-smokers their dose of nicotine, but without the tar, carbon monoxide and dozens of other poisons contained in cigarettes. Once they have got used to living without cigarettes, they can then begin to phase out the NRT. NRT products are available over the counter from a pharmacist or on prescription.

Another option your GP might suggest is a medicine called bupropion (better known by the trade name Zyban), which also works by reducing the symptoms of nicotine withdrawal and, like NRT, can double your chances of successfully giving up smoking, although some people may experience unpleasant side effects.

Related problems

People with addictions often have a previous history of **depression**, **anxiety**, **worry**, **stress** and **trauma**. And it is frequently a vicious circle, because addiction can cause and intensify these problems too.

Drug use can also create susceptibility to feelings of **paranoia** and **hallucinations**.

Where to go for more information

Changing for Good (Avon, 1998) by James Prochaska, John Norcross and Carla Diclemente provides step-by-step guidance on how to transform your life – including overcoming addiction.

Controlling Your Drinking (Guilford Press, 2005) by William Miller and Ricardo Muñoz is an excellent guide for those who want to control, rather than cut out, drinking.

Three titles in Constable & Robinson's 'Overcoming' series highlight the potential of Cognitive Behaviour Therapy (CBT) in dealing with addictions: Marcantonio Spada's *Overcoming Problem Drinking* (2006), Alex Blaszczynski's *Overcoming Compulsive Gambling* (1998) and David Marks' *Overcoming Your Smoking Habit* (2005).

The following are just some of many useful websites:

- ⓘ www.addaction.org.uk, the website of 'Britain's largest specialist drug and alcohol treatment agency'
- ⓘ www.adfam.org.uk provides support for families coping with drug and alcohol addiction
- ⓘ www.smartrecovery.org runs free online and face-to-face support meetings for people with addictions
- ⓘ www.nida.nih.gov, the website of the US National Institute on Drug Abuse
- ⓘ www.ukna.org is the website of the UK branch of Narcotics Anonymous
- ⓘ www.alcoholics-anonymous.org.uk
- ⓘ www.nicotine-anonymous.org
- ⓘ www.gamblersanonymous.org
- ⓘ www.gamcare.org.uk provides support, information, and advice to people with gambling problems
- ⓘ www.quit.org.uk, the website of the UK charity Quit, which helps people to stop smoking; you can also phone the Quitline on 0800 00 22 00
- ⓘ www.givingupsmoking.co.uk is an NHS initiative; their helpline number is 0800 169 0 169.

Anger and Irritation

Holding anger is like grasping a hot coal with the intent of throwing it at someone else; you are the one who gets burned.
The Buddha

Most of us are very familiar with anger and irritation. Anger is a perfectly normal and absolutely fundamental emotion. As every parent knows, even the tiniest baby gets angry – it is part of being human.

Anger takes many forms, of course, from mild irritation to wild rage and all points in between. Generally we get angry with people and irritated by objects and institutions (the tax office, perhaps, as a random example). And, like all emotions, anger affects us on a basic, physiological level: blood pressure and heart rate increase, muscles become tense and we feel 'on edge'.

Everyone has their own ways of expressing anger, but people generally tend to fall into one of two categories. The 'anger-in' person keeps their anger to themselves. While it may sound as though this is a case of admirable self-control, they may well be seething inside – even to the extent of constructing elaborate fantasies of revenge. Anger-ins might also sulk or hide away. 'Anger-out' people, on the other hand, prefer to let rip. They have rows, shout and may even be physically violent.

Whether you're an anger-in or an anger-out person, the crucial thing is to control your emotions. Everyone gets annoyed from time to time, but it is you that must be the boss, not your anger. If not, you run the risk of some unpleasant consequences. Anger can play havoc with your physical health, making you more susceptible to heart disease (see p. 64) and stroke, and it dramatically increases the chance of you having an accident in the car (see p. 56) or at work (one study found that around a third of people injured at work were angry immediately before their accident). It can also ruin relationships at home and at work – all too often it is loved ones who bear the

'You give me road rage ...'

'It's all over the front page, you give me road rage' – so sang the Welsh band Catatonia in 1998.

Aggressive driving is nothing new, but road rage does seem to have been on the increase over the past decade or so. More than 1000 people die each year in road-rage incidents in the US, with aggressive driving cited as a factor in a third of all accident injuries and two-thirds of all fatalities. In the UK, 60 per cent of drivers have admitted to losing their temper while behind the wheel. In one survey, Britain emerged as the worst country in Europe for road rage.

But what is it that turns the average citizen into a raging maniac when they get behind the wheel? Researchers have identified a number of 'risk' factors. Men are more likely to drive aggressively than women, and people under 45 are more prone to road rage than older drivers. Rush hour is a prime road-rage period, and heat, noise, air pollution, road quality and stress all contribute to temper tantrums while driving. Then there is the anonymity of the car, which makes it the perfect vehicle (excuse the pun) in which to take out our frustrations on the world.

Sadly, with car travel continuing to increase around the world, road rage is unlikely to diminish, but here are some things you can do to protect yourself:

- Reduce your stress levels by allowing plenty of time to make your journey.
- Stay calm and polite, no matter how other drivers are behaving.
- Never retaliate.
- Avoid eye contact with an angry driver.
- Apologize if you have annoyed another driver.
- Practise the anger-management skills described on pp. 60–64.

brunt of a temper, sometimes through physical injuries, but more often emotional and psychological problems that persist for years.

Almost all of the problems covered in this book include, at the most severe end of the spectrum, a 'clinical disorder' – something that needs professional help. Interestingly, there is no such thing as 'anger disorder'; extreme anger tends to be seen as a symptom of other problems or, when it spills over into violence, as a matter for the police. But that may change:

anger-related issues are so widespread, and often so serious, that a significant number of mental health professionals are now arguing that it deserves attention in its own right.

How common are anger problems?

We all get annoyed from time to time – as the following statistics amply demonstrate:

- Forty-five per cent of us regularly lose our temper at work.
- Over 80 per cent of British drivers have been involved in road-rage incidents.
- One in 20 of us has had a fight with our neighbours.
- The period from 1997 to 2000 saw a 400 per cent increase in 'air rage' incidents.
- Twenty per cent of Britons have behaved aggressively while shopping. (The figure rises to 33 per cent for young people.)
- Problems with our computer have prompted half of us to hit the machine, throw bits of it around or shout at colleagues.

The most common way of expressing anger is shouting and screaming – 50 per cent of us do this – but only about 5 per cent of people get physically aggressive when they're angry. Men and women get angry just about as often as each other, but men's reactions tend to be more extreme and they're much more likely to fly into a real rage.

Self-assessment

If you're concerned about your levels of anger, have a go at the statements below.

1. A. I do not feel angry.
   B. I feel angry.
   C. I am angry most of the time now.
   D. I am so angry and hostile all the time that I can't stand it.

2. A. I am not particularly angry about my future.
   B. When I think about my future, I feel angry.
   C. I feel angry about what I have to look forward to.
   D. I feel intensely angry about my future, since it cannot be improved.

3. A. It makes me angry that I feel like such a failure.
   B. It makes me angry that I have failed more than the average person.
   C. As I look back on my life, I feel angry about my failures.
   D. It makes me angry to feel like a complete failure as a person.

4. A. I am not all that angry about things.
   B. I am becoming more hostile about things than I used to be.
   C. I am pretty angry about things these days.
   D. I am angry and hostile about everything.

5. A. I don't feel particularly hostile towards others.
   B. I feel hostile a good deal of the time.
   C. I feel quite hostile most of the time.
   D. I feel hostile all of the time.

6. A. I don't feel that others are trying to annoy me.
   B. At times I think people are trying to annoy me.
   C. More people than usual are beginning to make me feel angry.
   D. I feel that others are constantly and intentionally making me angry.

7. A. I don't feel angry when I think about myself.
   B. I feel more angry about myself these days than I used to.
   C. I feel angry about myself a good deal of the time.
   D. When I think about myself, I feel intense anger.

8. A. I don't have angry feelings about others having ruined my life.
   B. It's beginning to make me angry that others are ruining my life.
   C. I feel angry that others prevent me from having a good life.
   D. I am constantly angry because others have made my life totally miserable.

9. A. I don't feel angry enough to hurt someone.
   B. Sometimes I am so angry that I feel like hurting others, but I would not really do it.
   C. My anger is so intense that I sometimes feel like hurting others.
   D. I'm so angry that I would like to hurt someone.

10. A. I don't shout at people any more than usual.
    B. I shout at others more now than I used to.
    C. I shout at people all the time now.
    D. I shout at others so often that sometimes I just can't stop.

11. A. Things are not more irritating to me now than usual.
    B. I feel slightly more irritated now than usual.
    C. I feel irritated a good deal of the time.
    D. I'm irritated all the time now.

12. A. My anger does not interfere with my interest in other people.
    B. My anger sometimes interferes with my interest in others.
    C. I am becoming so angry that I don't want to be around others.
    D. I'm so angry that I can't stand being around people.

13. A. I don't have any persistent angry feelings that influence my ability to make decisions.
    B. My feelings of anger occasionally undermine my ability to make decisions.
    C. I am angry to the extent that it interferes with making good decisions.
    D. I'm so angry that I can't make good decisions any more.

14. A. I'm not so angry and hostile that others dislike me.
    B. People sometimes dislike being around me since I become angry.
    C. More often than not, people stay away from me because I'm so hostile and angry.
    D. People don't like me any more because I'm constantly angry all the time.

15. A. My feelings of anger do not interfere with my work.
    B. From time to time my feelings of anger interfere with my work.
    C. I feel so angry that it interferes with my capacity to work.
    D. My feelings of anger prevent me from doing any work at all.

16. A. My anger does not interfere with my sleep.
    B. Sometimes I don't sleep very well because I'm feeling angry.
    C. My anger is so great that I stay awake 1–2 hours later than usual.
    D. I am so intensely angry that I can't get much sleep during the night.

17. A. My anger does not make me feel any more tired than usual.
    B. My feelings of anger are beginning to tire me out.
    C. My anger is intense enough that it makes me feel very tired.
    D. My feelings of anger leave me too tired to do anything.

18. A. My appetite does not suffer because of my feelings of anger.
    B. My feelings of anger are beginning to affect my appetite.

C. My feelings of anger leave me without much of an appetite.
D. My anger is so intense that it has taken away my appetite.

19. A. My feelings of anger do not interfere with my health.
B. My feelings of anger are beginning to interfere with my health.
C. My anger prevents me from devoting much time and attention to my health.
D. I'm so angry with everything these days that I pay no attention to my health and well-being.

20. A. My ability to think clearly is unaffected by my feelings of anger.
B. Sometimes my feelings of anger prevent me from thinking in a clear-headed way.
C. My anger makes it hard for me to think of anything else.
D. I am so intensely angry and hostile that it completely interferes with my thinking.

21. A. I don't feel so angry that it interferes with my interest in sex.
B. My feelings of anger leave me less interested in sex than I used to be.
C. My current feelings of anger undermine my interest in sex.
D. I'm so angry about my life that I've completely lost interest in sex.

© Snell (1995)

Now add up your score. You get zero for each A, one for B, two for C and three for D.

A score of between zero and 13 indicates that your anger is minimal; between 14 and 19 suggests mild levels of anger. If you've scored 20–28, your anger is at a moderate level; a total of between 29 and 63, on the other hand, suggests severe anger.

HOW TO OVERCOME PROBLEMS WITH ANGER AND IRRITATION

Watch your mood

Keeping your mood happy and positive is a great defence against anger. And you can do a lot to take charge of your own moods, including making

Problems with anger: a personal account

My dad was an angry man and I took after him. I believed I was being strong, standing up for both myself and my family, and not taking any rubbish from anyone. I saw myself as tough but fair, but I found out later that other people just thought I was an aggressive bully. When my wife eventually lost patience and told me a few home truths, I was shocked, but not altogether surprised. I'd begun to realise just how angry I was. I had no close friends, I was too rough on my wife and kids, some nights I couldn't sleep because I was so tense and I knew that if I drank, I was a fist-fight waiting to happen. I knew I couldn't go on like that. I had to find out why I was so furious all the time – and do something about it. I did some reading on the subject, and finally enrolled in an anger-management course. That course was a revelation. After all these years, I finally felt that I was in charge of my anger, and not the other way round.

Doug, aged 40

sure you get enough good-quality sleep, taking regular exercise, avoiding too much alcohol, caffeine or other drugs, eating regularly and well, learning how to cope with stress, having fun and maintaining a strong social life. (Take at look at pages 6–24 for more on these key strategies for a happy and healthy mind.)

Keep an anger diary

Most people are not angry or irritable all the time, but become aggravated by particular events in their daily lives. So if you want to deal with your anger, you need to understand just how and why you get annoyed. The best way to do this is to keep a diary. As soon as you can after any incident, write down what it was that made you angry (the trigger), the thoughts you had at the time and how you acted.

It is also a good idea to include in your diary how you were feeling before you got angry, because your moods play a big part in your reaction to events. The remark from your partner that would have made you furious one day, for example, might hardly make an impression on another occasion, depending on your mood at the time.

Identify the triggers for your anger

One of the benefits of keeping an anger diary is that it will help you to uncover your triggers – the things that drive you to distraction.

Once you have highlighted these triggers you can take steps to tackle your anger, and the first is to explore ways of nipping the offending behaviour in the bud. So if, for example, you identify a colleague's rather blunt way of making a point as a trigger for your anger, you could calmly and assertively (but not aggressively) talk it through with them.

However, being aware of a trigger does not just give you the chance to change other people's behaviour; it also allows you to alter your own response. If you can spot a trigger while it is happening – and also recognize the physical signs of your growing irritation – you can mentally guard yourself against anger. It is much easier to deal with anger in the early stages than once you're fuming.

Work out why a trigger makes you angry

Everyone gets angry, but some people get very much angrier and much more often than others; also, events that would drive some people mad seem utterly trivial to others. This directs us towards a crucial point – that what is most important about anger isn't the situation that provokes it, but the interpretation of that situation.

When you look at your diary entries, see if you can work out what is really behind your reaction to events. Ninety-nine times out of a hundred it's because of taking other people's behaviour personally. If, for example, a person gets angry when someone bumps into them on a station platform, it is probably because they feel the person has been rude and inconsiderate towards them (as opposed to just being in a rush to catch their train). Or if a colleague is late for a meeting, they take it as a sign of disrespect, rather than an indication that the colleague is simply a terrible timekeeper.

Challenge your view of an annoying situation

Once you have identified the thoughts underlying your anger, you can set about challenging them and the errors of interpretation that follow.

Here are some tips on how to do that:

- Review the evidence for and against your view of an annoying situation.
- Ask yourself what other conclusions you could come to.
- Try to be more accepting of other people. Accept life as it is, develop your tolerance and focus on the good things in life rather than the annoying ones.
- Imagine what a trusted friend would tell you, or how you would advise a friend in a similar situation.
- Talk it over and let it go; dwelling on it only keeps it alive, and that does no one any good. The time to get your anger off your chest is once you have calmed down. By then you'll probably find that it has disappeared completely, but if something is still bothering you it is often a good idea to talk it over with the person who made you cross. When you have that conversation, you need to stay calm. Try not to blame the other person; concentrate on helping them to see what irritated you and discussing with them how it can be avoided in the future. Of course, it isn't always possible to have this type of talk. So speak to friends about the situation, learn whatever lessons you can from it, and then let your anger go.

Once you have thought of a more positive way to interpret a given trigger, make sure you try it out the next time you're faced with it.

Change your response

Anger involves a chain reaction. First of all something happens (the trigger). Then an interpretation of the situation is formed, usually drawing on some pretty deep-rooted views of other people and the world in general. Then comes the response, perhaps in the form of shouting or throwing things.

If you're unable to defuse your anger by dealing with the trigger, you need to make sure that your response is as constructive as possible. So before you wade in, take 'time out'. Some people do this by visualizing a big red 'Stop!' sign, or you could try a relaxation exercise (see p. 359) or repeating a calming phrase to yourself (maybe 'Relax' or 'Don't rise to the bait'). Imagine how someone you admire would behave, or try and do something distracting – perhaps going for a run or a swim, getting on with some chores or even going somewhere quiet and private and having a good old yell!

Curb your temper and save your life

We all recognize the stereotype: the red-faced, overweight, bad-tempered businessman struck down by a deadly heart attack in the middle of his latest (and last) rant.

But as it turns out, there is more than a little truth in this image, and numerous research projects have revealed a link between excessive anger and coronary heart disease. In fact, it's been argued that anger is more of a risk than smoking, high blood pressure and high cholesterol. Anger stops the heart working efficiently, possibly because it overstimulates our immune system, causing inflammation and clogging of the arteries.

One study tracked 374 young US adults over a 10-year period and found that those with high levels of anger and hostility showed early signs of heart disease. Another study, this time involving medical students, suggested that individuals who were often angry were seven times more likely to die by the age of 50 than students with lower levels of anger.

Incidentally, and contrary to popular belief, 'venting' your anger at the person who has annoyed you is not a great idea. Rather than calming you down, it will only intensify your feelings.

Related problems

Anger is a factor in a range of problems, either contributing to or resulting from **stress, insomnia, addictions, trauma, depression** and **relationship difficulties.**

Where to go for more information?

Anger Management for Dummies (Wiley, 2007) by W. Doyle Gentry is an entertaining and very accessible guide to the topic.

William Davies' excellent *Overcoming Anger and Irritability* (Constable & Robinson, 2000) takes you through anger-management techniques drawn from Cognitive Behaviour Therapy (CBT).

On the Internet, check out:

ⓘ www.angermanage.co.uk, a site run by the British Association of Anger Management.

Anxiety

In this section you'll find information about all the major anxiety problems. For general advice on when to consult a therapist, medication for anxiety and related problems, turn to p. 124.

FEARS AND PHOBIAS

Aretha Franklin has a fear of flying; Madonna is scared of thunder; and Johnny Depp is afraid of spiders, ghosts and clowns...

Nearly everyone is afraid of something, but for some of us that fear can develop into a phobia – an intense feeling of fright and anxiety that is out of all proportion to the reality of the threat that faces us.

A phobia will strike each time a sufferer is faced with the situation (or object) they dread – or even when they just think about facing it. They might worry about being harmed – for example, falling from a great height or being bitten by a dog; or they might be terrified of how they will react (perhaps by panicking or losing control) – afraid, that is, of the fear itself.

Consequently, they will do all they can to avoid the situation in question.

Fears can be pretty unpleasant, and you may well want to tackle yours using the techniques below, but a phobia can really interfere with day-to-day life.

There are hundreds of different fears and phobias but they all fall into one of five main categories:

- **Animal phobias** – these include insects and usually start in childhood.
- **Natural environment phobias** – for example fear of storms, heights, water. Again, these normally begin in childhood.
- **Blood/injection/injury phobias** – these include fear of seeing blood or an injury, or of having an injection or similar medical procedure. People who panic when afraid often feel as though they're going to faint when, in fact, they won't: fainting happens when our blood pressure drops and panic *raises* our blood pressure. Not so, however, for blood/injection/injury phobias, which do actually lower our blood pressure and often result in fainting. This type of phobia very often runs in families.
- **Situational phobias** – for example fear of flying, enclosed spaces, public transport, tunnels, bridges, elevators and driving. Situational phobias tend to take hold in childhood or in our mid-twenties.
- **Other phobias** – which include everything else! Common phobias in this category are fear of choking and of catching an illness – as opposed to hypochondriasis, the fear of actually being ill (see pp. 119–23).

What causes a fear or a phobia? In some cases, there may be an evolutionary basis; an acute fear of wild animals, for example, might have made the difference between life and death for our ancestors. Closer to home, a phobia is sometimes triggered by a bad experience – such as a dog bite in childhood or a frightening plane trip. Or it may have its roots in something observed: maybe a family member has panicked in a particular situation or actually come to harm. Fears and phobias can be the product of our upbringing: we learn from our parents to be wary of animals, or storms or – in some cases – everything. And sometimes we pick up on whatever is scaring society at the time. Cases of illness phobia, for instance, increased significantly in the wake of the AIDS epidemic.

How common are fears and phobias?

Most of us are afraid of something: around 25 per cent of people are afraid of snakes, 12 per cent have a fear of heights and about 11 per cent are scared of flying. When it comes to phobias, the numbers are smaller, but they're still pretty significant. Eleven per cent of us will suffer from a phobia at some point in our lives, making it one of the most widespread psychological problems in the world.

Women are twice as likely as men to develop phobias. No one knows why this is, although it has been suggested that the apparent imbalance between the sexes is due to men's reluctance to admit to their fears.

The most common phobias are:

- Animals (zoophobia): 5.7 per cent
- Heights (acrophobia): 5.3 per cent
- Blood (haemophobia): 4.5 per cent
- Enclosed spaces (claustrophobia): 4.2 per cent
- Water (hydrophobia): 3.5 per cent
- Flying (aviophobia): 3.5 per cent

As you may have spotted, the percentage of sufferers in this list alone adds up to more than 11 per cent – that is because having one phobia makes it much more likely that you'll have others.

Problems with fears and phobias: a personal account

Near where I grew up was a Norman castle, which I visited with my class when I was eight. It had three enormous towers and you could climb up one of them, via a long, spiral stone staircase. My best friend started to panic as we went up. By the time we got to the top, she was crying and moaning – really hysterical. I was shocked. I thought she might throw herself off or something. I think that's what triggered my fear of heights. I was terrified that I'd react in the same way. Even the sight of a tall building upset me. I thought I was going to freak out. I wouldn't visit friends who lived

*in flats. I had to sit in the stalls at the cinema or theatre. But when
I left a job because I couldn't bear working on the fifteenth floor,
that was the last straw for me. I plucked up courage to go and see
my GP, and she recommended a really good therapist. It only took a
few sessions, but gradually the therapist got me used to being up
high. It's incredible, but all that fear has completely left me now.*
Lisa, aged 29

Self-assessment

How can you tell whether a fear is actually a fully fledged phobia? A good
way to start is by answering the following questions:

Do you experience intense fear when you are in certain situations,
or when you think about being in those situations?   Yes/No

Do you immediately become anxious when you are in these
situations?   Yes/No

Do you think your fear is excessive or unreasonable?   Yes/No

Do you try to avoid the situation you are afraid of?   Yes/No

Does your fear or anxiety interfere significantly with your
day-to-day life?   Yes/No

If you answered 'Yes' to all five of these questions, you probably have a
phobia.

HOW TO OVERCOME FEARS AND PHOBIAS

Fears and phobias are widespread, but they're also very treatable. In fact,
we now have a method of dealing with them that is almost always successful. It's called 'exposure' and involves getting you to spend time in precisely
the situations you dread the most.

An A–Z of phobias

… or almost – there are literally hundreds of phobias, but we're not aware of any beginning with the letters Q or Y. If you can fill those gaps, do write and let us know! In the meantime, here's a small but entertaining sample, courtesy of www.phobialist.com:

PHOBIA	FEAR OF
Arachibutyrophobia	Peanut butter sticking to the roof of your mouth
Batrachophobia	Frogs
Consecotaleophobia	Chopsticks
Decidophobia	Making decisions
Epistaxiophobia	Nosebleeds
Febriphobia	Fever
Genuphobia	Knees
Hippopotomonstrosesquippedaliophobia	Long words
Iatrophobia	Visiting the doctor
Japanophobia	Japan and Japanese people
Kenophobia	Empty spaces
Liticaphobia	Lawsuits
Musophobia	Mice
Nomatophobia	Names
Odontophobia	Teeth
Panophobia	Everything
Rhytiphobia	Getting wrinkles
Soceraphobia	Parents-in-law
Thalassophobia	Sea
Uranophobia	Heaven
Venustraphobia	Beautiful women
Wiccaphobia	Witches
Xyrophobia	Razors
Zoophobia	Animals

Exposure

The idea of exposure may sound scary, and you may well have a few uncomfortable moments along the way. But if you stick with it, you will learn to cope with your fear and, in time, conquer it. (Exposure isn't always practical for some phobias – like long-distance flights, for instance. But there are very successful alternatives, based on the exposure model, including virtual reality, visualization and specially designed courses.)

To work properly, exposure needs to be done regularly, for at least 45 minutes 3–5 times a week, and systematically. Begin by drawing up a list of the situations you find frightening, and rank them in order of how stressful they are for you. So if, for example, you have a fear of spiders, your list might run like this:

Least stressful	Looking at pictures of spiders
	Looking at small spiders in a jar
	Having a small spider on my hand
	Looking at a large spider in a jar
Most stressful	Having a large spider on my hand

Start with the least frightening task on the list and, when you're comfortable with it, move on to the next one. Give each task a score from 0 to 10 for scariness before you do it, and then update that score after you have accomplished it. (You'll probably be surprised at how different the two scores are.) You may find it helpful to have a friend work through the list with you, so that they do the task first and you follow.

You're bound to feel some anxiety at each stage, but try to stick with it. If you feel your fear is getting out of hand at any point, take a break from that particular task. Maybe go back to the previous task, or try an intermediate one. And don't feel like you have failed: almost everyone finds it tough from time to time. Move through the list as fast as you feel able to, and no quicker.

As you work through the exposure (sometimes known as desensitization) process, ask yourself what it is that you dread most about the situations you're afraid of. Are you worried about fainting, losing control or, perhaps, dying? After a few exposure sessions, you'll see that those things are not going to happen.

Avoid safety behaviours

Generally, people with fears and phobias 'deal' with them simply by avoiding the situation or object that scares them. But what about when you simply have to fly or you really need that injection? Most people have a range of 'safety behaviours' that they adopt to get them through the experience – they might have a couple of drinks and take a Valium before getting on the plane and pray constantly when they're in the air; or maybe they will persuade a friend to come with them to the doctor.

Work out what your safety behaviours are and try not to use them in your exposure sessions. This will help you to learn that it isn't your safety behaviours that prevent you from coming to any harm; it's the fact that the situation isn't a dangerous one in the first place.

Instead of using your safety behaviours, try to ride out your anxiety. Keep on reminding yourself that you're perfectly safe – that it is just your phobia up to its usual tricks. Aim to become a detached observer: you could even make notes on how you're feeling, as if you were conducting a scientific experiment (and in a sense you're doing just that). Watch the waves of your anxiety build and then, steadily, recede. This can be tricky at first but you will get the hang of it.

If you have a blood/injection/injury phobia and are liable to faint, you need to combine exposure with exercises designed to raise your blood pressure, known as applied muscle tension. It's a good idea to learn these with a therapist and to do so before embarking on exposure. Applied muscle tension involves tensing your arm muscles for 20 seconds, then your chest for another 20 seconds, stopping for 30 seconds, then tensing your leg muscles for 20 seconds. You repeat the cycle for five minutes. Once you have mastered it, this is a great way to combat feelings of faintness.

Reward yourself

Last, but definitely not least, give yourself a little reward each time you complete an exposure session; you will have earned it.

Where to go for more information

Warren Mansell's *Coping with Fears and Phobias* (Oneworld, 2007) is an excellent step-by-step guide to the topic.

The Anxiety and Phobia Workbook (New Harbinger, 2005) by Edmund Bourne offers comprehensive practical advice on coping with anxiety-related problems, including fears and phobias.

On the Internet, look at:

- ⓘ www.anxietyuk.org.uk and
- ⓘ www.adaa.org, which is run by the Anxiety Disorders Association of America.

ⓘ Triumph over Phobia, at www.topuk.org, organizes a UK network of self-help groups.

Also worth a look is www.algy.com/anxiety

ⓘ For a flying phobia, check out www.aviatours.indigo-2.com

ⓘ www.needlephobia.co.uk needs no explanation!

PANIC

Courage is resistance to fear, mastery of fear – not absence of fear.
Mark Twain

For most people, the word 'panic' describes a brief but disconcerting feeling of anxiety. It is a reaction to not being able to find your passport at the airport, for example, or on having deleted a crucial file on the computer.

Experiences like this are not a million miles away from true panic, but they're a watered-down version. Real panic involves intense fear and a horrible feeling of being on edge. There are usually lots of unpleasant physical sensations too, among them shortness of breath, sweating, chest pains, trembling, a choking sensation, dizziness, numbness, tingling in the limbs, nausea and chills and hot flushes. A heart rate might rise by up to 20 beats per minute.

As if that were not enough, panic brings with it a range of frightening thoughts – you might feel that you're about to faint or collapse, that you're going mad or even that you're dying. A panic attack can develop very quickly (which is scary in itself) and normally lasts for around 10 to 20 minutes, although it can seem, at the time, as if it will never end.

Clearly, panic is a very unpleasant experience. But it is not entirely without purpose: panic is the legacy of our ancient in-built response to danger, firing us up to run away or fight for our lives (the fight-or-flight response). But panic can also be the fear that grips us when there is really nothing to be afraid of. It's an early warning system gone wrong, like a fire alarm that goes off as soon as the sun comes out.

While many people experience the occasional panic attack, a small proportion develop what is known as Panic Disorder (PD). This involves recurring and unexpected panic attacks, followed by a month or more of:

- fear of another panic attack
- worry about what the attacks mean (concerns about a heart problem or brain tumour, for instance, or even of going mad)
- changes in behaviour because of the attacks (for example, giving up exercise because of associating the breathlessness it causes with panic).

Some people have panic attacks in particular situations – when they see a spider, or if they think about being at a great height. These attacks are, however, a symptom of their phobia, while those that strike people with PD are much less closely connected to specific triggers.

Agoraphobia is often a feature of PD. Most of us think of agoraphobia as a fear of open spaces, but in fact it covers any place or situation in which we worry that we will be unable to cope if we have a panic attack (some agoraphobics, for example, are afraid of being at home on their own).

Panic Disorder is no fun at all. Sufferers can become irritable and withdrawn. Frequently, they're depressed; they might be reluctant to leave the house, or will give up hobbies and social activities in case they have a panic attack – all of which can play havoc with their careers and close relationships.

How common is Panic Disorder?

Although around one in five of us has had an unexpected panic attack, generally at times of stress, Panic Disorder affects only about 2 per cent of the population at any one time. Roughly 5 per cent of people will go through a bout of PD at some point in their lives and it usually develops at a time of major challenges, such as bereavement, divorce or illness. Most PD sufferers also become agoraphobic.

Panic Disorder and agoraphobia are much more common in women (accounting for around two-thirds of cases), and PD is twice as common in the 25–44 age group as among people aged 45–64. People with PD often experience attacks at night, usually in the early hours of the morning.

PD seems to run in the family, with first-degree relatives of people with PD being up to eight times more likely to develop PD themselves. However, it isn't clear to what extent this is due to genetic influence as opposed to upbringing.

Problems with panic: a personal account

I started having panic attacks when I was 24. I'd feel a bit edgy and anxious. Then within a few seconds I couldn't breathe. I thought I was dying. It was terrifying. I'd have these panics a couple of times a week. I underwent medical tests which showed there was nothing physically wrong with me, but the next time I had an attack, I was still convinced I was about to die. I hated being on my own in case I fell ill. I dreaded being among a group of people in case they saw me having an attack. And I didn't like going out, so my social life petered out. Looking back, I think the panics were caused by intense stress. I was grieving for my mother, who'd just died, a close friend had been badly injured in a car accident and I was trying to make a go of a career as a teacher. It was only when I began to acknowledge all this that I began to get a hold on my panic.

Megan, aged 30

How fast is your heart beating?

People with Panic Disorder generally spend a lot of time monitoring themselves for the symptoms of an imminent attack (feeling hot or out of breath, for example). But are they any better than other people at sensing what is really going on in their bodies?

Psychologists Anke Ehlers and Peter Breuer decided to test this by asking a range of volunteers, including 120 PD sufferers, to count their heartbeat silently (they were not allowed to take their pulse). What they found was that those with PD were indeed much more accurate in their estimates than the other participants. And subsequent research has found that the same is true for children with panic problems.

But this is not necessarily a good thing. Because they're more sensitive to bodily sensations, people with PD may spot irregularities in their heartbeat that are perfectly normal and that most people never notice. And they're likely to misinterpret them too – as a sign of a heart attack, for instance. From there, it's just a short step to a full-blown panic attack.

Self-assessment

If you're worried that you might be suffering from Panic Disorder, have a go at this self-assessment exercise.

1. In the past 6 months, have you ever had a spell or an attack when all of a sudden you felt frightened, anxious or very uneasy?   Yes/No

2. In the past 6 months, have you ever had a spell or attack when for no reason your heart suddenly began to race, you felt faint or you could not catch your breath?   Yes/No

If you answered 'Yes' to question 1 or question 2, continue with the questionnaire. Otherwise, stop.

3. Did any of these spells or attacks ever happen in a situation when you were not in danger or not the centre of attention?   Yes/No

4. How many times have you had a spell or attack in the past month? (Select one.)
   - Hasn't happened at all in the past month.
   - Once.
   - 2–3 times.
   - 4–10 times.
   - More than 10 times.

5. In the past month, how worried have you been that spells or attacks might happen again? (Select one.)
   - Not at all worried.
   - Somewhat worried.
   - Very worried.

© Lippincott, Williams & Wilkins (1999)

People with Panic Disorder typically answer 'Yes' to questions 1–3, have had an attack at least once in the past month and have worried about another attack.

How to Overcome Problems with Panic

Panic attacks sometimes have physical causes (for instance, inner ear or thyroid problems), so start by seeing your GP to rule out any underlying medical issues.

Stress can play a big part in panic attacks; for information on how to cope with it see pp. 355–60. Make sure also that you follow the steps for happy and healthy living as outlined on pp. 6–24 – get plenty of good-quality sleep, take regular exercise and eat well. And avoid too much alcohol, caffeine and other drugs – overdoing them is sometimes enough to trigger panic attacks.

Now let's look at specific techniques to tackle panic attacks.

Get to know your panic

As with most of the problems discussed in this book, the first step towards tackling panic attacks is to understand them. And the best way to do that is to keep a panic diary. Write down when and where an attack took place, how intense it was, how you were feeling before the panic struck, and what you felt and thought during the attack and after it.

Try to pinpoint exactly what it was that you were afraid of, the worst-case scenario that you thought might happen. A heart attack? Making a fool of yourself? Losing control? Because the key lesson when it comes to coping with anxiety is realizing that these things won't happen.

When people panic, they misinterpret the physical signs (pounding heart, breathlessness and so on) as evidence of impending doom – which only makes them panic more. As you become familiar with the techniques in this section you'll gradually get used to these feelings and see that, unpleasant though they may be, they are temporary and harmless.

Identify your behaviours

Ask yourself why the thing you dreaded didn't happen. Why didn't you faint during your panic attack? How is it that you're still alive?

Many people with PD assume that disaster was only averted because they managed to take action in time – perhaps by getting out of the situation or calling a friend. These are what psychologists call safety behaviours. We may think they're helping us but, in fact, all they do is prevent us from finding out that we would have been fine without them.

If, for example, you're afraid that you're going to faint, you might sit down or hold on to something to avoid keeling over. And sure enough, you won't faint. But that isn't because you sat down; it's because you cannot faint in a panic attack. Fainting happens when your blood pressure drops, whereas in a panic attack your blood pressure rockets. But unless you drop your safety behaviours, you will never know. Many people also hyperventilate (or 'overbreathe') during an attack, which means taking lots of short, shallow breaths. This causes a reduction in the amount of carbon dioxide in the bloodstream and can make you feel dizzy or as if you're about to faint. Again, relax – it is not going to happen.

Using breathing exercises to calm yourself down is another safety behaviour – try to tough it out without them; otherwise you'll never see that your panic attack can't harm you.

Challenge your fears

Now that you have identified your fears, and spotted your safety behaviours, you can set about challenging them. Here are some tried-and-tested ways of doing this:

- Write down the evidence for and against your fears. For example, you might believe that you're going to have a heart attack because you feel chest pains. But what about the fact that you have been thoroughly checked out by a doctor and there are no signs of heart problems?
- Talk to other people about your experiences.
- Imagine what you would tell a friend in a similar position.
- Try to come up with alternative explanations for the way you think and feel during an attack.
- Find out as much as you can about panic attacks. The more you understand them, the less scary they will seem.
- Remind yourself that you're not going to come to any harm when you panic. As we have seen, you won't faint.

Learn to ride out a panic attack

Your panic attack is just a temporary blip. It doesn't mean you're ill or insane. And remember: the way you're feeling is solely the product of your panic – not of anything more sinister. You're not going to come to harm.

So when you feel panic building, don't try to escape the situation or let it overwhelm you, and don't resort to any of your safety behaviours. Instead, learn to face down your fears. Get used to the way you feel when you panic, ride it out and be confident that the attack will soon pass. It's not easy, and it takes practice, but you'll get there in the end.

Try talking yourself through a panic attack: 'Bring it on – I can cope'; 'I can do this – nothing is going to hurt me'. Become a detached observer or imagine that what you're going through is a harmless scientific experiment. You might even want to note down how you're feeling while it is happening – this is a great way of putting distance between yourself and the attack.

Some people find it helps to use what is called a 'mindful' approach. This means acknowledging your thoughts and feelings, but not dwelling on them; instead, you simply let them go.

Some therapy is based on deliberately provoking the sensations of panic; done gradually and systematically, this is a really effective way of getting people used to their panic and demonstrating that they can cope with it.

Combat your agoraphobia

Most people with serious panic problems also have to deal with agoraphobia. The way to beat it is to learn to cope with precisely the situations you have been avoiding.

Start by drawing up a list of places you find difficult to handle, and give each one a score for how stressful you find them. Then work your way through the list, starting with the least stressful, and gradually increasing the amount of time you spend in the situation. Try not to rush: it is better to make steady progress than to take on more than you're ready for.

Combine your trip out with a treat (maybe meeting a friend or buying something you want from the shops). That way it seems less like a chore and more like fun. And aim to be outside for at least 20 minutes. You're bound to feel some anxiety at first, so you need to allow enough time for that to die down.

(This technique can be used to help you deal with any situation you find stressful, not just agoraphobia.)

Reward yourself

Coping with a panic attack is a big achievement. So once you have done it, celebrate by doing something you enjoy. And after an attack has finished, don't try to escape: stay where you are and carry on doing whatever it was you were up to before you were so rudely interrupted.

Where to go for more information

Panic Disorder: The Facts (OUP, 2004) by Stanley Rachman and Padmal de

Silva provides lots of sensible advice on how to cope with panic attacks.

Overcoming Panic (Constable & Robinson, 1997) by Derrick Silove and Vijaya Manicavasagar presents a Cognitive Behaviour Therapy (CBT) approach to dealing with panic. CBT has proved highly effective at helping people with panic problems, and the advice in this book draws on it.

Among many useful websites are:

- ⓘ www.nopanic.org.uk
- ⓘ www.nomorepanic.co.uk
- ⓘ www.adaa.org (run by the Anxiety Disorders Association of America)
- ⓘ www.freedomfromfear.org
- ⓘ www.anxietynetwork.com.

OBSESSIONS AND COMPULSIONS

Obsession is the single most wasteful human activity, because with an obsession you keep coming back and back and back to the same question and never get an answer.
Norman Mailer

Have you ever left the house and then hurried back, maybe several times, to check that you locked the front door? Have you ever found yourself unpacking your bag – yet again – on the way to the airport in case you have forgotten your passport? How about strange thoughts that pop into your mind, as if from nowhere?

Nearly everyone has experiences like this from time to time, and usually they're not a problem. But for a small proportion of people, these thoughts and urges can really dominate their lives, developing into an incredibly powerful and distressing set of worries and rituals known collectively as obsessive–compulsive disorder, or OCD for short.

We all use the term 'obsession' quite loosely to describe a keen interest in something – 'he is obsessed with football', for example – but the obsessions involved in OCD are entirely different. They are upsetting and unwanted thoughts, images and impulses that recur over and over again, sometimes throughout the day and night. They are so upsetting, in fact,

Problems with obsessions and compulsions: a personal account

When I was 22, my mother was badly injured in a traffic accident. For two weeks, I spent almost every minute of the day at the hospital. I prayed, and also developed lots of counting rituals. First thing in the morning, I'd have to count to a thousand before I spoke to anyone. Every hour I had to count backwards from a hundred. I had sequences of numbers that I constantly ran through in my mind. I knew I was being daft, but I couldn't stop myself. I thought my mother might die if I did. Thankfully, she recovered. But I didn't stop praying or counting; in fact, the prayers and counting rituals grew so long that I had to write them down in a notebook! I got up at 5 a.m. so I could fit them in before work. I didn't go out in the evening because I didn't have time. Eventually, I went to see my GP because I was so exhausted and depressed, and I found myself telling her all about what had been going on. It was such a release finally to share my problems with someone!
Jane, aged 26

that people with OCD use a variety of elaborate and time-consuming rituals to make them go away: these rituals are called compulsions.

Obsessions typically involve:

- a fear of contamination from dirt or germs
- unwanted aggressive thoughts (perhaps about dropping or harming your baby, for example)
- upsetting sexual fantasies
- blasphemous thoughts
- worries about breaking social rules (shouting in church, for instance)
- doubts about whether you have done something properly (turned off the oven, written an email without spelling mistakes, spoken to someone without offending them)
- fears about losing things.

The most common compulsions are:

- washing and cleaning (generally as a response to an obsession with contamination)
- checking (usually because of obsessive doubts)
- arranging objects in a particular way
- repeating actions or thoughts (for example, counting or praying) a specific number of times
- hoarding (because of fears about losing things).

Sometimes, there is a logical connection between a compulsion and an obsession (as above), while in other cases there is no obvious rhyme or reason (for example, a person might perform counting rituals to prevent their loved ones from coming to harm). The vast majority of people with obsessions also have compulsions, but each can occur independently of the other.

Generally, obsessions revolve around fears about our own safety or the safety or feelings of others (people with OCD often have a really intense feeling of responsibility for the welfare of others). Instead of living with the small level of risk that's inevitable in life, sufferers become locked in a constant – and futile – battle to remove this uncertainty.

A person is likely to be diagnosed with OCD if:

- they regularly have unwanted and inappropriate thoughts, impulses or images, which:
  - are distressing, and not simply exaggerated worries about real-life problems
  - they try to ignore or suppress
  - they recognize as the product of their own mind
- they engage in repetitive and ritualistic actions or thoughts (compulsions, in other words) in response to their obsessions
- their compulsions are aimed at reducing the distress caused by the obsessions, or at preventing some dreaded event, but are excessive and unrealistic
- they have recognized that the obsessions or compulsions are unreasonable (this recognition often comes and goes, depending on how the person is feeling)
- their obsessions or compulsions cause significant distress, take up more than an hour a day or have a major impact on the person's normal life.

In its severest form, OCD can be devastating, taking up so much of the sufferer's time that they are unable to carry on their normal life. (It is not uncommon for someone with fears about contamination, for example, to spend many hours washing and showering each day.)

OCD can have a huge impact on loved ones too. Not only do people with OCD seek constant reassurance that things are all right – that the thing they fear is not going to happen – they can also seek to impose their rules and rituals on those they live with. The divorce and separation rates for people with OCD are some of the highest for any psychological problem. Happily, however, there is now a very successful therapy for OCD (as you'll see below).

How common are obsessions and compulsions?

There's nothing unusual about intrusive thoughts. In fact, 80 per cent of us have experienced them. It is estimated that the average person has around 4000 thoughts each day, of which 13 per cent are spontaneous (they just appear in our minds without us intending them to). Many of these spontaneous thoughts are similar to those that preoccupy people with OCD: they're bizarre, out of character and sometimes shocking. In one study, 50 per cent of people reported unwanted thoughts about hurting a family member, 32 per cent had imagined holding up a bank and 25 per cent had found themselves thinking about a 'disgusting act of intercourse'.

However, OCD is much less common, affecting around 3 per cent of people at some point in their lives. Generally it begins quite early, somewhere between early adolescence and the mid-20s. And unlike a lot of other anxiety problems, it affects men and women more or less equally.

Self-assessment

Everyone has obsessive thoughts from time to time, but if you're wondering whether you should talk to someone about OCD, have a go at this self-assessment exercise. When you answer the questions, think back to your experiences over the past month.

	Not at all	A little bit	Some-what	Very much	Extremely
1. I have saved up so many things that they get in the way.	0	1	2	3	4
2. I check things more often than necessary.	0	1	2	3	4
3. I get upset if objects are not arranged properly.	0	1	2	3	4
4. I feel compelled to count while I am doing things.	0	1	2	3	4
5. I find it difficult to touch an object when I know it has been touched by strangers or certain people.	0	1	2	3	4
6. I find it difficult to control my own thoughts.	0	1	2	3	4
7. I collect things I don't need.	0	1	2	3	4
8. I repeatedly check doors, windows, drawers, etc.	0	1	2	3	4
9. I get upset if others change the way I have arranged things.	0	1	2	3	4
10. I feel I have to repeat certain numbers.	0	1	2	3	4
11. I sometimes have to wash or clean myself simply because I feel contaminated.	0	1	2	3	4
12. I am upset by unpleasant thoughts that come into my mind against my will.	0	1	2	3	4

	Not at all	A little bit	Some- what	Very much	Extremely
13. I avoid throwing things away because I am afraid I might need them later.	0	1	2	3	4
14. I repeatedly check gas and water taps and light switches after turning them off.	0	1	2	3	4
15. I need things to be arranged in a particular order.	0	1	2	3	4
16. I feel that there are good and bad numbers.	0	1	2	3	4
17. I wash my hands more often and for longer than necessary.	0	1	2	3	4
18. I frequently get nasty thoughts and have difficulty in getting rid of them.	0	1	2	3	4

Questionnaire reproduced by permission of Edna B. Foa 2002.

Now add up your score. A total of 21 or above indicates possible OCD.

How to Overcome Obsessions and Compulsions

. . . .

The best way out is always through.
Robert Frost

. . . .

OCD is often so unpleasant that sufferers will do all they can to get rid of their obsessions. Which is where the compulsions come in, bringing short-term relief. Some people also avoid situations that trigger their worries, and try to distract themselves when their intrusive thoughts appear. They often try to stop or suppress the thoughts entirely. Unfortunately, not only do these strategies fail, they actually strengthen the obsessions' grip. One study, for example, found that some people with OCD spend upwards of three and a half hours a day trying to suppress their unwanted thoughts. Usually, these efforts are futile, and worse still, the failure makes them feel even more upset and down.

But there is a way out of OCD – a method that has proven extremely successful, even for people affected by the most debilitating form of the problem. You can use it on your own, but because OCD can be a severe problem it may be best to seek help from a trained cognitive behaviour therapist. (Your doctor may also suggest medication.)

By way of preparation for the therapy, start keeping a diary. Just note down each day – very briefly – how much time you have spent on your obsessions and compulsions. This is a great way to track your progress as you set about dealing with your OCD.

There are two parts to the therapy:

1. Understanding how obsessions and compulsions work

Obsessions and compulsions develop because we misinterpret an unwanted thought. Everyone has these thoughts, but few of us give them any attention. OCD begins when a person believes that a thought is actually significant – that they really might catch cancer if they don't wash thoroughly after coming into contact with other people, or that they're a risk to their child because they suddenly have an image of themselves striking him or her. These thoughts are so uncomfortable and distressing that, naturally, they will do anything to make them go away, for example by acting out their compulsions. But, as we have seen, these strategies only lock the person into the obsession and every attempt to forget the thoughts ends up being a reminder of them.

Having understood how obsessions and compulsions function, we can then set about changing the way in which we think about our unwanted thoughts. Remember that everyone has these thoughts: imagine that they're so much rubbish drifting through your mind. They are meaningless. You don't have to control them, and having them does not make you a bad person (if it did, we would all be bad). Having a thought does not mean you're going to act on it. There is a world of difference between doing something and just thinking about it.

And try not to take any notice of the thoughts predicting disaster if you don't shower eight times a day or check repeatedly that you have turned off all electrical appliances before you leave the house. None of us can ever be 100 per cent risk-free and no one can be 100 per cent certain that they have done a task perfectly. And it's not worth the time and trouble it takes to try. Once is enough.

OCD and the aviator

Howard Hughes (1905–76) was a colossal figure in the world of business, particularly aviation and Hollywood movies. He produced the seminal gangster film *Scarface*, set numerous air-speed records, designed ground-breaking aircraft and ran the giant US airline TWA. Hughes, who died a billionaire, has been the subject of dozens of books and several films, notably Martin Scorsese's Oscar-winning *The Aviator*.

But Howard Hughes is probably just as famous – or rather notorious – for his OCD. His mother – also apparently obsessed by cleanliness and disease – may have been an influence, but whatever the causes, in later life Hughes' OCD reached crippling proportions. Petrified by the threat of contamination, he insisted that any object he handled be covered with several layers of tissue paper and cellophane. Any aide who needed to wake him was instructed to do so by pinching his toes – but only through eight layers of tissue paper.

And the procedure for fetching his hearing aid cord was almost as complex as some of his aircraft designs. First, again using several layers of tissues, the bathroom door was opened and the taps turned on to draw warm water. More tissues were deployed to remove a new bar of soap from a cupboard. The aide was then required to wash his hands thoroughly, but without touching either the taps or any part of the sink. New tissues – and plenty of them – were used to open the cabinet where the hearing aid was stored in a sealed envelope. Nothing in the cabinet was to be touched except the envelope, which was to be removed using 15 tissues in each hand and with only the central part of the tissue coming into contact with the envelope...

2. Exposing yourself to the situations you dread ...

... without using any of the techniques you deploy to cope with them (your compulsions, for example). This sounds stressful, so why would you want to put yourself through it? Well, it is a brilliant way to learn that the situations you fear are in reality no threat at all. Gradually, you will see that your obsessive thoughts are not to be trusted: you're not in any danger. Your distress will ease, and with it, your need to tackle it using your compulsions.

Exposure has to be done in a controlled and systematic way, and it is often a good idea to have the support of a trusted friend or family member. Draw up a list of the situations that you find difficult, and rank them in order of stressfulness. Here's an example for someone who is afraid of catching an illness from dirt and germs:

Least stressful	Touching a door handle
	Sharing a seat on public transport
	Shaking hands with a stranger
	Having a stranger come into my home
Most stressful	Using a public toilet

Start with a task that you find challenging but bearable and expose yourself to it repeatedly without resorting to your compulsions or any other behaviour that makes you feel safer. You need to meet your fear head on – it's the only way you'll break through it – and once you have mastered one task, work your way through the list. But don't stop doing the easier ones.

It is really important that you stay with a task long enough for your anxiety to subside. That way you'll learn that the situation is not really threatening. And the exposure sessions need to be regular – aim for at least four times a week.

If real-life exposure is not practical, imaginary exposure is a good option. Try describing in writing a stressful situation and reading it through repeatedly to stimulate the feelings you would have if you were actually there. Even better: make a recording of your description and play it back to yourself.

Exposure works, but it can be difficult, especially at first – after all, you're facing down your fear. Move through your list at your own pace and stick with it.

Reward yourself

Make sure you reward yourself when you complete an exposure session – you will have earned it. Oh, and give some thought to what you're going to do with all the extra time you'll have once you have completely conquered your OCD.

Where to go for more information

There are a number of excellent self-help titles for OCD sufferers, including:

Obsessive–Compulsive Disorder: The Facts (OUP, 2004) by Padmal de Silva and Stanley Rachman; *Overcoming Obsessive Thoughts* (New Harbinger, 2005) by Christine Purdon and David Clark; *Overcoming Compulsive Checking* and *Overcoming Compulsive Washing* (New Harbinger, 2004 and 2005 respectively) by Paul Munford; *Stop Obsessing!* (Bantam, 2001) by Edna Foa and Reid Wilson.

On the Internet, have a look at:

ⓘ www.adaa.org (run by the Anxiety Disorders Association of America)
ⓘ www.freedomfromfear.org
ⓘ www.ocdaction.org.uk
ⓘ www.ocduk.org
ⓘ www.ocdfoundation.org.

SHYNESS AND SOCIAL ANXIETY

Shyness is nice and shyness can stop you
From doing all the things in life you'd like to.
The Smiths, 'Ask'

Everyone knows what it means to feel shy. It's a shrinking away from other people and withdrawal; a sense of not being up to coping with certain social situations; the feeling that people will think us inept, stupid or foolish, or that they'll see how anxious we are.

Shyness is absolutely normal. Lots of people – generally those with relatively mild shyness – function perfectly well. But shyness can be quite

> ### The shy president
> Do you know, I've never really grown up? It's a hard thing for me to play this game. In politics, one must meet people, and that's not easy for me … When I was a little fellow, as long ago as I can remember, I would go into a panic if I heard stranger voices in the house. I felt I just couldn't meet the people and shake hands with them. Most of the visitors would sit with Mother and Father in the kitchen and the hardest thing in the world was to go through the door and give them a greeting … I'm all right with old friends, but every time I meet a stranger, I've got to go through the old kitchen door, back home, and it's not easy.
> **Calvin Coolidge, US President (1923–9)**

severe, and when it really gets out of hand, psychologists call it 'social anxiety' (or social phobia).

Social anxiety comes in all manner of guises. Some people find all social situations stressful, while for others the fear only kicks in when they have to perform a particular activity in public. Most often, it's public speaking but social anxiety covers everything from dating to eating in front of other people to using a public toilet. (This last one is called paruresis and it mainly – but not exclusively – affects men.)

As with shyness, the thing that all types of social anxiety have in common is the sufferer's fear that others will think badly of them. And, again as with shyness, social anxiety can have a big impact on sufferers' lives. They spend their time worrying about events coming up and working out how to avoid them. If they don't manage to get out of attending a party or giving a presentation at work, they're consumed with anxiety. Their heart races, their face flushes and they may feel faint or dizzy. Later, they spend hours absorbed in gloomy post-mortems, convinced that they made a fool of themselves and sure that everyone could see how anxious they were. They are unassertive, apologetic, and consumed by nerves – and, not surprisingly, feel terrible about themselves.

When doctors assess whether someone has social anxiety, they look for all of the following symptoms:

* A marked fear of a social situation in which the person is exposed to unfamiliar people or in which other people might judge them.

The person is afraid that they will show their anxiety or do something humiliating or embarrassing.
- Almost always getting anxious in particular situations.
- Recognition that the fears are unreasonable or exaggerated.
- Avoidance of the feared situations or enduring them with distress.
- Difficulty in functioning normally because of the anxiety.

A memory for faces

What are you like at remembering faces? Some lucky people seem to have total recall; while others often find themselves staring blankly at someone they met just the other week. Research has shown that however efficiently our memory functions, we're much better at remembering faces if, instead of simply noting a person's features – the colour of their eyes, for example, or the line of their jaw – we also make a judgement about their personality.

But what about that judgement? Does our sense of a person's personality have a bearing on how likely we are to remember their face? And what if we suffer from social anxiety: does that affect our memory for faces? It was these questions that the Swedish psychologists Lars-Gunnar Lundh and Lars-Göran Öst set out to answer in an experiment they carried out in 1995.

Lundh and Öst showed 40 volunteers – 20 with social anxiety and 20 without significant psychological problems – photographs of 20 strangers and invited them to rate how accepting or critical they found each face. A little later, the volunteers were presented with 80 photographs of faces, including the 20 they had seen earlier. This time they were asked how many of the faces they recognized.

Fascinatingly, the volunteers without psychological problems were more likely to remember the faces they thought were accepting. But the opposite was true of those who suffered with social anxiety: they recognized more of the faces they'd judged to be critical. This is a striking demonstration of the way social anxiety skews our sense of the world. What remain in our memory are the negative views we imagine others to have of us. And this, of course, only reinforces our anxieties.

How common are shyness and social anxiety?

Forty per cent of people describe themselves as shy. And almost everyone has felt shy at some point, especially as children or young adults.

If you're struggling with social anxiety, take heart: you're not alone. In fact, it's one of the most common psychological problems, affecting around 13 per cent of the population at some stage of their lives. Like shyness, social anxiety often begins when we're young.

Self-assessment

Shyness is normal. But what if it's getting out of hand? The exercise below is a good way to tell whether your shyness has grown into social anxiety; base your answers on your experiences over the past week.

	Not at all	A little bit	Some-what	Very much	Extremely
1. I am afraid of people in authority.	0	1	2	3	4
2. I am bothered by blushing in front of people.	0	1	2	3	4
3. Parties and social events scare me.	0	1	2	3	4
4. I avoid talking to people I don't know.	0	1	2	3	4
5. Being criticized scares me a lot.	0	1	2	3	4
6. Fear of embarrassment causes me to avoid doing things or speaking to people.	0	1	2	3	4
7. Sweating in front of people causes me distress.	0	1	2	3	4
8. I avoid going to parties.	0	1	2	3	4

	Not at all	A little bit	Some-what	Very much	Extremely
9. I avoid activities in which I am the centre of attention.	0	1	2	3	4
10. Talking to strangers scares me.	0	1	2	3	4
11. I avoid having to give speeches.	0	1	2	3	4
12. I would do anything to avoid being criticized.	0	1	2	3	4
13. Heart palpitations bother me when I am around people.	0	1	2	3	4
14. I am afraid of doing things when people might be watching.	0	1	2	3	4
15. Being embarrassed or looking stupid are my worst fears.	0	1	2	3	4
16. I avoid speaking to anyone in authority.	0	1	2	3	4
17. Trembling or shaking in front of others is distressing to me.	0	1	2	3	4

The Social Phobia Inventory © 2000 Royal College of Psychiatrists

A total score of 19 or more is a sign of possible social anxiety.

How to Overcome Shyness and Social Anxiety

....

I was the shyest human ever invented, but I had a lion inside me that wouldn't shut up!
Ingrid Bergman

....

There is no cure for shyness any more than there is a cure for other normal human feelings. But although you can't eliminate shyness from your life, you can certainly learn to cope with it and, over the next couple of pages, you'll find out how. Social anxiety, on the other hand, you can get rid of, using just the same techniques.

When you boil them down to the basics, social anxiety and shyness are the products of a straightforward process. You have negative thoughts. These negative thoughts change the way in which you behave. This, in turn, produces more negative thoughts. And so on … So if you want to tackle your shyness and social anxiety, you need to examine your thinking and change your behaviour.

Reassess your thinking

First, let's focus on thoughts. A person's shyness or social anxiety is based on the belief that others will think badly of them because of the way they behave. Then, regardless of how things have actually gone, they're convinced that they have made a fool or an embarrassment of themselves. When it comes to shyness and social anxiety, reality does not get a look in.

These feelings are not, however, a reflection of what others think. What they reveal is how people view themselves. And, in fact, when they are in stressful social situations, people's thoughts often immediately turn inwards. They become extremely self-conscious, concentrating on their anxiety, petrified that the people they're with will pick up on it. It is this negative thinking that needs to be challenged.

As with overcoming other problems with anxiety, it helps to keep a diary. Note down the situations that trigger your shyness or social anxiety, as well as your thoughts and feelings. Ask yourself these key questions:

• Do people actually think of me like that?

- Is my anxiety really that noticeable to others?
- Does it matter if my anxiety shows, if people think my conversation is dull, if I think I'm inferior or if I'm not perfect in every situation?

As you set about trying to answer these questions, think of all the evidence – positive and negative – you can use. Talk to someone you trust. Do they know how others see you? Do they notice your anxiety?

Some therapists get their clients to act out scenarios they dread – for example, appearing in public with a wet shirt, as if it were soaked with sweat, or giving a speech with exaggerated pauses throughout. (This is called 'shame-busting'.) This helps people to realize that no one thinks anything of their anxiety, if they even notice it at all.

Negative thoughts often take the form of 'mental images' – vivid pictures in your mind of how terrible you look or how awful you sound in a given social situation. These images only increase anxiety and so you need to replace them with positive or more realistic alternatives. Focus on your alternative images as preparation for a stressful situation, and use them whenever a negative image pops up. Therapists often video their clients in social situations and then show them the film; this is a great way of demonstrating how negative images are not a reflection of reality.

Change your behaviour

Now let's look at the way negative thoughts affect behaviour. People often resort to avoiding situations that they expect to find difficult due to shyness and social anxiety. They may also adopt a range of 'safety behaviours' in order – they believe – to help them cope with certain social events. There are countless safety behaviours, but common ones include rehearsing what you're going to say, avoiding eye contact, monitoring performance and anxiety symptoms, hiding behind your hair, always agreeing with what others say, not venturing an opinion, only talking to people you know and holding on to things to stop others noticing that you're shaking.

Safety behaviours have a number of major drawbacks, not least that you don't learn that you can cope perfectly well without them, and that they don't improve the way you come across in social situations. After all, it's hard to have a good conversation with someone who never looks you in the eye, or who is so busy deciding what they're going to say next that they don't seem to be listening to what you're saying. Safety behaviours make people seem remote and self-absorbed, and send out all the wrong signals to others.

So you need to change the way you behave in social situations and confront your fears. You need to learn to face the situations you dread without using your safety behaviours. That way, you'll find out whether these behaviours are helping you or not. Start by drawing up a list of the situations you find stressful, and rank them in order of difficulty. For example, if you're anxious about going to social gatherings where you don't know most people, your list might run something like this:

Least stressful	Attending a party with a friend and feeling comfortable being there
	Talking to someone you don't know while your friend is with you
	Talking to someone you don't know on your own
	Attending a party on your own, talking to three people you don't know, and staying for 45 minutes
Most stressful	Attending a party on your own, talking to five people you don't know and staying for 90 minutes

Rate from 0–10 how distressing you think you'll find each task, then work your way through the list, starting with a situation you find challenging but tolerable. Don't use any of your safety behaviours to get you through the task. Alternatively, you could try doing the task with and then without them. After completing each assignment, write down how it went, rating how distressing you found the experience and comparing how this score measures up to the rating you gave earlier. How did not using your safety behaviours compare to using them? You'll soon see that you can manage just fine – or probably even better – without them.

To finish, here are four tips on coping with social situations without resorting to safety behaviours:

- Act as if you are a confident person.
- Fight the urge to focus on your own feelings by concentrating on the person you're with.
- Don't worry about a social event in advance. Focus on reasons for going to the event, whether it's having fun or getting to know

Problems with social anxiety: a personal account

I didn't have any girlfriends in school. I fancied girls, but there was no way I could speak to any of them. I felt like I was different – a misfit. By the time I was twenty-four, I'd had one girlfriend; and I married her. I couldn't face going through the whole dating thing again, and I was grateful someone would have me. But my wife wanted to visit friends and go to parties and restaurants and all that stuff, and I just couldn't handle it. I knew I was terrible in social situations and I thought people would instantly pick up on my worries. They'd see me as I saw myself: as a pathetic loser. I'd try to avoid social events; if I couldn't, I'd just grit my teeth and count down the minutes till I could get out. Not surprisingly, my marriage didn't last. But the break-up was so painful that I finally talked to my doctor about my shyness. He recommended a couple of really helpful books, and also gave me the details of a therapist. I'm still no extrovert, but now my shyness isn't ruining my life.

Rick, aged 33

colleagues, rather than on how you can avoid getting anxious. And don't bother with a post-mortem: learn whatever positive lessons you can from the experience and move on. (See pp. 109–12 for advice on dealing with worry.)

- Develop your assertiveness skills (see pp. 16–18); this will help you to deal more confidently with social situations.

Where to go for more information

Gillian Butler's *Overcoming Social Anxiety and Shyness* (Constable & Robinson, 1999) sets out a practical self-help programme for people struggling with shyness and social anxiety.

Triumph Over Shyness (McGraw-Hill, 2002) by Murray Stein and John Walker is a witty and accessible guide to the topic. It is co-published with the Anxiety Disorders Association of America.

On the Internet, check out:

- ⓘ www.anxietynetwork.com
- ⓘ www.freedomfromfear.org
- ⓘ www.social-anxiety.org.uk
- ⓘ www.phobics-society.org.uk
- ⓘ www.adaa.org, the website of the Anxiety Disorders Association of America.

TRAUMA AND POST-TRAUMATIC STRESS DISORDER

Give sorrow words: The grief that does not speak
Whispers the o'erfraught heart, and bids it break.
William Shakespeare, *Macbeth*

Life, as we all know, is full of stresses and strains. But the term 'trauma' refers to the really difficult ones, such as rape, violent physical assault, serious illness, natural disasters, a bad car accident, the sudden death of a loved one, a terrorist incident, combat, torture or physical and sexual abuse.

No one takes this kind of event in their stride and anybody who experiences them is bound to feel more than a little shaken up as a result. They might try to deny that the event happened. They will probably find it difficult to sleep and, when they do manage to fall asleep, they may be plagued by nightmares. They might spend hours thinking about what has happened to them, or distressing thoughts and images may keep popping into their heads. They might do all they can not to be reminded of the traumatic event, and will most probably feel upset, depressed and maybe angry or guilty too.

All of these reactions are completely normal and natural: it's the way people deal with horrible events, working them through in their minds until they get closure and can move on. Generally, these unpleasant feelings pass after a few weeks. But for a minority they remain and may even get worse. When these feelings go on for more than a month, and when they cause real problems, they're known as post-traumatic stress disorder (or PTSD).

When human beings find themselves in very stressful situations, they

97

become fearful and anxious. This is an ancient, in-built biological process that gears us up to fight or flee. Once we have dealt with whatever is causing us distress, the fear and anxiety disappear. But in cases of PTSD the fear and anxiety remain, even though the stressful situation has passed, rather like a fire alarm that never stops ringing.

PTSD has three main features:

Reliving the traumatic event. This can take the form of nightmares or sometimes flashbacks, when the person feels as though they're right back in the middle of the horror. Thoughts of the trauma repeatedly barge their way into the person's mind, no matter how hard they try to forget it. Distressing memories can be sparked off by the smallest things, such as a particular sound or smell, a place or the look on someone's face.

Avoiding any reminder of the traumatic event. PTSD makes the memory of the trauma so upsetting that sufferers will go to any lengths to avoid triggering it. They try desperately to keep any thoughts of the event out of their mind, steering clear of people and places that might be reminders of what happened. Understandably, they don't want to talk about their

Problems with PTSD: a personal account

A few years back, I was badly beaten up in the street. For a long time afterwards, I never went out alone at night. In fact, if it wasn't for the fact that I had to go to work, I probably wouldn't have ventured out at all. I shopped online. My social life shrank to nothing. I wanted to move to a different area so I never had to see the place where I was attacked, or any of the places I visited that night. I had terrible insomnia, and then horrible nightmares when I did eventually fall asleep. The assault was always on my mind, although I tried desperately to forget it. I was a bag of nerves, full of rage towards the people who attacked me and full of contempt for myself. If I hadn't eventually plucked up the courage to talk to my GP, I dread to think where I'd be now.

Phil, aged 28

experiences, to the extent that loved ones often find them detached, remote and closed off to them. It is as if the person finds the emotions caused by the trauma so distressing that they try to suppress all their feelings. To this end, PTSD sufferers often use alcohol or drugs to try to numb their feelings.

Feeling constantly on edge. This is what psychologists call a state of 'arousal', and it means being anxious, irritable and tense all the time. People with PTSD are forever on the alert for any thought or reminder of the trauma: it dominates their world, day and night (sleep problems are a typical symptom of PTSD).

PTSD makes people feel utterly crushed. As well as the features described above, sufferers often experience intense feelings of guilt, anger and sadness. It isn't surprising, therefore, that PTSD can lead to a variety of other problems, from addiction and depression to physical ailments and self-harm.

Interestingly, PTSD was not officially recognized as a condition until 1980. The symptoms had been spotted long before (known, for example, as 'shell shock'), but were usually attributed to physical causes or preexisting psychological problems. The Vietnam War generated many thousands of PTSD cases, and lobbying on the part of veterans' organizations proved influential in the struggle to have PTSD taken seriously as a condition in its own right.

Of course, while millions in the world suffer trauma, only a minority go on to develop PTSD. Why is this? It's partly to do with personality and life history. People are more susceptible if they have previously experienced traumatic events, and if they have existing psychological problems like depression and low self-esteem. There is a greater risk too among those who are not good at expressing their emotions, and those who don't have a strong social support network.

But the main factor in determining whether or not a person develops PTSD is the nature of the trauma itself. PTSD is more likely to strike if the trauma is particularly severe, long lasting or unpredictable, or if it happens at an early age. Harm suffered at the hands of other people (for example, rape or torture) can be particularly damaging. And the closer you are to a disastrous event, the greater the chance of experiencing PTSD. For example, one study of New Yorkers in the aftermath of the 9/11 attacks found that 7.5 per cent of people living below 110th Street in Manhattan reported symptoms of PTSD. But that figure rose to 20 per cent for people living close to the World Trade Center.

How common is PTSD?

About half of us will experience a severe trauma in our lives. And as we have seen, whether or not we develop PTSD-like symptoms depends largely on the sort of trauma suffered. In the case of most bad reactions, symptoms clear up after a few weeks, but in around a third of cases there are lasting problems, and about 5 to 10 per cent of us are likely to suffer from PTSD at some stage during our lifetime.

Self-assessment

If you're concerned that you might be suffering from PTSD, try this questionnaire. Base your responses on your reaction over the past seven days to the traumatic event.

	Not at all	A little bit	Some- what	Very much	Extremely
1. Any reminder brought back feelings about it.	0	1	2	3	4
2. I had trouble staying asleep.	0	1	2	3	4
3. Other things kept making me think about it.	0	1	2	3	4
4. I felt irritable and angry.	0	1	2	3	4
5. I avoided letting myself get upset when I thought about it or was reminded of it.	0	1	2	3	4
6. I thought about it when I didn't mean to.	0	1	2	3	4
7. I felt as if it hadn't happened or wasn't real.	0	1	2	3	4
8. I stayed away from reminders of it.	0	1	2	3	4

	Not at all	A little bit	Some-what	Very much	Extremely
9. Pictures about it popped into my mind.	0	1	2	3	4
10. I was jumpy and easily startled.	0	1	2	3	4
11. I tried not to think about it.	0	1	2	3	4
12. I was aware that I still had a lot of feelings about it, but I didn't deal with them.	0	1	2	3	4
13. My feelings about it were kind of numb.	0	1	2	3	4
14. I found myself acting or feeling like I was back at that time.	0	1	2	3	4
15. I had trouble falling asleep.	0	1	2	3	4
16. I had waves of strong feelings about it.	0	1	2	3	4
17. I tried to remove it from my memory.	0	1	2	3	4
18. I had trouble concentrating.	0	1	2	3	4
19. Reminders of it caused me to have physical reactions, such as sweating, trouble breathing, nausea or a pounding heart.	0	1	2	3	4

	Not at all	A little bit	Some-what	Very much	Extremely
20. I had dreams about it.	0	1	2	3	4
21. I felt watchful and on guard.	0	1	2	3	4
22. I tried not to talk about it.	0	1	2	3	4

Impact of Event Scale – Revised © Weiss, D. S., & Marmar, C. R. (1997).

Now add up your total score. Anything above 30 indicates possible PTSD.

How to Overcome Trauma and PTSD

Experiencing some of the symptoms of PTSD in the first few weeks after a trauma is normal. Generally they disappear of their own accord, but there are steps you can take to make sure they do.

In a nutshell, you need to take care of yourself. That means getting plenty of support from friends and family and lots of good-quality sleep, eating healthily and exercising regularly. Try to get back into your usual routine, but make time for fun and relaxation. Visit the place where the traumatic event happened if it is safe to do so – you don't want to get into the habit of avoiding things. Similarly, don't bottle up your feelings: share them with people you trust. If you're still at risk of something bad happening (for example, if you're in an abusive relationship), deal with that situation as your first priority.

Talk to your doctor so that they're aware of what you're going through. Take extra care doing day-to-day things, for example when you're driving: people often have accidents when they're very stressed. And go easy on yourself. The way you're feeling is not a sign of weakness, and you're not going mad. You should not expect that your difficulties will disappear overnight; but remember that they will in time.

If your symptoms are particularly severe, or if they have been going on for more than a month or so, you should consider seeing a PTSD cognitive therapist.

Cognitive therapy

PTSD has its roots in distressing memories of a traumatic event. These memories are so upsetting, and so at odds with people's view of themselves and the world, that they're unable to deal with them. So instead of being filed away with other memories, they hover at the forefront of their minds, keeping them in a state of perpetual fear and anxiety. Often these memories are fragmented, so that particular moments and specific details can be readily recalled, but the full picture is missing.

A PTSD cognitive therapist will help you to confront your memories and to put them into context. You will piece together the whole picture and finally be able to understand your experiences. During this process, you will also be encouraged to deal with any feelings of anger, guilt and shame. You will then find that you can file your traumatic memories away, just like any others and they won't keep bouncing back at you.

Trauma and sleep

Six months after the Great Fire of London in 1666, the diarist Samuel Pepys wrote:

It is strange to think how to this very day I cannot sleep a night without great terrors of fire; and this very night could not sleep to almost two in the morning through thoughts of fire.

Pepys' experience is typical of people with PTSD. Indeed, sleep problems are one of the most common symptoms. One study, for example, found that 70 per cent of the survivors of the 1995 Oklahoma City terrorist attack suffered disturbed sleep six months after the bombing and more than 50 per cent had nightmares. Research conducted in 1992 reported that 95 per cent of Holocaust survivors endured disturbed sleep and 83 per cent had nightmares.

Why it is that trauma should affect sleep so dramatically is not clear, although there are a number of theories. It may be because PTSD makes people so tense that they will naturally find it hard to sleep well. Or it could be that they fight sleep, whether consciously or unconsciously, in order to avoid the nightmares that are such a frequent feature of PTSD. Perhaps nightmares are so common because the phase of sleep that processes emotions and memories (rapid-eye-movement or REM sleep) is so often disrupted in PTSD. And some scientists have argued that when people are sleepy they're even more susceptible to their fears because they're not alert enough to use the strategies they would normally adopt to try to keep them at bay. As a result, not only does it take longer to fall asleep, a fear of feeling sleepy actually develops.

Whatever their causes, there is an effective treatment for nightmares. Imagery rehearsal therapy involves writing down your nightmare, changing it in any way you like, and then focusing on it for 15 minutes a day. As well as helping with nightmares in particular, research has shown that this technique seems to improve all aspects of PTSD.

Exposure

One of the key techniques used by therapists is exposure. What you'll be exposed to is your memories of the trauma, though in a very gradual and systematic way. This can be done either in 'real life' – for example, by visiting the location where the trauma took place – or by using the power of your imagination. You might, for instance, be asked to write an account of your experiences or to listen to a recording of your recollections. But whether the exposure is imaginary or real, the effect is the same. You'll piece together your fragmented memories and build a full account of the trauma. And you'll realize that your memories are only memories, and not a sign that you're still in danger. You don't need to suppress them and can think of them safely whenever you like, just like any other memory. But you're in control, not the bad memories.

Through this process, you will learn that all the strategies you have relied on to stop yourself thinking about your memories are unnecessary. In fact, not only are they unnecessary, they make matters worse. Numbing yourself with drugs and alcohol, for example, will increase your anxiety and depression. Being constantly on guard for any reminder of the trauma only means that it is always on your mind. And if you don't confront your fears, you will never see that actually you're no longer in danger.

Challenging thought patterns

Finally, your therapist will help you to deal with the thoughts and inter-pretations that underpin your fears.

Trauma can overturn in a moment the assumptions you have carried with you all your life. The world can suddenly look like an incredibly dangerous place, in which disaster is liable to strike at any moment. Other people can appear evil and untrustworthy, and you can suddenly feel intensely vulnerable, at the mercy of uncontrollable forces. On the back of these shattered assumptions, negative thoughts (and unpleasant memories) can creep in. You might blame yourself for the traumatic event, worry that PTSD symptoms are a sign of madness or be critical of yourself for not getting over things quicker. Your thinking is twisted by all manner of negative habits (or 'cognitive errors'), such as assuming the worst in every situation, focusing on the negative and dismissing the positive, mistaking the way you feel for facts about reality and over-generalizing – drawing big conclusions from isolated events.

Thoughts such as these need to be explored and challenged, and your therapist will give you some tried-and-tested techniques to do this. For example, weighing up the evidence for and against your thought, thinking about alternative ways of viewing the situation and asking yourself what you would advise a friend in a similar position. You will also spend time revisiting your original assumptions about yourself and the world around you, and will learn how to adapt them constructively to what you have been through.

Confronting your memories isn't easy. In fact, it can sometimes be upsetting as you dredge up into the light thoughts that you had tried to bury. But this way of treating PTSD is extremely successful. Stick with it and you'll put your fears firmly behind you.

Where to go for more information

Reclaiming Your Life From a Traumatic Experience (OUP, 2007) by Barbara Olasov Rothbaum, Edna Foa and Elizabeth Hembree is an excellent guide to overcoming PTSD, designed to be used as a workbook in combination with treatment by a therapist.

Glenn Schiraldi's *The Post-Traumatic Stress Disorder Sourcebook* (McGraw-Hill, 2000) provides comprehensive and accessible advice on the range of treatments available for PTSD.

Among several useful websites are:

- ⓘ www.adaa.org, run by the Anxiety Disorders Association of America
- ⓘ www.ncptsd.va.gov, the website of the US National Center for PTSD

- ⓘ www.anxietyuk.org.uk
- ⓘ www.uktrauma.org.uk
- ⓘ www.victimsupport.org.uk.

WORRY

Rule number one is: don't sweat the small stuff.
Rule number two is: it's all small stuff.
Robert Eliot

We all know what it's like to worry. We become preoccupied with an aspect of our lives, trying to second-guess what might go wrong and what will happen to us if it does. But worrying isn't a positive problem-solving exercise and is, in fact, more likely to make us become anxious, depressed and scared. And once we start worrying, it can be hard to stop; our worries can spiral out of control.

Often there is little rhyme or reason as to what people worry about. It need not be just the big issues in life, such as health, relationships or work. It can be minor day-to-day matters that others would find trivial. For those who are particularly prone to worry, everything can seem a potential cause for concern – which makes for an exhausting way to live.

A worrier tends to focus on the negative, spending considerable time dwelling on things that probably won't happen. They become very skilled (and imaginative) at 'What if?' thinking in which the worst possible outcome for any situation is always foreseen. Psychologists call this 'catastrophizing' and, not surprisingly, it can make a person anxious and depressed.

The most extreme form of worry is called Generalized Anxiety Disorder (GAD). This is characterized by:

- worry that is excessive, unrealistic and uncontrollable
- worry that has lasted for at least six months
- extreme anxiety
- worry having a big impact on the affected person's day-to-day life.

How common is worry?

According to the doctor and writer Lewis Thomas, 'We are, perhaps, uniquely among the earth's creatures, the worrying animal. We worry away our lives.' While this may be putting it a little strongly, it is true that almost

Problems with Generalized Anxiety Disorder: some personal accounts

I've always been a worrier, but I managed to keep things under control until a couple of years ago. Then I was hit by a series of stressful situations – mainly problems at work and the slow and painful disintegration of my relationship. That seemed to push me into the grip of a really vicious anxiety. I began to worry about everything, no matter how trivial. Even when good things happened, it felt as though disaster was always just around the corner. I couldn't concentrate and I couldn't sleep. I felt as though I were a total failure and that nothing would ever improve. The only break I got was sometimes when I first woke up. I'd have a few blissful moments to myself, and then the stomach-churning sense of dread would kick in again ...
Christina, aged 29

For several years I suffered from a range of problems – insomnia, stomach pains, headaches, loss of appetite, breathlessness, and feeling faint, to name just a few. And I was extremely anxious, pretty much all of the time. The GPs I saw were sympathetic, and checked out my physical symptoms, but things didn't improve – which only added to my anxiety and growing sense of hopelessness. And then, on yet another visit to yet another GP, the breakthrough: the doctor thought I might have something called Generalised Anxiety Disorder (I'd never heard of it) and referred me for a course of Cognitive Behaviour Therapy. I hadn't heard of CBT either, but those sessions were fantastic. I understood for the first time just how damaging my negative thought patterns were, and I learned how to change them. I haven't looked back.
Pete, aged 35

everyone worries from time to time. Some, however, worry more often and more intensely. In one study:

- Thirty-eight per cent of people reported worrying at least once a day, 19.4 per cent worried once every two to three days and 15 per cent worried approximately once a month.
- For 9 per cent of people, spells of worrying lasted for two or more hours, while 11 per cent worried for 1–2 hours, 18 per cent for between 10 and 60 minutes, 38 per cent for 1–10 minutes and a happy 24 per cent said they worried for less than a minute at a time.
- The 'peak periods' for worry are early in the morning and last thing at night – probably because these are the times when we're not busy with other things, and the most common topics for worry are work, health, money and relationships.
- About 3 per cent of people have GAD and women are twice as likely to be affected as men. People generally first notice the symptoms between their late teens and their late twenties, but they can remain for a long time.

Self-assessment

How often do you worry? Do you wonder whether your worrying might be getting out of control? Work your way through the exercise below for an assessment of just how much you're affected by worry.

Decide on a number that describes how typical or characteristic each of the following statements is of you, entering that number next to each one.

1	2	3	4	5
Not at all typical		Somewhat typical		Very typical

1. If I don't have enough time to do everything, I don't worry about it. _____
2. My worries overwhelm me. _____
3. I don't tend to worry about things. _____
4. Many situations make me worry. _____
5. I know I shouldn't worry about things, but I just can't help it. _____
6. When I'm under pressure, I worry a lot. _____

7. I am always worrying about something. _____

8. I find it easy to dismiss worrisome thoughts. _____

9. As soon as I finish one task, I start to worry about something else. _____

10. I never worry about anything. _____

11. When there is nothing more I can do about a concern, I don't worry about it any more. _____

12. I've been a worrier all my life. _____

13. I notice that I have been worrying about things. _____

14. Once I start worrying, I can't stop. _____

15. I worry all the time. _____

16. I worry about projects until they are all done. _____

Reprinted from Meyer, T.J., Miller, M.L., Metzger, R.L., & Borkovec, T.D. (1990). Development and validation of the Penn State Worry Questionnaire. *Behaviour Research & Therapy*, 28, 487-495 with the permission of Elsevier.

Now add up your scores for each statement. Questions 3, 8, 10, 11 are reverse scored, meaning that if, for example, you put 5, for scoring purposes that item is counted as 1. Scores can range from 18 to 80. People with worry problems usually score above 50 on the questionnaire. A score of over 60 may well indicate that the person has GAD.

Note: remember that the questionnaire above is not definitive; like all of the questionnaires in this book, think of it more as a guide in helping you to decide whether or not to look for additional help.

How to Overcome Worry

For many people, whether they're affected by GAD or are simply habitual worriers, worrying is so much a part of their make-up that the idea of stopping is scary.

Worrying feels like a way of coping, a way of anticipating and preparing for trouble. But in reality it is usually no help at all. Life will always throw up challenges, and the trick is to change the way in which we react to them.

Worry management

Worry needs to be managed – and here's how to do it.

Reduce the amount of time and effort you put into worrying

Worrying is negative thinking that only makes your troubles seem worse. It is also a notoriously unreliable guide to the future. How often have you spent days worrying about something that did not happen? Try to keep in mind how pointless worrying really is, as this will help you to overcome worries as and when they pop into your head.

Don't panic!

Worry about worry is a big problem for some people: they're frightened that their worrying may make them mentally or physically ill. But though worry in the short term is unpleasant and unproductive, it isn't actually dangerous. So don't add worry about worry to the list of issues troubling you – worry is normal, natural, and it can't hurt you.

Use worry periods

Save up your worrying for a designated daily 20-minute 'worry period'. If you find yourself worrying outside your worry period, just write down whatever it is that is bothering you and save it for later. Try to make your worry period at the same time each day (but not before bedtime when you're trying to wind down).

Focus on problem-solving

Start off with worry periods but then, when you're ready, try to turn these into problem-solving periods:

- Define the problem as specifically as you can.
- Think of all the possible solutions to the problem. What has worked for you in the past? What would you advise someone else with the same problem to do?
- Weigh up the pros and cons of each possible solution.
- Choose the solution you think is best and decide on how you're going to implement it. Try to guess what problems you might face with it and how you're going to deal with them.
- Try out the solution you've chosen and then have a think about how well it's worked. If things haven't gone to plan, try the next solution.

Don't fight your worries

This might sound a bit odd: isn't getting rid of worries the whole point? But fighting them won't help; they will only come back and you will be even more stressed and anxious about them when they do.

So, instead of fighting your worries, let them go. Don't dwell on them other than in your worry period. The rest of the time, just watch the worry come into your mind, acknowledge it, but don't let it distract you. Stay as calm as you can, focus on what you're doing and not what you're thinking, and watch the waves of your worries fade into the distance.

Accept uncertainty

As we have said, worrying can seem like a way of being prepared for the future – as if focusing on things that we dread will somehow make them less likely to happen. But of course worry can't do this.

You need to accept that life is made up of highs and lows, and no matter how much you worry, you can never know what is in store for you. So instead of dwelling on possible disasters in an uncertain future, you need to focus on the present – and especially on the positive things in your life right now.

Have more fun

You can dramatically change the way in which you think and feel simply by changing what you do. One of the most effective ways to combat worry is simply to add more enjoyable elements to your week. Spend time with your friends and family; go out to a restaurant or cinema; devote more time to your hobbies – whatever works for you. If you can find some physical activity you enjoy, so much the better: exercise is a great way of improving your mood and reducing worry and anxiety.

Learn from people around you

It's all too easy to allow yourself to get swamped by your problems, and it can often seem as if you're alone with your worries while everyone else is enjoying themselves.

But of course we all worry sometimes – and that means we all have experiences we can share. If you're having a tough time with worry, ask your trusted friends and family how they cope. The chances are that they will have some useful advice. It may also enable you to see your own situation more clearly – talking things over is often an excellent way to get some perspective on your problems.

Where to go for more information

The Worry Cure (Piatkus, 2006) by the American psychologist Robert L. Leahy provides very useful advice on identifying, understanding and overcoming worries.

On the Internet:

- ⓘ www.anxietyuk.org.uk offers information on a variety of anxiety problems including Generalized Anxiety Disorder.
- ⓘ Treatment guidelines for GAD are available from the National Institute for Health and Clinical Excellence (www.nice.org.uk).

. . . .

When I look back on all these worries, I remember the story of the old man who said on his deathbed that he had had a lot of trouble in his life, most of which had never happened.
Winston Churchill

. . . .

BODY IMAGE WORRIES

Most people dislike some aspect of their appearance. And almost everyone spends at least a part of the day making sure they look as good as they can. But for a small but significant proportion of people, concern over their appearance dominates their lives. They become convinced that a part of their body is deformed, ugly or somehow defective, although in reality any problem is actually minimal or even non-existent. When this kind of worry is severe it is known as Body Dysmorphic Disorder (BDD).

The most common complaints (in descending order) focus on the nose, hair, skin, eyes, chin, lips and overall body build. But people with BDD can worry about any part of the body – from their buttocks to their genitals and (literally) from their fingers to their toes. Very often, people are troubled by more than one aspect of their appearance. (If weight is the issue, the problem may be an eating disorder rather than BDD.)

BDD can lead to big changes in the way people behave. For example, people with BDD often:

Problems with body image worries: a personal account

By the time I was 17 it seemed like all the boys in my class had a girlfriend. I didn't, because I was too shy to ask anyone out. But I started to wonder whether I was repulsively ugly. I began spending hours every day in front of the mirror. I saw blotchy skin, horrible hair, a crooked nose. I hated going out. I hardly left my bedroom at weekends, and school was a nightmare. Half the time I was absent, pretending to be ill. Instead of studying, I'd be staring at myself in the mirror, trying to work out which hairstyle would best cover up my deformed features, or going through magazines trying to find someone who looked as bad as me. What turned it around was hearing a radio programme about teenagers with the same sort of worries. I realized that, whatever was going on with me, it had nothing to do with my appearance ...

Mark, aged 30

- avoid social situations or, when they do go out, feel extremely self-conscious
- camouflage their 'defect' – for example, by wearing heavy make-up or adopting a certain hairstyle
- constantly compare themselves to other people
- either spend hours checking how they look in the mirror or avoid mirrors altogether
- repeatedly pick their skin to make it smooth.
- engage in elaborate and lengthy 'grooming' rituals (for example, washing, applying make-up, brushing hair)
- continually ask for reassurance about their appearance from family, friends and sometimes doctors
- spend a fortune on clothes and beauty products
- undergo cosmetic surgery.

Like all the problems in this book, body image problems run from the relatively mild to the very severe. Doctors will only diagnose someone with BDD if their worries cause them real distress or have a big impact on their life, but even then, some sufferers are able to lead relatively normal lives. Others, however, find it extremely difficult to cope. Because social situations are so distressing, and they often spend several hours on their appearance, their education or careers are hugely disrupted. Relationships suffer and people can feel very isolated. Feelings of shame, guilt and depression

BDD: the secret illness?

Until very recently BDD had seemed a secret illness. Most of the medical profession knew little or nothing about it, and people suffering from the symptoms kept silent, partly from shame and embarrassment, but also in the belief that what they were going through was unique.

The term 'Body Dysmorphic Disorder' was officially introduced only in 1987, but the problem was in fact recognized by European psychiatrists as long ago as the nineteenth century. After seeing several patients with body image anxieties in the 1880s, the Italian psychiatrist Enrico Morselli introduced the term 'dysmorphophobia' – literally 'fear of ugliness' – still used by some health professionals in the UK today.

Not only does dysmorphophobia feature in the writings of some of the most influential figures in modern psychiatry, such as Emil Kraepelin (1856–1926) and Pierre Janet (1859–1947), it probably afflicted one of the world's most famous psychiatric patients, the Wolf Man. Sigmund Freud invented this name to protect his patient, Sergei Pankejeff's real identity when he published an account of the his case in 1918. Although Freud did not mention the Wolf Man's symptoms of dysmorphophobia, Pankejeff's subsequent psychoanalyst, Ruth Brunswick, certainly did in 1928:

[he] neglected his daily life and work because he was engrossed, to the exclusion of all else, in the state of his nose. ... His life was centred on the little mirror in his pocket, and his fate depended on what it revealed or was about to reveal.

Long before the term was invented, we have a perfect – and poignant – description of BDD: a life centred on a mirror.

are sometimes so intense that suicide seems the only way out. (A quarter of people with BDD try to kill themselves.)

Fortunately, however, therapy for BDD has come a long way in a short time (see pp. 116–19).

How common are body image worries?

There's nothing unusual about people taking an interest in the way they look. We all – or most of us – do it. A survey of 30,000 people, for example, found that 82 per cent of men and 93 per cent of women do what they can to improve their appearance.

And there is nothing unusual about disliking the way we look either. One study found that 43 per cent of men and 56 per cent of women were not happy with their overall appearance, and when asked about particular parts of their body, levels of dissatisfaction were even higher. And perhaps it is not surprising that so many people dislike their appearance, because lots of us seem to have a very inaccurate sense of how we look. A staggering 95 per cent of women in one research study overestimated their own body size, generally by around 25 per cent.

How often this body dissatisfaction escalates into Body Dysmorphic Disorder is very hard to say, however, because most people with BDD are too embarrassed or ashamed to talk about their problems or to seek treatment. One estimate though stands at 1 per cent of the population, with men and women equally affected. BDD can start at any age but usually begins in the teens through to the mid-twenties.

Self-assessment

Because more or less everyone is concerned with their appearance, it can be hard to know whether a person is just averagely anxious about the way they look or whether they may have a more serious problem. If you're not sure, the questionnaire below will give you some pointers.

Are you very concerned about the appearance of some part(s)
of your body that you consider especially unattractive?   Yes/No

Do these concerns preoccupy you? That is, do you think about
them a lot and wish you could think about them less?   Yes/No

---

If you answered 'Yes' to both of the above questions, continue on to the next ones.

Is your main concern with your appearance that you are
not thin enough or that you might become too fat?   Yes/No

Has your defect(s) caused you a lot of distress or emotional
pain?   Yes/No

Has it significantly interfered with your social life?   Yes/No

Has your defect(s) significantly interfered with your
schoolwork, your job or your ability to function
in your role (e.g. as a homemaker)?   Yes/No

Are there things you avoid because of your defect(s)?   Yes/No

Have the lives or normal routines of your family or friends
been affected by your appearance concerns?   Yes/No

How much time do you spend thinking about your defect(s)
per day on average? (Add up all the time you spend.)

Less than 1 hour a day

1–3 hours a day

More than 3 hours a day

Body Dysmorphic Disorder Questionnaire © 2005
By permission of Oxford University Press, Inc.

You may well be suffering from Body Dysmorphic Disorder if you answered:

'Yes' to questions 1 and 2 and
'Yes' to any of questions 4 to 8, and b or c to question 9.

If you also answered 'Yes' to question 3, it may be that you have an eating disorder rather than BDD.

How to Overcome Body Image Worries

BDD can be a debilitating illness, but huge strides have been made recently in its treatment. Strategies like the ones outlined below are now the standard therapy for BDD and usually they are very successful.

Challenge negative thoughts

The first thing you need to do is to find a positive alternative perspective on your worries, by ridding yourself of the upsetting thoughts that, for example, your skin is horrible or your nose is too big. To do this, write down one of your negative thoughts and rate how strongly you believe it (on a scale of 0–100 per cent). Then write down all the evidence you can think of to either support or contradict that thought. Try to imagine positive alternative explanations. Ask yourself what you would advise someone in your position. Talk through your fears with a trusted friend. Then, when you have weighed up all the evidence, have another go at rating how strongly you believe the negative thought.

Expose yourself to the situations you fear

This sounds scary, and you'll probably endure a few uncomfortable moments along the way, but it is a fantastic way of learning that there's nothing to fear in the situations you dread.

Exposure must be done in a gradual, thought-through way, so draw up a list of situations that you find stressful (going out without make-up, swimming or clothes shopping with friends, for example) and give each one a score for how distressing they seem. Start with the least frightening task on the list and, when you're comfortable with it, move on to the next one. When compiling your list, jot down what you think will happen (that people will stare at you or move away in disgust, for example). Later, you can compare these predictions with what actually happened. Give each task a score from 0 to 10 for scariness before you do it, then update that score after you have accomplished it. (You'll probably be surprised at how different the two scores are.)

You're bound to feel some anxiety at each stage, but try to stick with it. If you feel your anxiety is getting out of hand at any point, take a break from that particular task. Maybe go back to the previous task or try an intermediate one. And don't feel that you have failed; almost everyone finds it tough from time to time. Move through the list as fast as you're able to, and no quicker.

Drop your safety behaviours

It is really important that when you tackle these exposure assignments you don't resort to using 'safety behaviours' – the technical term for the variety of strategies people adopt to minimize the chances of the thing they fear occurring. It is especially crucial that you don't cover up the 'flawed' part of your body. You'll soon discover that you don't need these safety behaviours to cope, and that the reason why no one is staring at your lips isn't because you have kept your hands in front of your mouth, but because your lips look perfectly normal.

Some people find it helps to adopt a 'So what?' or 'Take me or leave me' attitude. 'OK,' you tell yourself, 'my nose may be a bit big, but who cares? If people don't like it, so what – that's their problem.' But the chances are that you'll find out that taking this stance is unnecessary, as no one is looking at your nose in any case!

Stop focusing on your body

Your rituals of checking, grooming, seeking reassurance and so on may seem like ways of coping with your anxieties. But in fact, all they do is reinforce them by keeping your mind on your body. Stopping these rituals is difficult – they're a habit, after all – but it is also really important. Choose those that you think you'll find easiest to give up and cut back on them, then stop them completely. Think about the situations that trigger your rituals and prepare a strategy for coping. Distracting yourself with something you find fun and interesting is a good tactic, for example.

Manage your worry

All of the techniques outlined above demonstrate that it isn't your appearance that is the issue, but your worry about it. Learn to keep your worrying under control by following the guidelines on pp. 109–12.

Have fun

As you gradually conquer your BDD, you'll find that you have a lot of extra time on your hands, as you regain all the hours you would normally spend on your appearance. So have a think about how you would like to use this extra time. Whatever you go for, make sure it is enjoyable. Not only do you deserve some fun, but it will help to keep your mind off any lingering body image concerns.

Where to go for more information

The Broken Mirror (OUP, 2005) by Katharine Phillips was the first book to be published on BDD. Now available in an updated edition, it is still a great guide to the topic.

Have a look also at *Overcoming Body Image Problems* (Constable & Robinson, 2008) by David Veale, Rob Willson and Alex Clarke and *Feeling Good about the Way You Look* (Guilford, 2006) by Sabine Wilhelm.

On the Internet, we recommend:

ⓘ www.thebddfoundation.org
ⓘ www.bddcentral.com.

Health Anxiety

> *It is a most extraordinary thing, but I never read a patent medicine advertisement without being impelled to the conclusion that I am suffering from the particular disease therein dealt with in its most virulent form. The diagnosis seems in every case to correspond exactly with all the sensations that I have ever felt.*
>
> Jerome K. Jerome, *Three Men in a Boat*

Most people fret about health from time to time, worrying that they might be suffering from a serious illness. When this anxiety is severe and long lasting, however, it is known as 'hypochondriasis'.

It is often thought that people with hypochondriasis are simply imagining their symptoms. But, in fact, it is more a case of misreading perfectly normal changes in the body as signs of a serious medical condition. For example, someone who has forgotten where they left their house keys may believe that they're developing Alzheimer's disease; or run-of-the-mill aches and pains in the chest or arms may be taken as symptoms of heart disease. And when, as a result, they get anxious, the physical symptoms that this brings with it – sweating, palpitations, breathlessness, for example – become yet another thing to worry about.

If it is not you who is affected, hypochondriasis might seem silly. But like all anxieties, it can play havoc with the lives of sufferers. They might spend hours checking their body for symptoms, reading about illnesses on the Internet and driving friends and family mad with a constant need

Problems with health anxiety: a personal account

I spent the best part of 40 years worrying about my health – I think because my dad died from a heart attack when I was 13. He was only 48, but he was a chain-smoker, never did any exercise and drank too much.

I was determined not to end up like my dad, so I've never smoked and hardly touched alcohol. But I've also been on the alert for any sign of health problems: headaches, tiredness, aches and pains, rashes, lumps and bumps and so on. Over the years I've imagined I was suffering from pretty much everything: heart disease, cancer, Parkinson's disease, a brain tumour, diabetes, pneumonia, even AIDS and Mad Cow Disease. I constantly examined myself – although usually I didn't know what I was looking for. Then one day my wife asked me how much more of my life I was going to waste worrying about dying and that really struck home. The next day, I went into town and bought a couple of self-help books. A few weeks later, after working through the exercises, my mindset had changed completely. **Brian, aged 55**

for reassurance that they're not ill. They may become fixtures in the doctor's waiting room, driven there again and again by a need to have their symptoms checked out. Or they might organize their lives around avoiding all reminders of illness and mortality. Unfortunately, although these habits might bring short-term relief, they don't help their anxiety in the long run; in fact, they keep it going.

A person is likely to be diagnosed with hypochondriasis if their anxiety has been going on for at least six months, despite reassurance from a doctor that there is no physical problem, and if it is causing them significant distress or interfering with their normal routine. (Incidentally, despite some similarities, we shouldn't confuse hypochondriasis with illness phobia, which is the fear that we may catch a particular disease; hypochondriasis, on the other hand, is the fear that we already have it.)

How common is health anxiety?

Almost everyone experiences some anxiety about their health from time to time. Around 3 per cent of people who attend GP surgeries, however, are suffering from hypochondriasis, the rates being the same for both men and women.

Self-assessment

Are you concerned that your health worries might be getting out of hand? If so, try the following questionnaire:

---

1. Do you often worry about the possibility that you have a serious illness? Yes/No

2. Are you bothered by many different aches and pains? Yes/No

3. Do you worry a lot about your health? Yes/No

4. If a disease is brought to your attention (whether via TV, radio, the newspapers or someone you know), do you worry about getting it yourself? Yes/No

5. Do you find that you are bothered by many different symptoms? Yes/No

6. Is it hard for you to believe the doctor when he/she tells you there is nothing to worry about? Yes/No

7. Do you think there is something seriously wrong with your body? Yes/No

Whitely Index © 1967 Royal College of Psychiatrists

Give yourself 1 point for each 'Yes' answer.

Like all the self-assessment exercises in the book, this one can't give you a cast-iron diagnosis, but if you scored 2 points or more and your doctor has ruled out any medical conditions, you may have hypochondriasis.

HOW TO OVERCOME HEALTH ANXIETY

Hypochondriasis is the result of misinterpretation. It occurs when people mistake perfectly harmless, normal bodily signs for symptoms of a dreaded illness. So, in order to overcome health anxiety, you need to tackle this misinterpretation.

Having said this, your first step should be to confirm that you really are not suffering from a physical illness. So talk to your doctor about the symptoms that are worrying you. Once you've done that and been given the all clear, you can start work on overcoming your problem.

Challenge misinterpretation

First of all, you need to challenge your own interpretation of what is going on in your body. It is much easier to get a clear idea of your thoughts if you write them down. So jot down on paper the illness you're afraid of, and rate how strongly you believe that you have it (on a scale of 0–100 per cent). Next, write down all the evidence you can think of in support of your fear and against it. To help you do this, imagine what your doctor might say, talk over your anxiety with someone you trust and consider what other explanations there might be for the way you're feeling. Could your fears be influenced, for example, by past experiences in your life, such as the illness of someone you've known? Once you've weighed up all the evidence, have another go at rating how strongly you believe that you're ill.

Change your behaviour

The misinterpretation of normal bodily sensations has a big effect on behaviour. As we've seen, people with hypochondriasis can spend enormous amounts of time reading about illness, seeking reassurance from friends, family and doctors and in checking themselves for signs of disease. But this only serves to reinforce their fears, and they become overly sensitive to normal changes in the body. This is always counterproductive. If they focus on swallowing, for example, their anxiety will inevitably make it seem more difficult, prompting fears that they have throat cancer. If someone continually prods and pokes parts of their body, they may well end up causing the rashes or bumps they're so afraid of finding. So it is essential to cut out these unhelpful behaviours.

Shift your focus away from your body

This doesn't mean that you shouldn't pay any attention at all to your health, but you do need to keep things in proportion. Discuss with your doctor a sensible check-up routine – maybe once a year – and back this up with a healthy diet and exercise programme. If you do find yourself checking your body again, or are tempted to read up about an illness, just be aware of what you're doing and then gently switch your attention to something else – ideally something enjoyable and absorbing.

Think about your wider views on health

People with hypochondriasis, for example, often assume that changes in their body are always a sign of a problem, and that they have to watch out for the slightest unusual symptom. They tend to feel that if they don't go to the doctor as soon as they suspect something is wrong, it will be too late. And trickiest of all, they want certainty: certainty that they're not ill; sometimes even certainty that they will never become ill.

All of these assumptions need challenging. Think them through and weigh up the evidence. Try to come to a balanced view – the sort of thing you would tell a friend with similar worries. We can't, for example, live our lives worrying about possible future problems. Instead, it's best to live a balanced, healthy lifestyle, and to concentrate on enjoying the present.

Exposure

It is common for people with health anxiety to avoid anything that could remind them of the illness they imagine they might have. They might, for example, turn off the TV if there is any mention of cancer, or avoid reading the papers in case they contain any discussion of health issues. If you're affected in this way, you need to expose yourself to the situations you're afraid of, and in doing so, you will learn that you have nothing to be afraid of. For more on exposure techniques, see pp. 87–8.

Finally, because hypochondriasis is essentially a specific type of worry, look at the strategies we suggest for dealing with worry in general (see pp. 109–12) – they should be extremely helpful.

Where to go for more information

An Introduction to Coping with Health Anxiety (Robinson, 2007) by Brenda Hogan and Charles Young is a very clear guide to what health anxiety is and how you can overcome it.

You'll also find plenty of useful information at:

- ⓘ www.nomorepanic.co.uk, which also offers a message forum and chat room
- ⓘ www.www.anxietyuk.org.uk

Anxiety: Therapy, Medication and Related Problems

Coping with anxiety is a challenge for us all. As we have seen, anxiety takes a variety of forms, from shyness to panic attacks, and from everyday worry to post-traumatic stress disorder (PTSD). But let's now take a look at anxiety across the board.

Can I tackle these problems on my own, or do I need a therapist? What about medication?

The techniques we have outlined are designed to help you overcome your anxiety problems on your own. And there is plenty of research evidence to suggest that self-help works. But as with virtually all of the issues covered in this book, anxiety problems run from the comparatively mild to the very severe. If you think that yours is towards the severe end of the spectrum – that is, if you're really struggling to cope and are experiencing quite a bit of distress – you would probably benefit from the help of a trained cognitive behaviour (CBT) therapist. There have been lots of very exciting advances in CBT over recent years, and it is now the standard treatment for anxiety problems (and many other psychological and emotional issues too). The advice in this book is based on CBT.

Start by seeing your GP and ask them to refer you to a CBT therapist. Your GP may also suggest medication. For many years, anxiety problems were treated with so-called 'minor tranquillizers', also called benzodiazepines, the best known of which is diazepam (Valium), but these are rarely used today. They only work in the short term and, because the body gets used to them, you need to take an ever-larger dose to achieve the same effects. People often become dependent on the drug and there can be some unpleasant side effects if you stop taking them too quickly.

These days the preferred drug treatment for anxiety problems is the new class of anti-depressants called SSRIs, the best known being fluoxentine (under the trade name Prozac). But there are numerous SSRIs on the market, and your doctor will try to find the one that works best for you. They have proved effective in treating anxiety problems, although there are side effects (usually minor) and people can sometimes find their problems return when they stop taking the drug.

If I have one anxiety problem am I likely to have others?
Just because you have one anxiety problem doesn't mean you will inevitably develop others. So try not to add that worry to those you're already dealing with!

Having said that, however, some people do have more than one anxiety problem. And that is not surprising, given that they're all quite closely related. Other common related problems are **depression, stress, insomnia** and **alcohol and drug abuse**.

Bereavement and Grief

It's so curious: one can resist tears and 'behave' very well in the hardest hours of grief. But then someone makes you a friendly sign behind a window, or one notices that a flower that was in bud only yesterday has suddenly blossomed, or a letter slips from a drawer … and everything collapses.
Colette

Few people manage to escape grief at some point in their lives and, painful though it can be, the alternative is probably worse. Grief after all is the normal human response to the death of someone we love. As the psychoanalyst Erich Fromm wrote: 'To spare oneself from grief at all cost can be achieved only at the price of total detachment, which excludes the ability to experience happiness.'

Of course, this doesn't make grief any easier to bear. Sufferers can become desperately sad or angry, fearful or guilty. They might find themselves wracked by anguish, dissolving into tears at any moment. They can feel intensely lonely and pine for their loved one. Often, it's a struggle to make sense of the fact that the person is gone. The world can suddenly seem a perilous, unpredictable place in which disaster may be lurking just around the corner.

Given the turmoil that bereavement can cause, it isn't surprising that people often find it hard to cope at work or in their social lives, and so become temporarily withdrawn and isolated. And as if all this were not enough, it isn't unusual for people to experience health problems after bereavement, since severe stress weakens the immune system.

But although grief can often affect people in the ways outlined above, there are plenty of exceptions. In fact, if there is one key message to take away from these pages, it is that everyone's experience of grief is different.

Problems with grief: a personal account

My husband, Alex, died very suddenly 18 months ago. We had been married for 29 years. I remember receiving a phone call at work but after that, until the funeral really, everything is very sketchy. It was as if I'd been anaesthetized. Most of the time I was completely numb, disbelieving. Then, after a week or two, I began crying and I didn't stop for what felt like weeks. I got through it by leaning very heavily on close friends, who must have been bored stupid listening to me going on about Alex and how unfair it all was, how I wished I were dead instead of him, but they never let it show. And of course I grieved with my son and daughter. We talked about their dad all the time, and it was so lovely. Alex's death has actually brought us much closer together. Now – and though I'd never have believed it 18 months ago – I have sort of reinvented myself. I'm a single woman, after all, and though of course I wish Alex were still here, I've come to enjoy lots of aspects of my new life.
Clare, aged 56

Six dimensions of grief

Everyone grieves in their own way. But what are those ways? What forms does grief take? It was precisely these questions that a research team in California set out to tackle when they followed the experiences of 350 widowed people in San Diego. They identified six 'dimensions' of grief (although it is important to remember that the precise way in which each person experiences them is likely to be different):

1. Emotions and thoughts

These include initial shock and then the – often – physical pain of grief, which is frequently triggered by a reminder of the loved one. Other typical emotions and thoughts are yearning, a sense of loss, anger, guilt, anxiety about the future, feeling overwhelmed, as well as positive feelings like relief.

2. Coping with emotional pain
The bereaved Californians did this in a variety of ways, including avoiding reminders of the deceased, using humour, religious faith, keeping busy, distracting themselves with TV or radio and taking a distanced, philosophical view of their experience.

3. A continued relationship with the deceased
Far from 'letting go', the bereaved tended to maintain their relationship with the dead, most powerfully by means of their memories. But many people dreamed of their deceased and – especially in the early days – hallucinations were common.

4. Changes in ways of functioning
Grief often disrupted the Californians' day-to-day routines, making it hard for them to function normally at work or in their social lives. It also sometimes affected their health.

5. Changes in relationships
Losing a partner, as the people in the San Diego research study did, not only takes away the most important person in your life, but also affects your relationships with other family members and with friends. The dynamic of the family, or the group of friends, changes. And friends and family have to learn how to support the bereaved person.

6. Changes in identity
The death of a loved one can shake up people's view of themselves and the world. For the widowed Californians, the biggest change was that they were now single. At first, they often found it difficult to get used to. But over time, people learned to cope – and felt good about themselves for doing so.

For some people grief comes as a hammer blow, while others may show few signs of distress. It can burn itself out very quickly or come and go for months on end, or even years. Most people work through their grief and are back to functioning normally within a year or so of their bereavement. But for a minority, grief can remain – for years in some cases – or be so tough to deal with that help from health professionals is needed. This is more likely to be the case in people who have had depression in the past, if the death was especially traumatic, or if the relationship with the deceased was a difficult one.

Because grief is such a personal response, it is important for us to rid ourselves of the idea that there is a right or wrong way to grieve. That can be difficult, because there are a number of persistent myths about grief. For example, it used to be thought that if you were not consumed by sorrow, you were abnormal; you were 'repressing' your grief. In fact, lots of people experience little or no distress, and it's completely normal. Not only that, it's a very healthy sign. Far from repressing their grief, they are actually dealing with it extremely well.

You shouldn't feel guilt-ridden if you find yourself enjoying positive thoughts and feelings after a bereavement. This is normal too. It's very common, for instance, for people to experience feelings of relief, especially if their loved one's death followed months of suffering. Bereaved people often find happiness in memories, or come to enjoy their new independence. These are not signs that they're not grieving properly; they show that they're healing – which is exactly the purpose of grief.

You may also have heard about the 'stages' of grief. It does certainly change over time, but the experience of grief is so individual that it isn't worth attributing too much importance to the idea of a 'normal' process. Whatever you're going through is normal. You may not grieve in the same way as your friends or other people in your family – or even in the way that you've grieved in the past. And that's fine; it's simply the way you're working through your feelings this time.

How common are bereavement and grief?

Bereavement is an inescapable part of human experience. In the UK, for example, around 360,000 people a year are widowed – approximately 1000 every day. Each year about 180,000 children lose a parent, and 12,000 children die.

Around 80–90 per cent of bereaved people are back on their feet, functioning at a relatively normal level, within a year, but 10–20 per cent are more severely affected by their grief and may need professional help in dealing with it.

Self-assessment

Remember that grief is not an illness, and there is no right or wrong way to feel after a bereavement. So unlike a lot of the self-assessment questionnaires in this book, this one isn't designed to diagnose a 'problem'. However, a score of 25 or above is an indication that your grief is particularly severe and that you might benefit from some professional help.

	Never	Rarely	Sometimes	Often	Always
1. I think about the person who died so much that it is hard for me to do the things I normally do.	0	1	2	3	4
2. I feel I cannot accept the death of the person who died.	0	1	2	3	4
3. I feel myself longing for the person who died.	0	1	2	3	4
4. I feel drawn to places and things associated with the person who died.	0	1	2	3	4
5. I can't help feeling angry about his/her death.	0	1	2	3	4

	Never	Rarely	Sometimes	Often	Always
6. I feel disbelief over what happened.	0	1	2	3	4
7. I feel stunned or dazed over what happened.	0	1	2	3	4
8. Ever since she/he died it is hard for me to trust people.	0	1	2	3	4
9. Ever since she/he died I feel like I have lost the ability to care about other people or I feel distant from people I care about.	0	1	2	3	4
10. I have pain in the same area of my body or have some of the same symptoms as the person who died.	0	1	2	3	4
11. I go out of my way to avoid reminders of the person who died.	0	1	2	3	4
12. I feel that life is empty without the person who died.	0	1	2	3	4
13. I hear the voice of the person who died speak to me.	0	1	2	3	4

	Never	Rarely	Sometimes	Often	Always
14. I see the person who died stand before me.	0	1	2	3	4
15. I feel that it is unfair that I should live when this person died.	0	1	2	3	4
16. I feel bitter over this person's death.	0	1	2	3	4
17. I feel envious of others who have not lost someone close.	0	1	2	3	4
18. I feel lonely a great deal of the time ever since she/he died.	0	1	2	3	4
TOTAL					

Inventory of Complicated Grief ©1995. Reprinted with permission from Elsevier.

How to Cope with Bereavement and Grief

Bereavement is difficult enough without worrying that you're not grieving 'properly'. But as we've seen, there is no 'proper' way to grieve. So give yourself the licence to mourn as you want to mourn. Follow your instincts, your gut feelings, and not what other people might tell you.

If you're finding it really difficult to cope, or if your grief has been bothering you for more than a year, don't be afraid to ask for help. Talk to your GP or get in touch with a specialist bereavement support group (see the list of organizations on p. 136). It is also a good idea to seek help if you have nobody to talk to about your feelings.

Strategies to help you through

If you have recently been bereaved, here are some steps you can take to help yourself through the grieving process:

Use the support of family and friends

Contrary to popular belief, you don't have to talk about your feelings if you don't want to. But many people do find it very helpful. In fact, just having a good cry with someone can be really therapeutic. (If you would rather not talk to other people, writing down your thoughts can be beneficial.) Make use of family and friends for help with practical arrangements too.

Look after yourself

Get plenty of rest and regular exercise. Try to eat well and avoid the temptation to use alcohol, drugs, caffeine or nicotine to help you cope. And give yourself a treat from time to time: buy yourself that CD or go and see a film.

Take things slowly

Go easy on yourself. Allow yourself to grieve in your own time and in your own way. Don't assume you should be 'over it' by now. If you're not ready to part with your loved one's clothes and other belongings, don't do it. Put off making any major changes in your life – like starting a new relationship or changing jobs – until you feel you have come to terms with your loss.

Make time for your memories

Many bereaved people derive much comfort and pleasure from happy memories of their loved one. So don't shy away from your memories, painful though they may be at times.

Put yourself first, not work

Don't allow yourself to be pulled back into the everyday hassles of work until you're ready for them. Let your employers know what you're going through. You'll need time off in the days immediately following your loved one's death, but you might also need a less pressured workload for a while once you're back. Talk to your manager to see what can be done to ease your transition back into the workplace.

Prepare for anniversaries and other difficult dates
The pain of bereavement is often sharpest on festive occasions and other special dates (the deceased's birthday, for instance, or the anniversary of their death). Think in advance about how you can best cope with these occasions. It is often a good idea to have the company of family or friends and to make these days a time for remembering your loved one.

Think about how you might commemorate your loved one
Commemoration can be a satisfying way of remembering the deceased, and of celebrating their life. There are many options, including holding a memorial service, planting a tree or cultivating a garden, or making a donation to a relevant charity.

Help your children to grieve
Children grieve in much the same way as adults. Explain – as honestly as you can and in terms they can understand – what is happening. Let your children attend the funeral if they would like to, and talk to them about how they can be involved (perhaps by writing a letter to go in the coffin, or by giving a reading). You can help your children by listening and allowing them to mourn in the way that feels most comfortable for them. Some children like to express their feelings by drawing or writing or acting out scenarios.

Just like adults, bereaved children can draw enormous comfort from memories. So make time to look through photograph albums with them, and to talk about the deceased. Encourage them to put together memory boxes of mementoes.

Helping the bereaved
A person never needs their friends and family more than when they have just been bereaved. As the actor Judi Dench commented after the death of her husband of 30 years Michael Williams: 'Friends and colleagues are very sustaining. They're the people who get you through it.' If someone you know has recently been bereaved, here are ways in which you can help them:

Be there for them
It can be hard to know what to say to the bereaved. What on earth do you say to comfort someone in this situation? In fact, it doesn't much matter.

The crucial thing is being there so that you can listen while they talk or put your arms around them when they need a hug. Don't be embarrassed or upset if the bereaved person cries – it's a natural part of the healing process.

Let someone grieve in the way that they want to
Remember that grief is a highly personal response to bereavement. Don't expect your friend to react in the same way that you would, or tell them how they 'should' be behaving. Just give them the freedom to express their feelings as they choose. And give them the time they need to grieve. Let them set the timetable for their mourning, not you.

Don't pretend it hasn't happened
It is natural to want to cheer someone up when they feel down, but if your friend needs to cry or talk about their experiences (even for hours on end), give them the space to do so. And don't avoid mentioning the dead person for fear that you'll upset the bereaved. The chances are that they'll find it comforting to talk about their loved one, and you wouldn't want them to think that you're ignoring what has happened.

Be around for anniversaries and festive occasions
These can be among the most distressing times for the bereaved, so make sure you're there for them on these occasions.

Offer practical help
Keeping a home running in the aftermath of a bereavement isn't easy, so try to help out with practical chores. Maybe you could do the supermarket run for a while, or lend a hand with childcare. If your bereaved friend or relative is elderly, they will probably need assistance with the chores their partner used to take care of, which may be anything from paying the bills to cleaning the bathroom.

Related problems
Feeling low and anxious after bereavement is normal, but occasionally grief can trigger **depression**, severe **worry**, and **Post-Traumatic Stress Disorder**. If you think you might be suffering from one of these problems, do consult your GP.

Where to go for more information

What to do Following a Death (Lawpack, 2007) is a very useful self-help kit put together by the charity Cruse Bereavement Care. It offers sensible advice on how to cope – both emotionally and practically – after the death of a loved one. Cruse also has a helpline (0844 477 9400) and an excellent website: www.cruse.org.uk. For young people dealing with bereavement, Cruse runs both a dedicated website – www.rd4u.org.uk – and a freephone helpline (0808 808 1677).

You can also find 24-hour support at Samaritans at www.samaritans. org or on 08457 90 90 90.

Several organizations provide specialized bereavement support and advice:

For road accidents: Brakecare (www.brake.org.uk; 0845 603 8570) and Roadpeace (www.roadpeace.org; 0845 4500 355).

For cancer: Cancer Backup at www.cancerbackup.org.uk or on 0800 800 1234; and Macmillan Cancer Support at www.macmillan.org.uk or on 0808 808 2020.

For stillbirth and neonatal death: SANDS at www.uk-sands.org or on 020 7436 5881.

For relatives/friends of people who have committed suicide: Survivors of Bereavement by Suicide at www.uk-sobs.org.uk or on 0844 561 6855.

For bereaved children and their families: Winston's Wish at www. winstonswish.org.uk or on 08452 03 04 05. Children and young people can also contact Childline at www.childline.org.uk or on their 24-hour helpline, 0800 11 11.

For families in which a child has died: Compassionate Friends at www. tcf.org.uk or on 0845 123 2304.

For widows and widowers: the National Association of Widows at www. nawidows.org.uk provides support for both men and women. The Way Foundation at www.wayfoundation.org.uk or on 0870 011 3450 is designed for those widowed under the age of 50, and their children.

Problems in Children and Young People

It is increasingly recognized these days that many of the emotional and psychological problems encountered by adults are also experienced by children and young people. In the following pages, we look at some of the most common ones affecting children and teenagers, but you should also read the entries on these problems in adults; the closer your child is to adulthood, the more useful the adult entries will be.

DEPRESSION, FEARS AND ANXIETY

The most important question in the world is, 'Why is the child crying?'
Alice Walker

Until very recently it was thought that children don't suffer from depression or anxiety or irrational fears. This type of problem was regarded as the product of long years of stress and hardship, and children – innocent and happy-go-lucky – had simply not lived long enough to develop them.

However, we now know better, and understand that these problems can strike at any age, although anxiety and depression tend to develop in adolescence, while phobias often start earlier in childhood. In fact, anxiety and depression are so alike in children and adults that you should read this section – which focuses on the 6–14 age group – in conjunction with the main entries on these topics (see p. 65 and p. 186).

There is one type of anxiety that specifically affects children. In separation anxiety, children become very distressed at the thought of being separated from their parents or loved ones, or sometimes even leaving the house. Separation anxiety is normal; all children go through it, generally as toddlers (although older children are susceptible, too). It is only regarded as a problem when it is particularly intense and distressing for the child and when it goes on for a month or more.

Generally, the symptoms of depression and anxiety in children are very similar to those experienced by adults. There are differences, though. Depressed children tend to be irritable and sometimes aggressive, rather than seeming sad. Anxiety in younger children often shows itself in tantrums, crying or being especially clingy and demanding.

Your child may have an anxiety problem if they:

- spend a lot of time worrying
- need constant reassurance
- develop an excessive perfectionist streak
- have sleep problems
- complain of frequent aches and pains
- cry a lot
- become distressed at the thought of being separated from their parents, or worry about losing them
- are extremely uncomfortable in social situations
- are very frightened by a particular object or situation – heights, for instance, or animals (this is a sign of a phobia).

Your child may be depressed if they:

- have trouble sleeping, or spend much more time asleep than usual
- no longer enjoy things that used to give them pleasure
- seem down most of the time
- are irritable or aggressive
- eat less, or more, than usual
- feel constantly tired
- seem preoccupied by death or dying.

Songs my mother taught me

What causes anxiety, irrational fears, and phobias? How do we end up scared of heights, or dogs or social situations? You probably won't be astounded to discover that there are no simple answers to these questions. Like most psychological problems, a combination of factors is usually involved. But we know now that the lessons we learn from our parents are often a factor.

This was nicely demonstrated in an experiment carried out by psychologists Friederike Gerull and Ronald Rapee. They showed 30 toddlers in Sydney, Australia a green rubber snake and then a purple rubber spider, and studied their reactions. While the toys were on display, the children's mothers were asked to react in a happy and encouraging way or in a frightened or disgusted manner. Later on, the snake and the spider were shown to the toddlers a couple more times, although their mothers' reactions were now strictly neutral.

What Gerull and Rapee noticed was that you could predict how a child would react to the toy when they saw it again, because they mimicked the initial response of their mother. If the mother had seemed to be afraid, the child was frightened. If the mother had been calm and happy, so too was the toddler.

As ever, more research needs to be done, but already we can see how crucial the example we set our kids can be. Children pick up anxieties, fears and phobias from their most influential teachers: their parents. But if that feels like a crushing burden of responsibility, remember that if our children copy our negative behaviour, it follows that we can help them to overcome their anxieties by maintaining a positive, relaxed attitude towards life's troubles in general and the situations they find scary in particular.

The problem is, of course, that most children – and especially teenagers – behave in these ways from time to time. How do you know if your perpetually bad-tempered fourteen-year-old is depressed, or simply being a teenager? And the fact that children and young people often find it difficult to talk about their feelings only makes it harder for parents to judge whether or not there may be a problem.

Just as in adults, children's experience of depression and anxiety varies hugely. For many, these feelings are not especially severe, and they come and go pretty quickly. But for a minority, they can be persistent and cause real distress, sometimes to the extent of provoking thoughts of self-harm or suicide.

Parents often assume that they're responsible for their child's anxiety or depression. This is a natural response, but although upbringing may have an influence, it is rarely as simple as that. Again, as with adults, psychological problems in children are generally the result of a complex interaction of multiple factors. That interaction varies from person to person, but somewhere in the mix are usually:

- personality and genetic make-up
- lessons learned from those around them – psychologists think children can pick up anxious or depressed behaviour from the people closest to them
- unpleasant life experiences, such as family conflict, bereavement or bullying

Children who are 'down' or anxious often come out of it fairly quickly and without outside assistance. But if things don't resolve themselves within a few weeks, their problems do need to be confronted. Apart from the impact on the child's current life, severe depression or anxiety can persist well into adulthood if they're not tackled promptly. However, the good news is that there are now some extremely effective psychological therapies to help you deal with them, as outlined on pp. 148–53.

Problems with depression, fears and anxiety in children: some personal accounts

I had a horrible time as a teenager. I think I spent at least a year of it on my own in my room. I was always quite shy, and I can remember when I was six or seven looking at the other girls in my class and thinking that they were all prettier than me. But basically I was fine till I got to about 13; then it was like someone turned the lights out. I felt

incredibly low most of the time. I hated the way I looked. I had absolutely no energy. Nothing was fun. Thankfully, my parents were incredibly patient with me – which can't have been easy because I was usually foul to them. My mum in particular used to drag me out to places with her. She didn't lecture me; she just let me whinge on at her, and I think that helped. Basically, my mum and dad pulled me out of a very deep hole, and I'll always be grateful to them for that.
Amy, aged 20

Ben was quite a fretful baby. He didn't like being put down, and he didn't like strangers. By the time he was 18 months old, he'd scream blue murder if I wasn't with him. Everyone told us he'd grow out of it, but things just got worse. Even at the age of five he'd have huge tantrums if he thought he was going to be separated from me or his dad. Getting him to school was horrific; he'd howl all the way and say he had a tummy ache or his head hurt and how he'd never be happy again if we didn't take him home. At night, we'd settle him in bed, stay with him for however long it took for him to drop off – and then 10 minutes later he'd be up, crying for us. We were at the end of our tether. But our GP was terrific; she referred us to a child psychologist and much to my surprise things got better very quickly.*
Dawn, aged 31

How common are depression, fears and anxiety in children and young people?

Every child goes through stages of feeling anxious, fearful or sad. Fifty per cent of teenagers say they feel low. Childhood fears are a normal part of our development, for sensible evolutionary reasons. For example, all babies have a spell during which they hate to be separated from their parents, and young children are usually wary of animals they're not familiar with. These normal feelings only become an issue when they go on for a long time or when they have a big impact on everyday life.

Anxiety, fears, and depression are the most common psychological problems faced by children and young people. At any one time, around 4 per cent of children and young people have a clinical anxiety disorder and about 1 per cent suffer from severe depression.

Assessment

Diagnosing any psychological problem is a job for a trained health professional, and that is especially true when it comes to children. If you're at all worried about your child, you should talk to your GP, but you can get an indication of possible problems from the two questionnaires below.

	0 – Not true or hardly ever true	1 – Somewhat true or sometimes true	2 – Very true or often true
1. When my child feels frightened, it is hard for him/her to breathe.			
2. My child gets headaches when he/she is at school.			
3. My child does not like to be with people he/she does not know well.			
4. My child gets scared if he/she sleeps away from home.			
5. My child worries about other people liking him/her.			
6. When my child gets frightened, he/she feels like passing out.			
7. My child is nervous.			
8. My child follows me wherever I go.			
9. People tell me that my child looks nervous.			
10. My child feels nervous with people he/she does not know well.			
11. My child gets stomach aches at school.			

	0 – Not true or hardly ever true	1 – Some-what true or sometimes true	2 – Very true or often true
12. When my child gets frightened, he/she feels like he/she is going crazy.			
13. My child worries about sleeping alone.			
14. My child worries about being as good as other children.			
15. When he/she gets frightened, he/she feels like things are not real.			
16. My child has nightmares about something bad happening to his/her parents.			
17. My child worries about going to school.			
18. When my child gets frightened, his/her heart beats fast.			
19. He/she gets shaky.			
20. My child has nightmares about something bad happening to him/her.			
21. My child worries about things working out for him/her.			
22. When my child gets frightened, he/she sweats a lot.			

	0 – Not true or hardly ever true	1 – Some-what true or sometimes true	2 – Very true or often true
23. My child is a worrier.			
24. My child gets really frightened for no reason at all.			
25. My child is afraid to be alone in the house.			
26. It is hard for my child to talk to people he/she does not know well.			
27. When my child gets frightened, he/she feels like he/she is choking.			
28. People tell me that my child worries too much.			
29. My child does not like to be away from his/her family.			
30. My child is afraid of having anxiety (or panic) attacks.			
31. My child worries that something bad might happen to his/her parents.			
32. My child feels shy with people he/she does not know well.			
33. My child worries about what is going to happen in the future.			

	0 – Not true or hardly ever true	1 – Some-what true or sometimes true	2 – Very true or often true
34. When my child gets frightened, he/she feels like throwing up.			
35. My child worries about how well he/she does things.			
36. My child is scared to go to school.			
37. My child worries about things that have already happened.			
38. When my child gets frightened, he/she feels dizzy.			
39. My child feels nervous when he/she is with other children or adults and he/she has to do something while they watch him/her (for example: read aloud, speak, play a game, play a sport).			
40. My child feels nervous when he/she is going to parties, dances or any place where there will be people that he/she does not know well.			
41. My child is shy.			

Screen for Child Anxiety Related Disorders (SCARED); Birmaher and colleagues (1999).

A score of 25 or more indicates a possible anxiety disorder.

The following questionnaire is designed to gauge depression in children and young people aged 6 to 17. It needs to be filled in by the child or teenager themselves.

During the past week	Not at all	A little bit	Some	A lot
1. I was bothered by things that usually don't bother me.				
2. I did not feel like eating, I wasn't very hungry.				
3. I wasn't able to feel happy, even when my family or friends tried to help me feel better.				
4. I felt like I was just as good as other kids.				
5. I felt like I couldn't pay attention to what I was doing.				
6. I felt down and unhappy.				
7. I felt like I was too tired to do things.				
8. I felt like something good was going to happen.				
9. I felt like things I did before didn't work out right.				
10. I felt scared.				
11. I didn't sleep as well as I usually sleep.				

During the past week	Not at all	A little bit	Some	A lot
12. I was happy.				
13. I was more quiet than usual.				
14. I felt lonely, like I didn't have any friends.				
15. I felt like kids I know were not friendly or that they didn't want to be with me.				
16. I had a good time.				
17. I felt like crying.				
18. I felt sad.				
19. I felt people didn't like me.				
20. It was hard to get started doing things.				

Center for Epidemiological Studies Depression Scale for Children (CES-DC); Weissman and colleagues (1980).

Each answer scores between 0 and 3 points:

0 – Not at all   1 – A little bit
2 – Some   3 – A lot

But questions 4, 8, 12, and 16 are reverse scored:
3 – Not at all   2 – A little bit
1 – Some   0 – A lot

A total score of 15 or above may be a sign of depression.

How to Help Your Child Overcome Depression, Fears or Anxiety

Finding the right tools to help your child

As a parent, you're in a great position to help your child overcome any emotional or psychological problems. After all – and even though it may not always feel like it! – no one understands them better or has such a huge influence on them. Use the following strategies to help your child.

Find out if something specific is troubling your child

It might be bullying or difficulty with an aspect of schoolwork. Talk to your child, and their teacher, to see whether you can identify the problem. And then help your child to work out how to solve it (see p. 110 for information on problem-solving techniques).

Note: although bullying is often a factor in childhood depression or anxiety, it's an extremely complex issue that goes beyond the scope of this book. If you think your child is being bullied, a good place to start is the Parentlineplus website (see p. 153).

Consider your child's diet

How many of us get grumpy when we're hungry? Food, and especially the lack of it, can have a massive impact on mood, and children are no exception. Make sure your children have regular, nutritious meals (for more advice, see pp. 18–21), don't let them skip breakfast and do give them healthy snacks between meals to keep up their blood sugar level. The occasional bag of sweets or bar of chocolate is fine, but save them for treats.

Encourage good sleep habits

Any parent who can recall their child's first few months in the world will know the effects of a lack of sleep. So it follows that plenty of good-quality sleep can work wonders if your child is feeling down or anxious. Children aged 5 to 12 need between 9 and 11 hours' sleep a night, while teenagers generally need about 9. Stick to a bedtime routine, especially for younger children, and make sure it includes winding-down time (a soak in the bath and a story are great for little ones). It helps too if your child goes to bed and gets up at roughly the same time each day.

Make sure your child gets regular exercise

There is evidence to suggest that regular exercise is a fantastic remedy for depression. Encourage your child to get at least 30 minutes exercise a day.

Develop a routine

Anxious children in particular find routines comforting because they don't have to worry about what might be happening next. This doesn't mean you have to plan their day in microscopic detail, and it's healthy to keep a degree of flexibility, but developing routines for, say, the start of the day, mealtimes, and bedtimes can make a big difference.

Practise your communication skills

This might be the most crucial advice of all. It can be tough to find out from your child how they're feeling; chatting about this sort of thing generally doesn't come easily to them. But you can help by making time to talk. Ask your child questions – and listen to the answers.

If there is bad news for your child, however minor it might seem to you, don't spring it on them at the last minute: give them some warning. Make sure the notice you give them is appropriate for their age. An hour or so is fine for under-fives (anything more and they'll probably forget) and children aged five to seven can handle a day or two's warning. Children aged eight to eleven will appreciate several days' notice; give older children as much warning as possible.

Talk to your child's teacher and to other parents

Teachers can often provide a different perspective on a child's behaviour. They also need to know your concerns about your child.

Other parents can be a great source of advice too, so share your worries with friends. Remember, whatever you have to cope with, the chances are that someone else will have gone through it before you.

Set clear and consistent boundaries

You might never guess it, but children love fair, clear and consistent rules. They need them to feel secure and, of course, to give them something to push against. (If they're pushing a little too hard though, see pp. 175–81 for advice on how to deal with tantrums.)

Try to involve your child when you define the boundaries – a little token negotiation and compromise can work wonders. And remember that everyone caring for your child needs to buy into the rules; if each parent follows their own, for example, it's a recipe for disaster.

Be a positive role model

Children pick up so much from their parents, including – sometimes – their anxiety and depression. If you have a serious problem, it's important that you get help, for your own sake as well as your child's. Children often end up sharing their parents' fears and phobias in particular, so turn to pp. 68–72 for advice on how to overcome them. And if you're just inclined to be a bit down or anxious, try to remain positive in front of your kids.

Boost your child's self-esteem

Almost by definition, a depressed or anxious child is not going to be feeling great about themselves. But if you can turn that around, you'll be going a long way towards helping them get over their problems. Try the following:

Set aside 10 minutes each day of 'special time'. This is a great way to show your child how much they mean to you. Drop everything else and make them the centre of attention. Let them decide how you spend this special time.

Give your child plenty of praise, several times a day. Concentrate on the activities your child enjoys and is good at, and on the behaviour you want to see more of – that way, you keep the focus positive.

Schedule in one interesting activity every day. This doesn't have to be a grand outing, just so long as it's fun (school doesn't count, and neither does watching TV). It could be a trip to the park or the swimming pool, or tea at a friend's house. Something involving exercise is always good. But whatever you opt for, it will take your child's mind off their worries and help them to feel more positive about themselves and the world.

Have fun as a family. This gives everyone a lift, and is another great way to show your children that you want to spend time with them.

Encourage your child to try new things. One of the consequences of low self-esteem is a lack of confidence. And when a person lacks confidence, they tend to restrict their activities to relatively easy things – which, in turn, confirms their sense that this is all they're good for. Encourage your child to have a go at new things – maybe trying out a new sport or an after-school club that you think they will do well at. They'll soon discover that they're capable of so much more than they realized, which will provide them with a much-needed confidence boost. And make sure you reward your child for their bravery. It doesn't have to be much, as long as it's something your child really wants. Try to give them their reward as soon after the new activity as you can.

Help your child to face their fears

Children, just like adults, try to avoid situations they find stressful. If they can't get out of them altogether, they'll use a range of tactics to help them cope. If they're anxious in social situations, for example, they might only go to a party with a close friend; if they're worried about participating in school, they might try to hide themselves at the back of the class. (These coping strategies are known as 'safety behaviours'.)

When people behave in this way, they might succeed in eliminating any distress in the short term, but at the same time they're not giving themselves a chance to find out whether or not their fears are justified. To do that, they must face the situations they dread – and without resorting to safety behaviours. This is called 'exposure', and you can read more about it on pp. 87–8. In a nutshell, however, you need to help your child identify and make a list of those activities they find frightening, then break each one down into small, manageable tasks. For example, if the problem is participating in class, the first step might be to move to a seat towards the middle of the room; the second might be to take a place at the front; the third to raise a hand to speak alongside other children; and the fourth to volunteer an answer when no one else has raised a hand.

Guide your child gently through their list of most-feared activities step-by-step, starting with the least stressful one. Your child will soon learn that the scary physical signs of fear – pounding heart, breathlessness, dizziness and so on – are not dangerous. Their anxiety will gradually decrease and, in time, they'll realize that they really can cope with these situations. (Exposure, incidentally, is the most effective way to treat separation anxiety.)

Work with your child to challenge their negative thoughts

The older a child is, the more likely it is that their depression or anxiety is fuelled by a host of gloomy thoughts about themselves and the world: 'Everyone hates me'; 'I'm ugly'; 'You can't trust other people'; 'Bad things are bound to happen to me'. Help your child to identify their negative thoughts, then work with them to assess the evidence for these thoughts and to come up with positive alternatives. (See pp. 9–12 for more information about challenging negative thoughts.)

Help your child manage their worrying
Worry is an integral part of depression and anxiety. See pp. 109–112 for advice on how to cope with it.

Therapy and/or medication
If your child is feeling very depressed or anxious, make sure you talk to your GP about it. You should contact them urgently if you suspect that your child might harm themselves.

The standard technique for treating childhood depression and anxiety is Cognitive Behaviour Therapy (CBT); much of the advice given here is drawn from this discipline and has proved very successful. Your GP may refer you to a specialist child psychologist for a full review and perhaps a number of CBT sessions.

In some instances, your GP may also suggest a child and adolescent psychiatrist. The psychiatrist may consider medication, but only if they think your child's problems are severe. The National Institute for Health and Clinical Excellence (NICE), the government body responsible for recommending the most effective forms of treatment for medical problems, has said that medication should only be used to treat mild depression after psychological therapies have been tried, and that even when medication is prescribed it should be used in combination with these therapies (of which, it says, CBT is the best). If your child is given medication it is likely to be the antidepressant fluoxetine, better known as Prozac.

Related problems
Relationship problems in a family or a parent struggling with **anxiety** or **depression** can have an impact on a child's emotional well-being. In a small proportion of young people, severe depression or anxiety can be reflected in challenging behaviour, including **drug** and **alcohol** problems, and in **self-injury**.

Where to go for more information
Coping with an Anxious or Depressed Child (Oneworld, 2007) by Sam Cartwright-Hatton is an excellent guide, full of sensible advice and written in a very accessible style.

The following are also worth looking at:

Happy Kids (Virgin Books, 2007) by Alexandra Massey; *Helping Your Anxious Child* (New Harbinger, 2000) by Ronald Rapee, Susan Spence, Vanessa Cobham and Anne Wignall; *Overcoming Your Child's Fears and Worries* (Robinson, 2007) by Cathy Cresswell and Lucy Willetts.

And several books are aimed specifically at children and young people:

Mr Jelly and Little Miss Shy (both Egmont, 2003) by Roger Hargreaves (pre-schoolers); *I Don't Know Why ... I Guess I'm Shy* (American Psychological Association, 2000) by Barbara Cain and J. J. Smith-Moore (4–8 years); *No Worries!* (Walker, 2000) by Marcia Williams (4–8 years); *Up and Down the Worry Hill: A Children's Book about Obsessive–Compulsive Disorder and Its Treatment* (Lighthouse Press, 2004) by Aureen Pinto Wagner; *Think Good – Feel Good* (John Wiley, 2002) by Paul Stallard (older children and teenagers); *How to be a Friend* (Little, Brown, 1998) by Laurie Krasny Brown and Marc Brown; *The Willow Street Kids Beat the Bullies* (Macmillan, 1997) by Michele Elliott (7–11 years); *Bullying* (Hodder, 2005) by Michele Elliott (older children and teenagers); *Bullying: How to spot it and how to stop it* (Rodale, 2006) by Karen Sullivan.

On the Internet, parents can find support and advice at:

- ⓘ www.parentlineplus.org.uk
- ⓘ www.anxietyuk.org.uk (the Anxiety UK website) which includes information for young people struggling with anxiety
- ⓘ www.youngminds.org.uk which has dedicated sections for parents, younger children and teenagers.

Bedwetting

Conventional wisdom used to regard bedwetting as a symptom of underlying emotional or psychological problems. What we know now is that it is usually nothing of the sort. For most children, bedwetting is simply the result of the brain and bladder not communicating properly. As children get older, these two parts of the body start working together as a team and the bedwetting stops.

Bedwetting can mean lots of extra work for parents, not to mention anxiety. And, as children get older, it can bring shame, worry and guilt.

Because bedwetting – for understandable reasons – is not the sort of thing most parents or children are comfortable talking about, it is easy to think that you're the only ones affected. So it's important to remember that bedwetting, even in schoolchildren, is normal. They grow out of it.

Bedwetting is so common that doctors don't regard it as a problem until children are at least five. If after that a child wets the bed at least twice a week for three consecutive months, they would be classed as suffering from 'nocturnal enuresis', which is just the medical term for bedwetting. That does not mean a child must have 'treatment'. There are lots of things parents can do to help them become dry – as you'll see. But if parents and child prefer, simply waiting for brain and bladder to start talking to one another is a perfectly reasonable option.

How common is bedwetting?

Until they're about two, almost all children wet themselves: they're too young to have bladder control. Over the two or three years that follow, most preschoolers learn to be dry at night. But around 1 in 7 five-year-olds wets their bed regularly. By age 10, that figure is around 1 in 20. And by the time they're 15, 99 per cent of young people are dry at night.

I was a bedwetter, and I married an ex-bedwetter, so I guess neither of us was surprised that Mattie took so long to be dry at night! He didn't wet the bed every night – maybe twice or three times a week, but more often if he was really tired or away from home. I can't pretend it was a joy, but we decided early on to downplay it with Mattie as much as possible. We'd put him in trainer pants at night; take them off for a while every couple of months; and then try again for two or three weeks. Things carried on like that until Mattie was seven. Then one evening he announced at supper that he didn't want to wear his pants in bed any more – and lo and behold he was dry that night. We had a few accidents after that but within a couple of months he had it sorted.
Jan, aged 32

Among younger children, boys are more likely to wet the bed, but in the 12–16 age group it is more common in girls. Bedwetting runs in the family: children are much more likely to wet the bed if a parent did likewise.

How to Overcome Bedwetting

Actually, you don't have to 'overcome' bedwetting at all. You could just wait for it to stop (and 99 times out of a hundred it does). As children get older, and it dawns on them that their peers are dry at night (or claim they are), dealing with bedwetting often becomes a more pressing issue. But even then you can wait. Just make sure you're relaxed and that you don't make an issue of it. If your child is a bit older, talk things through with them. You're much more likely to be successful if they really want to sort things out.

If you and your child do decide to tackle their bedwetting, this is what you need to do:

Keep a diary
This will give you an accurate sense of how frequently, and how severely, your child wets the bed. It will also help you to track their progress, which can really boost morale if it seems like it's taking for ever to get them dry.

Bedtime routine
Don't be tempted to restrict your child's fluid intake during the day, or you run the risk of them becoming dehydrated, but avoid drinks close to bedtime. And make sure they go to the toilet before bed.

Encourage and praise your child
Every time your child has a dry night, let them know how pleased and proud you are of their achievement.

Don't criticize your child
If your child has wet the bed, don't criticize them or show any frustration or unhappiness. And you should definitely not punish them. They're not wetting the bed on purpose, after all. Besides, your disappointment will

do nothing to help them stay dry; if anything, it'll just make them more anxious about the whole situation.

Make sure the toilet is within easy reach

If your toilet is up a flight of stairs, for example, it may be difficult for your child to get there in time – in which case consider putting a potty in their room. Similarly, keep the house at a reasonable temperature – no one likes getting up in the middle of the night when it's freezing. And if your child is scared of the dark, use a night light. (See also pp. 157–164 for more information on children's sleep problems.)

Wake your child up and take them to the toilet

This is probably worth a try if the tactics above don't work. It can't teach your child to be dry, but it may save you from having to deal with yet another wet bed. Take your child to the toilet when you go to bed, but try to vary the precise times. Make sure your child is fully awake, and get them to use the toilet even if they're already wet.

Medical help

If there's no improvement, talk to your GP who will be very used to dealing with these issues. They'll be able to check for any physical problem, such as a urinary tract infection, although in 99 per cent of cases there isn't one. Your GP may put you in touch with a specialist, who is likely to recommend a urine alarm. These go off when they detect urine, prompting the child to go to the toilet. It can take three or four months, but eventually the child learns to wake up before the alarm sounds. The success rate for alarms is very high – around 60–80 per cent of children who use them learn to become dry at night. (To find out more about alarms, have a look at the websites listed below.)

Related problems

In a relatively small proportion of children, bedwetting is caused by **anxiety**, **worry**, **fears** or feeling miserable.

Where to go for more information

Waking Up Dry (American Academy of Pediatrics, 2005) by Howard Bennett sets out a practical programme to overcome bedwetting. It is designed for children (roughly aged 6–11) to read through with their parents.

The Complete Bedwetting Book (PottyMD, 2006) by D. Preston Smith is a short and sensible guide to the topic.

On the Internet:

- ⓘ www.eric.org.uk offers information and support for parents, children and teenagers
- ⓘ There is a wide range of urine alarms and other accessories at www.bedwettingstore.com.

SLEEP PROBLEMS

Yes, there is a Nirvanah; it is leading your sheep to a green pasture and in putting your child to sleep, and in writing the last line of your poem.
Khalil Gibran

For many parents, the phrase 'sleeping like a baby' will seem like savage irony. Lots of infants don't appear to sleep very much at all, and never when their exhausted parents want them to. Things don't always improve as your little one gets bigger either. In fact, children and teenagers can be affected by most of the same sleep problems as adults, so it is also worth looking at the general sleep problems entry on pp. 334–52.

Top of the list for children, just as it is with adults, is insomnia. This means taking longer than half an hour to fall asleep and problems with staying asleep – in both cases, often accompanied by crying, protests or repeated trips out of bed in babies and young children. Sleepwalking, nightmares and night terrors (in which the child screams and cries inconsolably, though deeply asleep) are common, especially in younger children.

When your child is a teenager, they may also experience a strange resetting of their body clock, which means they want to go to sleep and, most crucially, get up later than they did previously. And because school starts at the same time for fourteen-year-olds as it does for everyone else, this can soon lead to your teenager being sleep deprived.

How much sleep does your child need?

The table below suggests average requirements, of course: each child is different. But if children don't get enough good-quality sleep they all react in the same way. Like adults, they become grumpy and sleepy and are unable to concentrate or function properly.

Age	Average amount of sleep needed (including naps)
Birth–2 months	10.5–18 hours
2–12 months	14–15 hours
12–18 months	13–15 hours
18 months–3 years	12–14 hours
3–5 years	11–13 hours
5–12 years	9–11 hours
Teenagers	8–10 hours

This, of course, is no fun for the other members of the family. As every parent knows, children's sleep problems affect the whole household. Apart from their exhausted behaviour during the day, if your child isn't sleeping well, the chances are that you won't be either. If this is the case, you need to take action.

How common are children's sleep problems?

At least a quarter of children experience sleep-related problems at some stage, with insomnia being the most common. Lots of children sleepwalk, particularly in the 4–8 age group. Only 2–3 per cent sleepwalk regularly, but 40 per cent take an occasional midnight stroll. Around 5 per cent of children suffer night terrors, although (as with sleepwalking) they generally grow out of it by the age of eight.

How to Overcome Children's Sleep Problems

The techniques for improving children's sleep are very similar to those we recommend for adults, so read the advice on pp. 340–52 as well.

Here, we're going to focus on the most common problem facing parents: how to teach your child to fall asleep easily and, just as importantly, to stay asleep. In other words: how to tackle childhood insomnia. And it is a question of teaching. Good sleep habits are learned, which is great news for tired parents, because although it may take a bit of perseverance, you really can train your child – no matter how old they are – to sleep well.

Start by keeping a sleep diary. Jot down what kind of a night your child has had. Sleep problems can take a while to sort out. So when you're feeling as if things are not getting any better, a record of the progress you and your child have actually made can provide a big morale boost.

Teaching techniques

Now you can get to work on teaching your child those good sleep habits. Some of the following strategies are particularly relevant to babies and preschoolers; much of it, with a little tweaking, is applicable to children of all ages.

Develop a bedtime routine
The final hour before bed should be winding-down time. A nice, warm bath and some happy, relaxing stories is a tried-and-tested formula for younger children.

Keep to specific times
Put your child to bed at the same time each night, and stick to the same getting-up time. Older children may want to lie in at weekends, but keep this to a minimum (an hour or so), otherwise you run the risk of disrupting the body clock you have worked on setting all week.

Make your child comfortable
Ensure that your child's bed is comfortable, and that their room is dark, warm and quiet.

No television in bed
Do not allow your child to watch television in bed. In fact, many experts recommend that children don't even have televisions or other electronic equipment (such as computers or PlayStations) in their room at all; it is too much of a temptation at bedtime.

Monsters, Inc.?

Is your little one afraid of the dark? Do they worry about wild animals under the bed? Or furry blue monsters with purple spots in the wardrobe?

It used to be thought that only very young children had anxieties like these. But recent research has shown that much older children also have night-time fears (although furry blue monsters tend not to figure). In fact, these worries affect an astonishingly large proportion of children of all ages.

One fascinating study looked at 176 children aged 4 to 12 in the Netherlands. Almost three-quarters of the kids experienced night-time fears. And these didn't diminish as the children got older. In fact, more of the over-sevens had worries like these than the under-sevens.

What exactly were the children afraid of? Intruders (for example, burglars and kidnappers) came top of the list, followed in descending order by ghosts and monsters, frightening dreams, fear of the dark and thunderstorms, animals and upsetting thoughts about something horrible happening to themselves or their parents. The younger children tended to be scared of monsters and ghosts and frightening dreams, whereas older children were more prone to upsetting thoughts.

When asked where their fears had come from, the children overwhelmingly pointed to things they had seen, read or been told, with television being the principal culprit.

Most interesting of all, however, was the contrast between what the Dutch children reported about their experiences and what their parents said. Seventy-six per cent of the children reported night-time fears. But only 34 per cent of parents said their children had them. Not only that, but the parents thought that night-time fears decreased with age, which is not, as we have seen, the case.

Restrict fluid intake before bedtime

Cut down on the amount your child drinks before bedtime so that they don't need to get up in the night for the toilet. Drinks with caffeine in them (tea, coffee, cola, etc.) are a particular no-no. Make a trip to the toilet part of their bedtime routine.

Children's sleep problems: a personal account

Grace had always been a great sleeper but that all changed soon after she started school. She'd lie awake for an hour or more, constantly calling for us, and getting out of bed repeatedly. She'd come into our bedroom three, four, even five times a night. It didn't take long before we were all exhausted. Whenever we asked her what was wrong, she'd just say she wasn't tired or there was too much noise, or too much light – whatever popped into her head. It was driving us mad. But a friend suggested we stay really calm, not make a big deal out of it, and see what happened. Well, what happened was that Grace told us one day – slipped it into conversation while we were in the supermarket, in fact – that she was scared of going to school. After that, it was easy. We had something we could deal with. And within a few weeks Grace was sleeping as well as she ever had.

Philippa, aged 28

Make sure your child is tired at the end of the day

Has your child had enough exercise? (Thirty minutes a day is a minimum requirement, although this shouldn't be at the end of the day.) Have they napped too long?

Consider your own role in your child's sleep habits

You also need to think about the part you play in your child's sleep habits. This includes:

Teaching your child to fall asleep on their own and in their own bed. This is crucial, because children (like everyone else) wake periodically in the night. The trick is getting them to settle themselves back to sleep. But if your child is used to going to sleep with you beside them, or holding them, or feeding them, that is what they will want in the middle of the night.

There are a number of ways to sort this out; choose the one that is right for you and your child. You could try what is known as 'controlled crying', whereby you let your child cry for a limited time and they soon learn to settle themselves.

Or you might prefer to leave the room but return to check on your child at progressively increasing intervals. Finally, you could opt for 'gradual withdrawal', in which you might start by holding your child as they fall asleep or by lying next to them, but over a number of nights you gradually move further away.

Being clear, firm and consistent in your night-time rules. Once you have explained to your child what is going to happen at bedtime (and during the night), don't give in to pleas for yet another story or for you to lie down next to them. Children sometimes act up at bedtime because they love the special one-to-one attention they get from their parent and they don't want it to end. If you think this could be a factor with your child, try to make time for them earlier in the day.

Taking your child straight back to bed if they get up in the night. This can be tough at 2 a.m. and even tougher if it happens again at 3, 4 and 5 a.m. But don't let your child sleep in your bed – unless you want them there all the time.

Rewarding good behaviour. Like most of us, children respond much more positively to praise and encouragement than they do to criticism and punishment. So when your child behaves well at night, let them know how pleased you are – and resist the temptation to rant and rave if they don't, as this will only make a stressful situation worse. Sticker charts and little rewards are often very effective.

What if your child's sleep problems are caused by worries or fears?

As we have seen, it is very common for children of all ages to have certain anxieties that can affect their sleep. The following techniques can be helpful if you think this may be the case with your child:

- Talk to your child – and listen to their answers. Be understanding, sympathetic and reassuring.
- Teach them positive thoughts they can use: 'Nothing is going to hurt me', 'There is no such thing as monsters'.
- A soft toy to cuddle can be a big help for little ones, and if they're scared of the dark, use a night light.
- Avoid scary stories or films before bed.
- Older children are often worried by things they read or see on television. Again, talk through their worries with them and help them to get some perspective on their anxieties. If they're fretting about a problem closer to

home – a situation at school, for example – help them to work out how to solve it (see p. 110 for information on problem-solving techniques).

- Praise your child for their bravery.
- Teach your child tricks to take their mind off their worries. Word-based activities are great, if they're old enough – for example, thinking of animals beginning with each letter of the alphabet. If your child is too young for this sort of thing, get them to visualize, for example, all the animals they can think of that live in the jungle. In fact, visualization is a terrific way for children (and adults) to relax: ask your child to imagine a waterfall, or waves washing up on a beach.

What about sleepwalking and night terrors?

Both of these are less likely to occur if you can teach your child good sleep habits (see the advice above for dealing with insomnia on p. 158). If your child is affected, however:

- Don't wake them up. Both sleepwalking and night terrors happen during the very deepest stage of sleep – so deep, in fact, that your child will have no memory of what has happened in the night. Waking them up is incredibly difficult, but also not worth the trouble. You'll only add to their distress or agitation if you do. If your child is sleepwalking, gently lead them back to bed.
- Make sure they're safe. If your child is a sleepwalker, try to make the house as safe as possible for them. Don't leave windows open or the front door unlocked, and consider using a stair gate. If your child is having a night terror, just stay with them to make sure they're all right.
- Try scheduled waking. (This strategy can be used to tackle either sleepwalking or night terrors, although it's really only suitable if they occur frequently and at roughly the same time each night.) Very gently rouse your child about 30 minutes before their sleepwalking or night terrors usually start. There's no need to wake them up completely; what's important is to stop them going into the very deep sleep that leads to these night-time episodes. Do this every night for a week and then take a break.

Medical help

If you're still worried about your child's sleep after trying these techniques, talk to your GP. They will be able to rule out any physical cause and may refer you and your child on to a sleep specialist.

Note: you should definitely see your GP if your child snores or has breathing problems when they're asleep.

Related problems

Don't forget to look at the general **sleep problems** section (pp. 334–52) where there is plenty of information and advice that is relevant to children as well as adults. Similarly, if you think your child's sleep problems might be caused by **anxiety**, **worry**, **fears**, or **depression** have a look at the entries on those topics.

Where to go for more information

There are dozens of books on children and sleep, which just goes to show how common these problems are – and how desperate parents can become. Two that are particularly helpful are Tanya Byron's *Your Child, Your Way* (Penguin, 2007), which includes a useful section on sleep problems, and *Take Charge of Your Child's Sleep* (Marlowe, 2005) by Judy Owens and Jodi Mindell, which covers teenagers as well as younger children.

HYPERACTIVITY, IMPULSIVENESS AND INATTENTION

. . . .

By the time I think about it, I have done it!
Dennis the Menace

. . . .

Does your child have a short attention span? Are they always on the go? Do you have trouble persuading them to do what you say? Does your child sometimes seem to be in a world of their own?

Did you answer 'Yes' to any of the above? Well, of course – that's what children are like. But in a small proportion of cases, this kind of normal behaviour becomes exaggerated and really difficult to deal with. This is known as Attention Deficit Hyperactivity Disorder – or ADHD.

A child with ADHD typically finds it difficult to concentrate on a task for any length of time. They're hyperactive: restless, fidgety and always flitting from one thing to another. Children with ADHD are often extremely boisterous, charging around in the most inappropriate situations and talk-

ADHD in adults

Most people think of ADHD as a childhood problem. But in fact a sizeable proportion of children – some studies put the figure as high as 30–50 per cent – never grow out of their ADHD and take it with them into adulthood.

Relatively little research has been done in this area, but one notable exception is a US study of 172 people diagnosed with ADHD at a specialist clinic. The researchers compared them to another 30 adults who had been referred by their doctors to the same clinic, but who had turned out not to have ADHD.

The contrast was startling in that the adults with ADHD:

- had much higher rates of drug and alcohol problems
- were nearly twice as likely to have been fired from a job
- frequently quit jobs on an impulse
- were more likely to be antisocial, aggressive or difficult
- had been involved in more driving accidents and received more speeding tickets
- were much more likely to have dropped out of college or performed poorly at school
- had been married more often
- reported more difficulties with relationships, and more emotional problems such as anger, depression, anxiety and phobias.

Bear in mind that these are people at the relatively severe end of the ADHD spectrum – the ones who seek professional help – and that many more adults cope well with their hyperactivity and impulsiveness. But the study suggests that ADHD may lurk behind all kinds of personal problems in adults.

ing a mile a minute. They're impulsive, seeming to act first and think later. Waiting for someone else to finish talking or to take a turn is torture for a child with ADHD. And they can seem dreamy and vague (or 'inattentive'), always forgetting what they have been asked to do and easily distracted from the task in hand.

As all parents know, every child is like this from time to time. A doctor will only diagnose a child with ADHD if the behaviour has been going on for at least six months, if it is unusually severe for a child of that age and if it is causing significant problems at school and at home. Sometimes a child just has the inattentive type of ADHD, while other children may be hyperactive and impulsive but not inattentive. In most cases, however, children with the disorder have the full range of ADHD behaviours.

ADHD is usually spotted when a child goes to school, although the signs are often there well before then. It can persist right through to adulthood (see p. 165).

Bringing up a child with ADHD can be an extremely stressful and utterly exhausting experience for parents. And life with ADHD can be very tough for the sufferer too. School, in particular, is usually a real challenge. Many children with ADHD don't achieve the academic success of which they're

Problems with ADHD: a personal account

Josh was always a live wire. He didn't sleep much as a baby, and once he started to crawl he was constantly on the go and into everything. We were exhausted, and a bit concerned, but our friends said Josh was just a typical boy. However he had only been at school a few weeks when his teacher asked us in for a chat. She said Josh was very bright, but hopeless at concentrating on a task. He was also becoming disruptive, running around the classroom, distracting the other children and generally acting the clown. He seemed happiest at playtime, when he'd charge around the playground – on his own – like a mad thing. The teacher wondered whether Josh might have ADHD. I remember how upset and worried we were when we left that meeting. But it was actually the best thing that could have happened. It made us seek expert advice, and the strategies we learned for dealing with Josh's behaviour have helped enormously.

Cathy, aged 33

capable. They also tend to struggle in social situations and find it hard to make friends. Underachieving in school, ostracized by their peers and often constantly arguing with parents – it's no wonder that many children with ADHD also have low self-esteem.

It can be difficult for an anxious parent to get some perspective on their child's behaviour, so if you're worried that your child may have ADHD get as much input as you can from school, family and friends. If you still have concerns after that, have a chat with your GP.

Note: ADHD can also be known as hyperkinetic disorder, hyperactivity and attention deficit.

How common is ADHD?

ADHD affects around 3–5 per cent of children. It is much more common in boys, although there is less of an imbalance between the sexes when it comes to the inattentive form of ADHD.

Assessment

Gauging whether or not your child might have ADHD is difficult because so many of the characteristic behaviours are often displayed by children who do not have the disorder. Obviously, making a diagnosis should be left to a trained professional. But the following questionnaire may give you some helpful pointers.

The questionnaire is designed for parents of children aged 6 to 12. This is a fairly wide age range, so when you answer the questions, try to keep in mind what is appropriate for a child of his or her age.

Part 1 . My child:	Never	Occasionally	Often	Very often
1. Does not pay attention to details or makes careless mistakes, for example in homework.	0	1	2	3
2. Has difficulty sustaining attention to tasks or activities.	0	1	2	3

	Never	Occasionally	Often	Very often
3. Does not seem to listen when spoken to directly.	0	1	2	3
4. Does not follow through on instructions and fails to finish schoolwork.	0	1	2	3
5. Has difficulty organizing tasks and activities.	0	1	2	3
6. Avoids, dislikes, or is reluctant to engage in tasks that require sustained mental effort.	0	1	2	3
7. Loses things necessary for tasks or activities (school assignments, pencils or books).	0	1	2	3
8. Is easily distracted by extraneous stimuli (i.e. things going on around them).	0	1	2	3
9. Is forgetful in daily activities.	0	1	2	3
Part 2. My child:	**Never**	**Occasionally**	**Often**	**Very often**
10. Fidgets with hands or feet or squirms in seat.	0	1	2	3
11. Leaves seat when remaining seated is expected.	0	1	2	3
12. Runs about or climbs excessively in situations when remaining seated is expected.	0	1	2	3

13. Has difficulty playing or engaging in leisure/ play activities quietly.	0	1	2	3
14. Is 'on the go' or often acts as if driven by a motor'.	0	1	2	3
15. Talks too much.	0	1	2	3
16. Blurts out answers before questions have been completed.	0	1	2	3
17. Has difficulty waiting his/her turn.	0	1	2	3
18. Interrupts or intrudes on others (e.g. butts into conversations or games).	0	1	2	3

Vanderbilt ADHD Diagnostic Parent Rating Scale; Wolraich et al. (2000).

If you answered 'Often' or 'Very often' to at least six of the questions in Part 1, your child may have the inattentive type of ADHD; if you answered 'Often' or 'Very often' to at least six of the questions in Part 2, it is possible that your child has the hyperactive/impulsive type of ADHD.

How to Overcome ADHD

Raising a child with ADHD is no picnic. But take heart – you can do a lot to help your child (and to preserve your own sanity).

Get the basics right

As with adults, all children need plenty of good-quality sleep, regular exercise and a healthy diet, and those with ADHD are no exception. If you take your eye off just one of these balls you'll see how their mood changes. Some experts think that certain foodstuffs may contribute to ADHD; artificial food colourings and sodium benzoate (a preservative used in some ice creams and confectionery) have been linked to increases in hyperactivity.

General strategies for living with ADHD

Once you have established a healthy overall regime for your child, there are a number of other things you should keep in mind. Again, these are guidelines we would recommend for all parents in general, but they can make a particularly big difference if your child has ADHD.

Aim for clear, fair and consistent parenting

Set out a limited number of rules to follow and explain to your child what will happen if they don't comply. Equally, be sure to praise them when they observe the rules, using rewards or star charts, for example (see opposite).

If your child won't do as they're asked, you must keep calm, speak in short, clear sentences and give them a warning; tell them you will count to three, for example. If that doesn't work, use the time-out technique (see p. 178) or withdraw a privilege, such as watching the TV one evening – this is particularly effective for older children. Ignoring unwanted behaviour is also a useful tactic.

Highlight the positive

Don't let your child's difficult behaviour dominate everything. Try to focus on the good things. Make sure you set aside regular one-on-one time for them doing something you both enjoy. And don't allow yourself to be consumed by guilt; you're not to blame for your child's ADHD.

Choose your battles

Some children with ADHD, as well as many without, have a wearing habit of nagging, whining and generally appearing to be doing all they can to wind their parents up. Try to ignore these relatively minor irritations and save the confrontations for things that are really important.

Use your support network

Share your experiences with friends and family. Keep in close contact with your child's teacher. And investigate the support groups listed on p. 173.

Look after yourself

Bringing up a child with ADHD can be extremely demanding, so it's crucial that you find time for yourself – and for the other important people in your life.

Improving concentration

Alongside the strategies outlined above, there are a number of techniques you can use specifically to develop and increase your child's levels of concentration.

Set goals and use rewards

Rather than focusing on stopping 'bad' behaviour try to concentrate on increasing 'good' behaviour. A great way of doing this is to set your child clear and achievable goals, such as working on their homework alone for 15 minutes, for example. Then reward them when a goal is achieved. The rewards need not be extravagant or expensive – just a hug or some words of praise will generally do the trick. You could then build up to a bigger reward using a star chart, so that every time your child achieves a goal (or tries really hard), they get a star to stick on the chart. Once they have collected an agreed number, they earn themselves a treat.

Play to your child's strengths

Everyone responds better to praise than they do to criticism. And all of us are prepared to work harder at something we enjoy and feel confident about than an activity we hate. So think about the sorts of things your child is good at and which you would like to see more of. This may be playing a musical instrument or helping you in the garden – whatever it is, encourage more of it and give your child lots of praise for their efforts.

Teach your child organizational skills

It's difficult to get things done when you're unable to concentrate for long. So work with your child to identify all the steps they need to take to accomplish a task. Help them to break down a complex assignment, such as a piece of homework, into manageable short-term goals. You may need to give your child clear instructions and repeated reminders. For little ones, it can be helpful to verbalize the steps: 'What do we need to do? We have to draw a picture. We'll hold the pencil and work slowly. We'll ignore that noise and carry on drawing ...'

If your child is impulsive, show them how to control their behaviour, by counting to ten, for example, before they act. This shouldn't make you feel that you're spoon-feeding your child; what you're doing is teaching them vital life skills, and helping to boost their self-esteem when they actually complete a task.

Learn from the good things

Children with ADHD can be challenging, but they're also sometimes a joy to be around. Think about the times when your child's behaviour is good: are there any patterns or possible explanations for this? Often children with ADHD (just like most children) are better in the morning than in the afternoon or evening. And they respond much more positively to varied, interesting and entertaining activities than to comparatively boring and repetitive tasks. Once you've identified any positive influences on your child's behaviour, try to build them into your regular family routine.

Encourage structure and routine

Again, this goes for most children, but for those with ADHD in particular, as these things don't come naturally to them. It isn't necessary to run your life to a strict timetable, but it will help your child if there is a basic routine to their day – one that includes regular mealtimes and times for getting up and going to bed. Try to make your home relatively structured too, with a specific area for play, another for homework and so on.

Plan ahead

There are few things more stressful for a parent than their child creating havoc in public or on a long car journey. Try to anticipate the sort of problems you might encounter and how they can be avoided – by making regular stops if you're in the car or by using rewards, for example. Let your child know your expectations in advance, and what will happen if these aren't met.

Medication

Children with severe ADHD are often prescribed stimulants, of which the best known is Ritalin. But medication does not offer a permanent cure and its use is controversial.

Professional help may be useful in some cases; your child's school may be able to recommend someone.

Related problems

Children with ADHD can be prone to **tantrums** or, in **teenagers, difficult behaviour, insomnia, depression, fears** and **anxiety**.

Where to go for more information

Understanding ADHD (Vermilion, 1997) by Christopher Green and Kit Chee is accessible and comprehensive, although – like many books on ADHD, especially those published in the US – it does focus on medication as the best way of treating affected children.

Harvey Parker's *ADHD Workbook for Parents* (Specialty, 2005) offers a sensible overview, with lots of information on how to manage your child's behaviour. You will find more on dealing with challenging behaviour in Thomas Phelan's very popular *1–2–3 Magic: Effective Discipline for Children 2–12* (Child Management Inc., 2003) and *Try and Make Me! Simple Strategies that Turn Off the Tantrums and Create Cooperation* (Rodale, 2004) by Ray Levy, Bill O'Hanlon and Tyler Norris.

Useful websites include:

ⓘ www.addiss.co.uk, the website of the UK National ADHD Information and Support Service

ⓘ www.add.org, which is run by the US Attention Deficit Disorder Association

ⓘ www.mind.org.uk (search for information on ADHD)

Tantrums in Preschool Children

> *There are three ways to get something done; do it yourself, hire someone, or forbid your kids to do it.*
> Mona Crane

It probably won't seem like it as you watch your little one roll around on the floor in fury, but tantrums are one of the ways in which your children try to communicate with you. They might be bored or tired. Perhaps they want to carry on covering themselves in paint rather than have their tea. Or maybe their little brother is driving them crazy.

Young children often find it very difficult to explain how they're feeling. Even if your child can speak, they may not have learned to explain how they're feeling or what they're thinking. By having a tantrum, your child is trying to get your attention and express their feelings.

Unfortunately, it's not much fun for anyone – parent or child. Tantrums can encompass a range of behaviours, from simple crying to screaming, stamping, falling to the ground, stiffening, breath-holding, kicking, hitting, throwing and running away. And though a child can get over a raging tantrum amazingly quickly, the anger and frustration of the parent – not to mention the embarrassment if your child has a full-scale tantrum in public – is often longer lasting.

People often use other terms to describe tantrums, including temper tantrum, tizzy or hissy fit, or they might describe their child as strong-willed, defiant or uncontrollable.

How common are tantrums?

Tantrums are absolutely normal in preschool children, often starting at around 18 months. Here are some figures from a study of 1200 families:

Age of child	Number of tantrums per month	Average number of tantrums per month	Average length of tantrums in minutes
1	0–19	9	2
2	0–14	6	4
3	0–12	5	5
4	0–14	6	5

During a tantrum the most common behaviours are crying (reported in 86 per cent of tantrums), screaming (47 per cent), shouting (39 per cent), falling to the ground (37 per cent), kicking (27 per cent), hitting (26 per cent), pulling and pushing (23 per cent), running away (23 per cent), stiffening (19 per cent), stamping (17 per cent), whining (13 per cent), throwing (12 per cent) and holding on to a parent's leg (11 per cent). A short tantrum usually includes two of these sorts of behaviours, while a longer one might have about four.

Giving challenging behaviour in young children a medical or psychological diagnosis is a contentious area. But when the challenging behaviour is really severe doctors might use the name 'oppositional-defiant disorder' or OPD (for older children, the term is 'conduct disorder'; for more on difficult behaviour in teenagers, see p. 181). A child might be diagnosed with oppositional-defiant disorder if, over the past six months or more, they've been doing *at least four* of the following things much more often than is normal for a child of their age:

- losing their temper
- arguing with adults
- ignoring adult requests or rules
- deliberately annoying other people
- blaming other people
- being angry and resentful
- being spiteful or vindictive
- being touchy or easily annoyed.

Oppositional-defiant disorder is quite rare, affecting around 2 per cent of children. The figures are a little higher for severe instances of individual behaviours (OPD involves a combination of challenging behaviours). For example, 8 per cent of children are exceptionally defiant of adult rules and requests, 4 per cent lose their temper much more often than normal and 4 per cent are especially angry and resentful.

How to Cope with Tantrums

Preschool kids will always have tantrums from time to time. But that's not to say you just have to put up with it. There are steps you can take to reduce the number of tantrums your child has, and their intensity. And there are strategies you can learn to help you cope when your child throws that inevitable wobbly.

Remember that your child's tantrum is an attempt to communicate

The first step in dealing with a tantrum is to work out what exactly your child is trying to tell you. Usually it's one of the following:

- I want your attention.
- I'm tired.

- I'm hungry.
- I'm bored.
- I want my own way.
- I'm not getting what I want.
- I can't tell you what I want.
- I don't want to stop what I'm doing.

To help you figure out what your child is trying to tell you, keep a tantrum diary. Write down when the tantrum occurred, the events immediately before it, what the tantrum was like, and what happened afterwards. This will help you to identify the sort of things that cause the tantrum (i.e. the triggers), which, in turn, will shed light on what it is really about. If your child starts howling when their friend takes one of their toys, for instance, you'll know that they find it difficult to share.

Pinpointing your own reactions to a tantrum can also be really instructive. You might discover, for example, that you give your child a lot of attention when they have a tantrum – which may be exactly what the tantrum is designed to achieve.

Reduce tantrum triggers

Once you've got some insight into the sorts of things that trigger your child's tantrums, you can try to avoid these situations or at least deal with them in a different way.

If your child wants more attention, for example, think how you can give them this before things escalate into a tantrum. If the tantrum is a result of boredom, see whether you can make activities a bit shorter or more fun.

The supermarket is, of course, a favourite place for tantrums. Not only is it likely to bore your child, but it also diverts your attention away from them, towards your shopping. So, make your supermarket trip as quick as possible. If you can't shorten it, take along a toy or book for your child.

Tantrums are often triggered when you say 'No' to your kids. To combat this, offer your child a couple of choices. For instance, when you tell them they can't watch television, suggest something else they enjoy instead – a story, perhaps, or some time in the garden. This will help your child to feel they have some control.

If your child tantrums when it's time to stop doing something, introduce five-minute warnings, so they can prepare for the transition. And if the tantrum is the result of your child not being able to tell you what they want, see whether you can help them express their feelings – perhaps using a picture.

Use distraction

When you spot a tantrum brewing, distraction can be a great way to stop things getting out of hand. Do something fun with your child – and make

Problems with tantrums: some personal accounts

Our three-year-old Jack is a master of the tantrum – screaming, throwing things, rolling around on the floor – we've had it all, including one famous shopping trip when he lay in the middle of a department store and howled as if he'd been told he could never play with his toys again (actually we'd just mentioned that we'd be going for lunch in a minute). Often Jack tantrums when it's time to stop doing something and start doing something else. I used to find it really stressful. I'd look around the playgroup and see all these other mums with their perfectly behaved kids and wonder what I was doing wrong. Now I try really hard not to let it stress me out. I think you have to avoid getting sucked into the same kinds of feelings that are making your child have a tantrum. Generally, I just leave Jack to it – he prefers an audience! Afterwards we have a little chat and a cuddle and that shifts the mood very quickly.
Kate, aged 28

My daughter was particularly bad at about age two. She'd get very angry and frustrated and sometimes we wouldn't have a clue what had sparked her off – which made it all the more difficult to deal with. Our strategy was just to give her lots of quality time – to make her day as full of fun as we could. Easier said than done, but it really helped. In retrospect I think some of her behaviour stemmed from the fact that she didn't have the language skills to tell us what she wanted – as she got older and her vocabulary increased she was happier and we had fewer tantrums.
Pete, aged 42

sure you give them your full attention. If you can make them laugh, so much the better – even the most obstinate three-year-old finds it hard to wail and laugh at the same time …

Don't give in to a tantrum

Learning to obey the rules is an essential part of every child's development. And because that's a lesson the average preschooler would happily do without, tantrums are inevitable.

But don't let your child use a tantrum to get what they want. Instead, try to ignore it (ensuring first that they are safe – if, for example, they're rolling around on the floor). Move away, or simply look on with a relaxed and detached expression. Don't talk to your child while they're having a tantrum. You want your child to learn that a tantrum won't make you change your mind, or get them your attention – even your angry, frustrated attention.

Try time outs

If all else fails, and if the tantrum gets really out of control or your child becomes aggressive, you may want to use a time out. Give them a very clear warning and then, if the unwanted behaviour goes on, take your child to their room for a set period of time (one minute for each year of their life is the usual recommendation). After the time out is up, explain to your child why they were put in their room.

Reward your child for calming down

Once the tantrum is over, give your child lots of loving attention (even though you might not feel like it, having spent five minutes listening to their impression of an air-raid siren). But remember that you're not giving them a hug because they've had a tantrum, but because they've stopped having one, so make this distinction clear to them too.

And this doesn't mean you should simply brush the tantrum under the carpet. Talk through with your child what's happened and tell them how you'd like them to behave instead. For example, if your child's tantrum was triggered by asking them to clear away their toys, explain to them why you made the request, how you'd like them to react in future and ask them to clear up while you watch.

Some parents try to show children the consequences of a tantrum by sending them to their room or taking away a favourite toy, for example. If you go down this route, take the action immediately after the tantrum

Tantrums: hidden patterns and secret signs

A tantrum can look like total chaos. But research has shown that the way children behave when they have a tantrum is actually determined by the particular feelings that fuel it. So what a child does when they're really angry is different, for example, from what they do when they're distressed.

There seem to be five main groups of tantrum behaviours, each provoked by a different emotion:

Distress – crying, whining, holding on to a parent.
High anger – hitting, kicking, screaming, stiffening. These kinds of behaviours are more likely to happen the longer the tantrum goes on, and the angrier the child gets.
Medium anger – throwing, shouting.
Mild anger – stamping.
Trying to cope – going to the ground, running away.

And there are other patterns and signs amid the chaos. For example, when they're having a tantrum, children's anger generally peaks very quickly, often after only 30 seconds. Distress, on the other hand, slowly increases as the tantrum goes on: the longer the tantrum, the more chance there is of the child becoming distressed. If your child goes to the ground or stamps in the first 30 seconds of their tantrum, the chances are the tantrum will be a short one. On the other hand, a tantrum that starts off with relatively low levels of anger can all too often last much longer.

Try to analyse your child's behaviour during their next tantrum. Look for the signs and patterns – they'll help you to understand what your child is thinking and, in turn, deal with the tantrum as painlessly as possible.

so your child can clearly see the connection, and make sure you remain nice and calm. You want your child to understand that there are rules (no tantrums) and consequences when they break them (ten minutes in their room) – rather than just seeing it as an arbitrary punishment handed out by a furious parent.

Similarly, avoid spanking or hitting – these are usually a sign of an adult's own temper tantrum, and they won't teach your child how to behave, either.

Be firm, fair, and consistent

You can't expect kids to obey the rules if you're not absolutely clear and consistent in your handling of their behaviour. So, take the time to explain to your child what you'd like them to do and why.

Handle tantrums in the same way each time. And don't send mixed messages: if you let your child eat a bag of sweets on Monday, they're not going to understand why they can't eat another on Tuesday.

You may find that as your child adapts to the 'new regime' the tantrums get worse; this is because they're testing the boundaries. Once they learn that those boundaries won't shift, no matter how hard they push, their behaviour will improve.

Don't let tantrums change the way you feel about your child

Dealing with constant tantrums can be really stressful. But if you start to blame your child or feel that there must be something 'wrong' with them – or with yourself as a parent – you can end up not enjoying any of the time you spend with them.

So, remember: a tantrum is an isolated incidence of bad behaviour and not a sign that the child is bad, or that you're a lousy parent. Tantrums are normal – and because they're normal, every parent will have had to deal with them. Talk about your experiences with your friends and family; you'll probably pick up some useful tips, and you'll definitely have the consolation of realizing that you're not alone.

To ensure that tantrums don't define your relationship with your child, focus on the good stuff. Give them lots of praise and attention when they're behaving well. See if you can identify the sorts of situations that bring out good behaviour, and try to do more of them.

Related problems

All children have tantrums, but they're more frequent (and sometimes more intense) in children who are also dealing with **stress**, **anxiety** and **depression**, or who are **hyperactive**.

Where to go for more information

Among the useful books on dealing with tantrums are Christopher Green's *New Toddler Taming: A Parent's Guide to the First Four Years* (Vermilion, 2006) and *Toddler Tantrums* by Penney Hames (National Childbirth Trust, 2002).

Thomas W. Phelan's *1–2–3 Magic: Effective Discipline for Children 2–12* (Child Management Inc., 2003) presents a programme designed to deal with challenging behaviour in children. You can find more information at the accompanying website, www.parentmagic.com.

Good advice on dealing with difficult behaviour in older children (up to teenage) is offered by *Try and Make Me! Simple Strategies that Turn Off the Tantrums and Create Cooperation* by Ray Levy and Bill O'Hanlon with Tyler Norris (Rodale, 2004).

Parentline offers advice to parents on a range of issues including tantrums. Call them on 0808 800 2222 or check out their website, www.parentlineplus.org.uk.

> *You can learn many things from children. How much patience you have, for instance.*
> Franklin P. Jones

DIFFICULT BEHAVIOUR IN TEENAGERS

Seesawing emotions, self-absorption, a steely determination to do things their way and titanic tantrums if thwarted ... don't tell your kids, but parenting teens can sometimes seem remarkably similar to parenting toddlers!

Bringing up teenagers can be tough. Not only are they prone to behave in all kinds of ways you'd rather they didn't, but you also have to get used to the idea that your little ones are now well on the way to adulthood. And that's a tough lesson to learn.

Managing your teen's behaviour isn't made any easier by the fact that many of the methods you've used in the past will no longer work. The days of the naughty step are long gone. You'll need to rely now on communication, compromise and empathy. Here's how:

Think back to your own teen years

For most kids, being a teenager is a decidedly mixed bag: hugely exciting but also full of bewildering new responsibilities and problems. They're desperate for independence, but still hugely dependent on the love and support of their parents. Add to this dramatic physical changes and wildly fluctuating hormones, and it's not surprising that teens can sometimes be less-than-perfect company. Remembering how you felt as a teenager will help you to understand what your own child is going through.

Keep going with the basics

They may dispute it, but it's still really important for teenagers to exercise, eat regular, healthy meals and get plenty of sleep. You'll soon see the effect on their mood if they don't.

Stay positive

Don't let your teen's occasional temper tantrums or sulks drive a wedge between you. Try to spend regular one-on-one time with them, preferably doing something you both enjoy. And include them in at least some family activities. Focus on getting more of the behaviour you like rather than less of what you don't. Like everyone, they'll respond much better to positive feedback than criticism. So give them lots of praise and encouragement and don't run down their clothes or haircut, their friends or their political opinions. Accept your teenager for who they are.

Talk to them ...

... but make sure you also listen. Good communication is probably the most valuable tool you have in your relationship with your teen, not least when it comes to crucial issues such as drugs, alcohol and sex. So, make time for regular chats, and try not to dominate the conversation (you probably do know best, but your teenager won't appreciate hearing it). Talk to them as if they were an adult – after all, they soon will be. Don't try to get them to tell you more than they want to: respect their privacy. And don't be afraid to give your teen an insight into your own thoughts and feelings: communication, after all, is a two-way street.

Choose your battles

Even older teenagers need a few basic ground rules. With luck, you'll be able to get their agreement on these rules – and the penalties for breaking them. Wherever possible, be open to negotiation and compromise. And focus your energies on the stuff that really matters. The alternative is far too exhausting and demoralizing.

When you do find yourself embroiled in an argument, keep calm – someone has to, and it's unlikely to be your teenager. Be firm, but try not to make threats or issue orders; offering choices and explanations for why you'd like them to do something will be much more effective. And don't personalize the argument: by all means tell your teenager you don't like their behaviour, but don't make them feel you don't like them.

If you're losing your cool, or if your teen is behaving really unacceptably, leave the room. Once the argument is over, the two of you can sit down and talk things over. Sometimes you may simply have to agree to disagree. If your teenager flies off the handle regularly, show them some anger-management techniques (see pp. 60–64).

Look after yourself

Parenting teens can sometimes seem an impossibly gruelling yet thankless task. So it's really important that you make time for yourself. And do talk to other parents and friends about their own experiences. Remember, too, that what you're experiencing is absolutely normal. However implausible it may occasionally seem, your teenager will soon become a pleasant, communicative and responsible adult. At which point, of course, they'll leave home!

Where to go for more information

For more on raising teenagers, check out these three really useful books. All three also contain details of relevant websites.
Coping with Teenagers (Sheldon, 2003) by Sarah Lawson
The Teenager Manual (Haynes, 2007) by Pat Spurgin
Whatever! (Piatkus, 2006) by Gill Hines and Alison Baverstock

Child Abuse

This entry will help you to understand what child abuse is, how to recognize the signs, what to do if you suspect a child is being abused and where to go for more information and advice.

What is child abuse?

There are four types of child abuse:

Physical – hurting a child, for example by smacking, hitting, kicking, or
shaking them.
Emotional – constantly criticizing, telling off or humiliating a child.
Neglect – denying a child proper food, clothing, housing or medical
care and failing to keep them safe from harm.
Sexual – involving a child in sexual activities, regardless of whether the
child seems to be willing.

Parents are often terrified of strangers harming their children, and these
cases tend to get lots of media coverage. But, in reality, the vast majority
of abusers are known to the child and, very often, are family members.

How common is child abuse?

No one knows for sure how widespread child abuse is. Many children don't
tell anyone, and certainly not the authorities, what they're going through.
And there isn't always agreement among experts about the precise definition of child abuse. But one UK survey of more than 2800 randomly
selected young adults (aged 18–24) found that 21 per cent had been physically abused by parents or carers, over a third had suffered some form of
emotional abuse, 17 per cent had experienced neglect and 16 per cent had
been sexually abused.

How you can tell if a child is being abused

Some of the signs of abuse are relatively obvious – bruises, black eyes,
burns and problems in the genital areas are clear warning flags. But look
out too for the child who is:

- unusually sad, withdrawn or aggressive
- suddenly unhappy at school
- having problems sleeping
- frightened of certain adults
- often dirty, hungry or not properly dressed
- using inappropriate sexual language or behaviour
- often left alone or in charge of younger siblings.

None of these proves that a child is being abused, of course. But they do mean it's worth further investigation.

What to do if you think a child might be being abused

The suspicion that a child you know may be experiencing abuse is bound to be distressing. But don't ignore it. Get in touch with the NSPCC (see below) or with your local social services. If you think sexual or physical abuse may be occurring, you need to act especially fast: call the police if you believe a child is in immediate danger.

If a child confides in you, make sure you listen and take them seriously. Don't force them to reveal more than they're comfortable doing. Reassure them that they're not to blame for the abuse, and give them lots of praise for being brave enough to speak out. And don't be tempted to confront the abuser yourself: leave that to the authorities.

Where to go for more information

The NSPCC website (www.nspcc.org.uk) offers lots of useful information and helpful links. They also run a helpline on 0808 800 5000. Children and young people can contact the NSPCC's free, confidential Childline on 0800 1111.

NAPAC, the National Association for People Abused in Childhood, runs an excellent website – www.napac.org.uk – and a support line on 0800 085 3330.

Among the many books published on child abuse, we particularly recommend:

When Your Child Has Been Molested (Jossey Bass, 2004) by Kathryn Brohl; *Helping Your Child Recover from Sexual Abuse* (University of Washington Press, 1992) by Caren Adams and Jennifer Fay; *Overcoming Childhood Trauma* (Robinson, 2000) by Helen Kennerley.

Depression

In fourteen months I've only smiled once and I didn't do it
consciously.
Bob Dylan, 'Up to me'

We all feel low occasionally. Sadness, like happiness, is simply part of life. Generally, it lifts pretty quickly; but sometimes it takes root and deepens into depression.

Depression can hit hard, distorting the way you feel – both physically and emotionally – the way you think and the way you behave. The writer William Styron offered a powerful insight into his own severe depression in *Darkness Visible*:

The pain is unrelenting and what makes the condition intolerable is the foreknowledge that no remedy will come – not in a day, an hour, a month, or a minute. If there is mild relief, one knows that it is only temporary … One does not abandon, even briefly, one's bed of nails, but is attached to it wherever one goes.

Like Styron, people with depression feel down pretty much all the time. Life becomes an ordeal, devoid of interest or pleasure. Depression has been likened to wearing a pair of glasses that make the world look blue, filtering out the good stuff and leaving only the very worst. Or, as the Rolling Stones put it, painting everything black.

When someone is depressed, energy drains from their body. They feel exhausted, plagued by aches and pains and unable to concentrate on anything for very long. Making decisions becomes a nightmare. Completing the most basic task – washing the dishes, phoning a friend, even getting out of bed – seems beyond them. Sleep and appetite are affected – generally people

Problems with depression: a personal account

I became depressed a couple of months after a messy break-up. Shortly after everyone had been complimenting me on how well I was coping, I ground to a halt. I stopped going to work. I stopped seeing friends. I wouldn't even answer the phone. I hardly ate anything. I'd burst into tears for no apparent reason. Most of the time – even during the day, while the sun streamed through the curtains – I stayed in bed. But I couldn't sleep. I couldn't read. I couldn't even bear to watch TV or listen to the radio. Instead I spent hours obsessing over the past. Life seemed incredibly bleak – like there was nothing at all to look forward to. I wasn't suicidal, but I did think I'd be better off dead. It was only because work needed a medical certificate that I plucked up the courage to see my GP, but [just 10 minutes talking to her] was the first step in my recovery from depression.
Kevin, aged 28

with depression don't feel like eating much (resulting in marked weight loss) and have problems sleeping; but sometimes they find themselves sleeping much more than usual and comfort feeding (and you can imagine the effect that the extra weight has on their already battered self-esteem).

Negative thoughts fill the mind: feelings of worthlessness, that the world is horrible and that the future is unremittingly bleak. Sufferers of depression are plagued with guilt – for past failings and, most especially, for the way they feel now. Life may start to seem not worth living and some people do consider, and even attempt, suicide when in the depths of depression.

Not surprisingly, this mass of negative thoughts and feelings can have a big impact on behaviour. People with depression often withdraw into themselves, avoiding social contact and generally doing as little as possible. They might be irritable and agitated or, on the other hand, noticeably sluggish in their thought, speech or movements. Tears and long bouts of anguished brooding are typical.

Depression, like almost all the problems in this book, varies in its severity. To make a diagnosis of depression, a doctor will look for several of the symptoms mentioned above occurring pretty much all the time for at least two weeks and causing a lot of distress or interfering with day-to-day life. (A less severe but longer-lasting form of depression is known as Dysthymic Disorder.)

The causes of depression are generally pretty complex. It's thought that some people are more vulnerable either because of their genetic make-up, their early experiences, the way they tend to think about themselves and the world – or, most probably, a combination of all three.

But what triggers an episode of depression is almost always a particularly stressful experience – divorce or other relationship problems, unemployment, bereavement, serious or long-lasting illness are common culprits. Two other triggers for depression are childbirth, which can spark postnatal depression in women, and changes in the seasons (generally the onset of autumn or winter), which can cause what's known as Seasonal Affective Disorder (SAD).

Even without treatment, depression usually passes after a while. A quarter of episodes last less than a month and half are over within three months. But around 25 per cent last at least a year – which will seem like a lifetime – and you can't know whether you'll be one of the lucky ones for whom it's all over quickly. Moreover, once you've had one bout of depression, you're more vulnerable to another at some stage. So make sure you take advantage of the very successful treatments available for depression, and particularly the techniques described below.

How common is depression?

According to the World Health Organization, depression is the number-one cause of disability in the world, with around 120 million people suffering from it at any one time. In fact, depression is so widespread that it's been called the 'common cold of the mind'.

In the UK, around 5 per cent of the population is clinically depressed and 10–20 per cent of us will experience at least one episode of depression at some point in our lives. One in 10 mothers develops postnatal depression. Around 2 per cent of people in the UK receive treatment for SAD, although up to 10 per cent are thought to suffer from a mild form of the illness. No one knows for sure why, but women are around twice as likely as men to develop depression.

Depression seems to be on the increase globally and certainly the average age at which it first strikes has come down dramatically. Forty years ago it was an illness of the middle aged, affecting people in their forties and fifties; these days depression generally begins in the mid-twenties.

Self-assessment

Everyone feels down from time to time, so how can you tell if what you're going through is just a spell of the blues or a bout of depression? The following exercises will help you to judge. The first is a general questionnaire and the second focuses on postnatal depression.

	Little or none of the time	Some of the time	A large part of the time	Most of the time	Score
1. I feel downhearted, blue and sad.	1	2	3	4	
2. Morning is when I feel the best.	4	3	2	1	
3. I have crying spells or feel like it.	1	2	3	4	
4. I have trouble sleeping through the night.	1	2	3	4	
5. I eat as much as I used to.	4	3	2	1	
6. I enjoy looking at, talking to, and being with attractive women/ men.	4	3	2	1	
7. I notice that I am losing weight.	1	2	3	4	
8. I have trouble with constipation.	1	2	3	4	
9. My heart beats faster than usual.	1	2	3	4	

	Little or none of the time	Some of the time	A large part of the time	Most of the time	Score
10. I get tired for no reason.	1	2	3	4	
11. My mind is as clear as it used to be.	4	3	2	1	
12. I find it easy to do the things I used to do.	4	3	2	1	
13. I am restless and can't keep still.	1	2	3	4	
14. I feel hopeful about the future.	1	2	3	4	
15. I am more irritable than usual.	1	2	3	4	
16. I find it easy to make decisions.	4	3	2	1	
17. I feel that I am useful and needed.	4	3	2	1	
18. My life is pretty full.	4	3	2	1	
19. I feel that others would be better off if I were dead.	1	2	3	4	
20. I still enjoy the things that I used to.	4	3	2	1	
TOTAL					

© Zung Depression Scale, American Medical Association (1965)

If you've scored 50–59, you may be mildly depressed. A total of 60–69 indicates moderate depression and a score of 70 or above suggests severe depression.

The next questionnaire is designed for women who've recently given birth. When you answer the questions, base your responses on how you've felt over the past seven days.

		Score
1. I have been able to laugh and see the funny side of things.	As much as I always could: 0 Not quite so much now: 1 Definitely not so much now: 2 Not at all: 3	
2. I have looked forward with enjoyment to things.	As much as I ever did: 0 Rather less than I used to: 1 Definitely less than I used to: 2 Hardly at all: 3	
3. I have blamed myself unnecessarily when things went wrong.	Yes, most of the time: 3 Yes, some of the time: 2 Not very often: 1 No, never: 0	
4. I have been anxious or worried for no good reason.	No, not at all: 0 Hardly ever: 1 Yes, sometimes: 2 Yes, very often: 3	
5. I have felt scared or panicky for no very good reason.	Yes, quite a lot: 3 Yes, sometimes: 2 No, not much: 1 No, not at all: 0	
6. Things have been getting on top of me.	Yes, most of the time I haven't been able to cope at all: 3 Yes, sometimes I haven't been coping as well as usual: 2 No, most of the time I have coped quite well: 1 No, I have been coping as well as ever: 0	

		Score
7. I have been so unhappy that I have had difficulty sleeping.	Yes, most of the time: 3 Yes, sometimes: 2 Not very often: 1 No, not at all: 0	
8. I have felt sad or miserable.	Yes, most of the time: 3 Yes, quite often: 2 Not very often: 1 No, not at all: 0	
9. I have been so unhappy that I have been crying.	Yes, most of the time: 3 Yes, quite often: 2 Only occasionally: 1 No, never: 0	
10. The thought of harming myself has occurred to me.	Yes, quite often: 3 Sometimes: 2 Hardly ever: 1 Never: 0	
TOTAL		

Cox, J.L., Holden, J.M., and Sagovsky, R. 1987. Detection of postnatal depression: Development of the 10-item Edinburgh Postnatal Depression Scale. *British Journal of Psychiatry* 150: 782–86.

If you've scored 10 or more, you may be suffering from postnatal depression.

How to Overcome Depression

Happily, there's much less stigma around depression these days than there used to be. The media regularly features celebrities – J. K. Rowling, Stephen Fry, Alistair Campbell, for example – talking publicly about their experiences. But when you're grappling with depression, it can still be hard to shake the feeling that you're somehow to blame. Depression isn't a sign of weakness – it's an illness – and there are now some really effective ways to overcome depression. But first, just as with any other illness, you need to allow yourself the time and space to recover.

Here are our strategies for beating depression.

Look after yourself

You probably won't feel like it, but now's the time to be particularly careful about what you eat and drink. Make sure you're eating regular, healthy meals (see p. 223 for specific guidelines) and steer clear of alcohol or other drugs: they may help you feel better temporarily but they definitely won't help in the long run.

Getting lots of good-quality sleep is important too, so check out our advice on p. 340. And aim for regular exercise – three sessions of around 45–60 minutes per week for 10–12 weeks will make a big difference.

Use your support network. Talk to someone you trust. Try to keep up contact with friends and family. Depression often makes you want to hide away, but the sense of loneliness and isolation that results only makes things worse.

Following these guidelines will not only help you overcome your depression; they'll reduce the chances of you becoming depressed in the first place.

Keep active

The feelings of exhaustion and listlessness that depression brings make doing anything seem impossible. Then the less you do, the less you'll want to do – and the more wretched and paralysed you'll feel. You can give yourself a huge morale boost by completing even the smallest of tasks – even domestic chores. If they seem scarily ambitious, break them down into manageable chunks. So instead of 'tidying the house', set yourself the goal of simply doing the washing-up. The positive feeling you will get from achieving that one, relatively small goal will inspire you to do more.

Aim to build into your routine activities that give you pleasure or a sense of achievement. Keeping a detailed schedule for your week will help you to make sure you don't forget.

If you're struggling to think of an activity you'll enjoy, ask yourself these questions:

- What could I do for an afternoon that I'd really find fun or satisfying?
- What could I do for an hour?
- Is there something good I could plan to do one weekend?

Mood music

Music can have a powerful effect on mood. Psychologists have done lots of research in this area, and the evidence is clear: sad music lowers our mood; happy music cheers us up.

It's definitely worth making a compilation CD for when you're feeling down or stressed. But what should you put on it? Well, you may want to avoid Samuel Barber's 'Adagio for Strings' – voted the saddest piece of music by listeners to BBC Radio 4's Today programme. When the mental health charity Mind carried out a similar survey, these were the songs that had the biggest emotional effect on people:

Happy	Sad	Chill out
'Let Me Entertain You' (Robbie Williams)	'Everybody Hurts' (REM)	'Thank You' (Dido)
'Walking on Sunshine' (Katrina and the Waves)	'Creep' (Radiohead)	'Bridge Over Troubled Waters' (Simon and Garfunkel)
'Shiny, Happy People' (REM)	'Candle in the Wind' (Elton John)	'Porcelain' (Moby)

All of which goes to show just how subjective, as well as powerful, the effects of music are!

- What can I do that costs money?
- What can I do for free?
- What could I do that will really stimulate my mind?
- What would give me a sense of achievement?
- Is there a course or evening class I'd find interesting?
- What physical activity would I like to do?
- What about learning a practical skill?
- If a friend was visiting, what would I suggest we do?
- Do I want to meet new people?
- Do I want to make new friends?
- What enjoyable activity could I do on my own?
- What could I do at home?
- Where would I like to go?

- What could I do that I've never done before?
- What have I enjoyed doing in the past?
- Are there any interesting events or activities listed in the paper?
- How about voluntary work?

When someone is down, they can easily find reasons not to do something (psychologists call this, 'Yes, but …' thinking). Don't let your depression put you off. For instance, you might feel you don't have the energy to go for a walk or a swim. Test this out by staying at home one time and then going out another. Chances are, you'll discover that you have much more energy and are less depressed after you've done some exercise.

Fight negative thoughts

How can you combat the negative thoughts that automatically come to mind when you're depressed – and which make your mood even lower? Well, you have to deprive them of their power over you. You need to recognize that they're only thoughts, and not a reflection of reality.

You can start to do this by keeping a record of your negative thoughts. Once you've identified them, you can set about challenging them. Write down the evidence for and against. What other ways are there to think about the situation? Are you taking things too personally or making too much of insignificant details? Imagine what you'd tell a friend in a similar situation. Are you being too hard on yourself?

A great way of challenging negative thoughts is to test them out. Ask someone you trust whether they share your view of a given situation. You can even conduct practical experiments. If you're afraid that your friends don't really enjoy your company, for example, suggest a trip out together – you'll be pleasantly surprised at their response.

Learn how to cope with worry

When someone is depressed they become preoccupied with their problems, trapped in a vicious circle of worry. The more they fret about things, the more anxious and upset they become, and thus the more they worry.

Try to get some perspective on your problems. Imagine how you'll feel about the situation in, say, five years' time. If you're lying awake worrying, think how you'll see things in the morning. If you're afraid you've messed up, does it really matter? Tell yourself it's so much water under the bridge, and let it go. And remember that we all – absolutely every one of us – make mistakes. The trick is to put them behind you and move on. As Samuel Beckett wrote: 'Ever tried. Ever failed. No matter. Try again. Fail again. Fail better.'

Have a look now at our suggestions for combating worry on pp. 109–112. If a specific event or situation has triggered your depression, the problem-solving techniques outlined on p. 110 may be especially relevant.

Medication and other approaches

There are four main types of antidepressant medication: tricyclics, MAOIs (monoamine oxidase inhibitors), SSRIs (selective serotonin reuptake inhibitors), and SNRIs (serotonin and noradrenaline reuptake inhibitors). They seem to work well with more severe depression, but they usually take a few weeks to kick in and can have side effects (although these are generally quite mild with the newer SSRIs and SNRIs). One downside to these drugs is a relatively high relapse rate in that once people stop taking the medication, their depression sometimes returns.

Doctors often suggest a combination of antidepressants and psychological treatments like Cognitive Behaviour Therapy (CBT), which is the type of therapy we've drawn on for the suggestions above, or Interpersonal Therapy (IPT), which starts from the insight that depression often has its roots in relationship problems. For both CBT and IPT, relapse rates are lower than for medication, even long after the therapy sessions have been completed.

A form of meditation called mindfulness has also proved pretty success-ful in preventing further bouts of depression. Mindfulness focuses on living in the present moment, cultivating a way of seeing negative thoughts as passing mental events, rather than necessarily reflecting truth or reality. (For more about mindfulness, see the excellent *The Mindful Way through Depression*, listed below.)

As for herbal remedies, St John's Wort seems to be quite effective for mild to moderate depression and is widely used in Germany. It can inter-fere with other medication though, so do discuss things with your doctor if you'd like to go down this route.

If you're suffering from postnatal depression, the kinds of suggestions we make for tackling depression in general should work well. But it's also a good idea to talk to your doctor, health visitor or midwife.

Light therapy – which, essentially, involves sitting in front of very bright lights for an hour or so every day – is very successful in the treatment of SAD.

Suicidal thoughts

Many people with depression think about killing themselves – so don't assume you're going crazy. The way you feel is a product of your illness. Things will seem very different once you're happier. But do tell someone you trust what you're going through or have a chat with your GP. You'll probably feel a whole lot better just for talking to someone. Make a point of deciding who you'll go to for help if your suicidal thoughts become so strong that you actually might harm yourself.

If you're worried that someone you know might kill themselves, don't ignore it. Generally, the danger is greatest if the person has made a previous suicide attempt. Other risk factors include:

- feelings of hopelessness and being trapped
- impulsiveness
- a poor track record at coping with stress or other problems
- drug or alcohol issues
- access to pills or weapons or other means of suicide
- a recent setback or serious disappointment.

But even if none of these factors applies, take your concerns seriously. Talk to the person. Don't beat around the bush: you need to ask them directly whether they've had suicidal thoughts and if so how likely they are to act on them. Have they planned a suicide attempt? If so, how detailed is it? (The more detailed the plan, the greater the danger.) Help them to get professional support and advice and remove anything they could use to harm themselves. If you think a suicide attempt is imminent, get them to a GP or to a hospital Accident and Emergency department.

Related problems

Depression is often a factor in many of the problems covered in this book, particularly **anxiety**, **worry** and **mood swings**.

Where to go for more information?

If you've ever doubted how widespread depression is, one glance at the dozens of books published on the subject should put your mind at rest!

Here's a selection of titles we've found particularly useful:

Feeling Good (Avon Books, 2000) by David Burns; *Cognitive Therapy and the Emotional Disorders* (Penguin, 1991) by Aaron T. Beck; *Depression after Childbirth* (Oxford, 2001) by Katharina Dalton with Wendy M. Holton; *Learned Optimism* (Vintage, 2006) by Martin Seligman; *The Mindful Way through Depression* (Guilford Press, 2007) by Mark Williams, John Teasdale, Zindel Segal and Jon Kabat-Zinn; *Overcome Your Postnatal Depression* (Hodder Arnold, 2007) by Denise Robertson and Alice Muir; *Overcoming Low Self-Esteem* (Robinson, 1999) by Melanie Fennell; *Overcoming Depression* (Robinson, 2000) by Paul Gilbert; *Seasonal Affective Disorder for Dummies* (Wiley, 2007) by Laura Smith and Charles Elliott.

You'll also find plenty of useful advice and information on the following websites:

- ⓘ www.depressionalliance.org (the Depression Alliance is a UK support group for people with depression)
- ⓘ www.nmha.org (the website of the US organization Mental Health America)
- ⓘ www.mind.org.uk (Mind is the UK's best-known mental health charity)
- ⓘ www.apni.org (the website of the Association for Postnatal Illness)
- ⓘ www.sada.org.uk (run by the Seasonal Affective Disorder Association)

Eating Problems

Binge Eating

> *I had bulimia for a number of years. And that's like a secret disease. You inflict it upon yourself because your self-esteem is at a low ebb, and you don't think you're worthy or valuable. When you have bulimia, you're very ashamed of yourself and you hate yourself ... so you don't discuss it with people.*
> Diana, Princess of Wales, 1995

In the mid-1970s doctors began to notice a new type of eating problem. Those affected – almost all women – were prone to regular bouts of frenzied, uncontrolled eating. After these binges, they would attempt to compensate by vomiting, taking laxatives or other medications, dieting, fasting or exercising excessively. And underlying this behaviour was an intense concern – an obsession, even – with weight and appearance.

Bulimia nervosa, as the illness was termed in 1979, is still making the news. But these days, it's generally because of the revelations of yet another celebrity. Elton John, Jane Fonda, John Prescott, Joan Rivers, Geri Halliwell and many others have followed the most famous bulimia sufferer of all, Princess Diana, in going public about their battle with the illness. Bulimia, like other eating disorders, is now acknowledged to be widespread among young women.

Bulimia is at the severe end of the binge-eating spectrum. To make a diagnosis, doctors will look for bingeing and the associated compensatory behaviour (generally vomiting) happening at least twice a week for three months. But many people who don't meet the official criteria for bulimia still have a problem with binge eating and vomiting.

Bulimia generally takes the form of a vicious circle. It starts with low self-esteem and develops into a belief that people are only successful and valuable if they're slim and attractive. This leads to dieting, but dieting that's so strict that failure is more or less inevitable.

When that happens, there's a tendency to go off the rails completely and binge eat. (The extreme hunger produced by dieting doesn't help here.) According to one study, the average binge lasts an hour and a quarter, contains 3415 calories and most often comprises (in descending order) ice cream, bread, sweets, doughnuts, salads, sandwiches, biscuits, popcorn, cheese and cereal.

A binge may provide some short-lived pleasure and relief, but shame and self-loathing soon set in. Most people with bulimia attempt to prevent the binge from leading to weight gain by making themselves vomit, others use laxatives or diuretics (water tablets) or they exercise frantically. Consumed by guilt at their lapse, they go back on their diet – and may even make it stricter. And so the cycle continues …

No one knows for sure why certain people are prone to this obsession with body image, but it's likely to be a combination of factors. What seems fairly certain is that society's preoccupation with appearance plays a major part (see the box on p. 208). From an early age, girls are given the message that the way they look is crucial. Exactly what constitutes female beauty changes from one historical period to another, but there's little doubt that in today's society we value physical fitness and, above all, slimness. For most people, it's an ideal they can never achieve, no matter how hard they diet and exercise.

Problems with binge eating: a personal account

As a teenager, I'd always been self-conscious about my weight and appearance and I was usually on some half-hearted diet (most of my friends were too). But things didn't get out of hand until I went to college. I shared a room with this amazingly beautiful and incredibly slim girl, and I realized I was ugly and fat. So I stopped eating. At first I felt wonderful – really proud of myself. But of course I couldn't keep it up. Eventually, I'd get so hungry I'd have a biscuit or something and, before I knew it, I'd be stuffing my face with anything I could get my hands on. I didn't even taste the food;

I was cramming it in like a robot. I can't tell you how much I hated myself after these binges. Total disgust. I'd make myself throw up, but that only made me feel worse. I told myself it'll never happen again; this time I'm going to stick to my diet. But of course I couldn't – and on and on it went until, three years later, I couldn't take any more. I told my mother everything, and that in itself was such a huge relief after all the years of secrecy. She came with me to the doctor – I couldn't face it on my own. My GP referred me to this brilliant therapist. After just a few sessions I was eating normally again for the first time in years. It was fantastic!
Hayley, aged 26

Interestingly, there may be another factor behind binge eating. Recent research has suggested that problems in dealing with emotions are often influential in bulimia. A person may be uncomfortable with strong feelings of any type, or struggle to cope with unpleasant emotions such as unhappiness, worry or boredom. Binge eating is a response to these problems – a distraction, for example, or a way of feeling in control.

Many people who binge eat, and even many people with bulimia, live relatively normal lives. But, for others, the illness can have far-reaching consequences, plunging them into depression and anxiety, and damaging relationships with friends and family. Thankfully, the treatment options available today are excellent.

Incidentally, there's another group of people who regularly binge eat, but who don't try to undo the effects of the food in some way afterwards. This behaviour is known as binge eating disorder. People with binge eating disorder are often overweight, whereas people with bulimia are generally normal weight.

How common is binge eating?

It's difficult to know for sure how widespread binge eating is, largely because it's very much a secret problem. People binge (and purge themselves) in private and often their friends and family are completely unaware of what's going on. Only a very small minority ever seek professional help.

None the less, it's estimated that around 5–10 per cent of women binge eat. About 1–2 per cent suffer from bulimia, but that figure jumps dramatically for young women (bulimia usually starts in the mid- to late teens). Roughly 4.5 per cent of women aged 18–24 are thought to be bulimic. And a quarter of people with bulimia have previously suffered from anorexia (see p. 211).

Bulimia seems to be overwhelmingly a female illness. Although eating disorders are thought to be increasing among men, they are still 10 times less likely than women to develop bulimia. The gender imbalance is less pronounced for binge eating disorder, which also seems to affect a greater number of older people.

Self-assessment

The Eating Attitudes Test is widely used by health professionals. Try it now to get a sense of whether you may have an eating problem (the test is designed for both bulimia and anorexia).

	Always	Usually	Often	Sometimes	Rarely	Never	Score
1. I am terrified about being overweight.							
2. I avoid eating when I am hungry.							
3. I find myself preoccupied with food.							
4. I have gone on eating binges where I feel that I may not be able to stop.							
5. I cut my food into small pieces.							

	Always	Usually	Often	Sometimes	Rarely	Never	Score
6. I am aware of the calorie content of foods that I eat.							
7. I particularly avoid foods with a high carbohy-drate content (i.e. bread, rice, potatoes, etc.).							
8. I feel that others would prefer it if I ate more.							
9. I vomit after I have eaten.							
10. I feel extremely guilty after eating.							
11. I am preoccu-pied with a desire to be thinner.							
12. I think about burning calories when I exercise.							
13. I know other people think that I am too thin.							

	Always	Usually	Often	Sometimes	Rarely	Never	Score
14. I am preoccupied with the thought of having fat on my body.							
15. I take longer than others to eat my meals.							
16. I avoid foods with sugar in them.							
17. I eat diet foods.							
18. I feel that food controls my life.							
19. I display self-control around food.							
20. I feel that others pressure me to eat.							
21. I give too much time and thought to food.							
22. I feel uncomfortable after eating sweets.							
23. I engage in dieting behaviour.							

	Always	Usually	Often	Sometimes	Rarely	Never	Score
24. I like my stomach to be empty.							
25. I have the impulse to vomit after meals.							
26. I enjoy trying rich, new foods.							
TOTAL							

The EAT–26 has been reproduced with permission. Garner et al. (1982). The Eating Attitudes Test: Psychometric features and clinical correlates. *Psychological Medicine*, 12, 871–8.

For questions 1 to 25, give yourself 3 points for each time you've selected 'Always', 2 for 'Usually', 1 for 'Often' and 0 if you've answered with 'Sometimes', 'Rarely' or 'Never'.

The scoring for question 26 is 3 for 'Never', 2 for 'Rarely', 1 for 'Sometimes' and 0 for 'Always', 'Usually' or 'Often'.

A total score of 20 or more suggests a high level of concern with body weight, body shape and eating. It also indicates a possible eating disorder – for example, bulimia or anorexia.

How to Overcome Binge Eating

Many people can get over their binge-eating problem simply by following the guidelines we set out below (and which you'll find in more detailed form in some of the books recommended on p. 210). But if you feel that you are really locked into your binge eating, are very depressed or don't have much of a support network, think about getting professional help. (A course of Cognitive Behaviour Therapy is the standard – and very successful – treatment for bulimia, and is what we base our suggestions on.) You must talk to your GP or an eating disorders specialist if you're significantly underweight (see p. 217).

Before you tackle your eating disorder, it can be really helpful to enlist the support of a trusted friend or member of the family – having someone you can chat to when you're going through a rough patch can make all the difference. It's also a good idea to talk regularly to someone who you're not quite so close to – your doctor perhaps. They'll be able to give you a more distanced view of things.

Now let's look at the main steps towards overcoming binge eating.

Get back to a normal eating pattern

This is vital. You need to stick to a planned schedule of three meals a day, plus two or three snacks. Keeping a diary of your current eating habits will help you: note down what, where and when you eat, whether you binge or vomit and your feelings at the time. This will help you to see exactly what changes you need to make and, as the weeks pass and you get more comfortable with your new eating regime, it'll provide a morale boost if you're finding things hard.

Work out in advance when and what you're going to eat, and don't go for more than three hours without food. Decide on one or two places in the house where you're going to eat and don't have your meals anywhere else. Make sure that the only food within reach is what's on your plate (that way you won't be tempted to eat more). Sit down to eat, and take your time over the meal. Focus on eating; try not to read or watch TV at the same time.

No vomiting (or laxatives or diuretics, etc.)

Once you've settled into a regular eating pattern you almost certainly won't feel as though you need to compensate for your food intake. Even so, it's worth bearing in mind that the sort of strategies that bulimia sufferers use – vomiting, for example – are harmful to health, as well as completely ineffective at preventing weight gain.

Regular vomiting can cause permanent dental problems, swelling of the salivary glands (making the face look puffy) and damage to the throat and intestines; it can even upset the chemical balance of bodily fluids, resulting in serious heart and kidney conditions. Taking lots of laxatives and diuretics can also play havoc with this balance of bodily fluids. And, the body becomes used to laxatives, so that you have to take more and more to achieve the same effect.

Moreover, they don't work. Diuretics reduce your weight because they make you lose fluid; but when your fluid levels come back up to normal, you put that weight straight back on. Laxatives act on the 'wrong' part of the gut; the calories have already been absorbed into the body. And vomiting only gets rid of around half of the calories you've just consumed. These methods are a trap. They seem to promise that you can eat what you like without putting on weight. In actual fact, they encourage overeating.

Conquer the urge to binge

Look through your eating diary to help you identify the sorts of situations and feelings that make you want to binge. Then draw up a list of activities you can use to distract yourself if the urge strikes. What generally work best are activities you can do with other people or ones that involve using your hands (for example, gardening or playing a musical instrument). Solitary, passive pastimes such as reading or watching TV aren't so effective.

Many people find that they binge more when they're very stressed, so have a look at the stress-management guidelines on pp. 355–9. If there's something in particular that's upsetting you and triggering your binges, make sure you read through the advice on problem-solving on p. 110.

Prepare for setbacks

Though you might doubt it right now, you can overcome your binge-eating problem, but it's not going to be easy. You'll need to be absolutely determined to make the change. And you'll also have to be prepared for the occasional setback. Changing deep-seated eating habits can take several weeks and you're bound to feel the occasional urge to binge. Sometimes you might give in. But it doesn't mean you've failed. Get back on track right away – don't be tempted to write off the whole day. If you're finding it particularly difficult to stick to your eating plan, start by focusing on the mornings (when most people are generally at their best) and build from there.

Say goodbye to dieting

Lots of people prefer to stick to low-calorie foods when they begin eating regularly. That's fine in the short term, provided you're getting at least 1500 calories a day (preferably closer to 1800). Ultimately though, you need to be eating a wide range of foods. Nothing should be taboo – even sweets and puddings – as long as they're in moderation.

Remember: dieting doesn't work. For one thing, your weight and body shape are partly the product of your genes, not just your lifestyle. As a result, it's hard to maintain long-term weight loss because your body adapts to its new diet. Moreover, and perhaps most tellingly, restricting your intake only makes you more preoccupied with food and desperate to eat (for a dramatic illustration of this, see the box on p. 200).

So, give up dieting. If there are foods you don't allow yourself at the moment, make a list and rank them in order of how stressful you find the thought of eating them. Introduce the least stressful ones into your diet and, once you're comfortable with them, work your way through the list.

Why do so many teenage girls and young women develop eating disorders?

A question of that magnitude is inevitably going to have a complex answer. Eating disorders are generally caused by a combination of factors including personality, family background and the attitudes of peers. But social and cultural influences are also hugely important, as two fascinating research studies have shown.

A survey of more than 500 girls aged 10–18 in the US found that almost 60 per cent were unhappy with their body shape and two-thirds wanted to lose weight. This is alarming enough, but the research also found that 69 per cent of the girls turned to fashion magazines for their idea of the perfect body shape, and almost half wanted to lose weight to look more like the models. The more often the girls read fashion magazines, the more likely they were to diet.

Another study tracked almost 7000 American girls aged 9–14 over the course of a year. Around 30 per cent had been on a diet, and 1 per cent had begun vomiting or using laxatives to control their weight. The girls who began purging were those who'd previously been most concerned about their weight and shape, who'd dieted most often and whose friends placed the greatest importance on being thin. They were also the girls who most wanted to look like the women on television, in the movies or in magazines.

Occasionally, we hear pleas for the media not to feature exclusively young, slim and beautiful women. These surveys provide an insight into what's at stake.

Only weigh yourself once a week

People with bulimia often weigh themselves obsessively, but all this does is stoke their anxiety. Weigh yourself once a week, on the same day and at the same time. Bear in mind that your weight is bound to fluctuate; you can only really draw any meaningful conclusions from four consecutive weekly readings. Don't try to check your weight or body size by looking in the mirror or judging how well your clothes fit: they're not reliable indicators.

Lots of people worry that they'll put on weight once they start eating regularly. In fact, you probably won't (unless you were underweight to begin with). But the real battle is to accept your natural weight for what it is. Perhaps it's a little higher than you'd ideally like, but that's a boat that most people are in. (If you're unsure what your natural weight is, a few weeks of eating properly should show you. The BMI calculator on p. 218 will also give you a rough indication.)

Challenge unhelpful attitudes

People with eating disorders generally believe that they're only as good as their appearance. Their sense of self-worth is determined entirely by their weight and body shape. And, because they tend to be perfectionists, given to setting themselves impossible targets, when they look in the mirror they can be incredibly hard on themselves.

As you've probably realized, these are attitudes you need to change. Write down your negative thoughts and try to challenge them. Ask yourself what evidence there is, for and against. Imagine what a friend would tell you, or what you'd advise someone else in the same position.

Make a list of the qualities you most admire in other people. And perhaps ask a close friend what they most like about you. You'll see that they value you for much more than your appearance. Talk to your girlfriends about the pressure on women to look 'good', and check out books like Naomi Wolf's *The Beauty Myth*. And, when you next see a woman you think is attractive (an ordinary woman, that is, not a model or film star), try to spot their 'imperfections'; you can be sure they'll have some.

Make time for fun

When you're preoccupied with worries about eating, it's easy to withdraw from friends and family and to give up the hobbies and interests you used to love. But if you can get out and about and enjoy yourself, you'll find that those worries weigh much less heavily.

Medication and/or other approaches

As we've mentioned, bulimia is generally treated very successfully with a course of Cognitive Behaviour Therapy (CBT). Excellent results have been achieved too with Interpersonal Therapy (IPT); this focuses on tackling problems in relationships, which often turns out to be the key to improving eating habits. Some people also find it helpful to talk to a dietitian about food issues.

Some doctors prescribe antidepressants, in particular the new SSRIs (selective serotonin reuptake inhibitors) like fluoxetine, better known by the trade name Prozac. These can be helpful, but there's doubt over how long the benefits last, even if the person keeps taking the medication.

What to do if a close friend or family member has an eating disorder

It can be tough, but you'll help most by being as positive and supportive as you possibly can. Don't try to force them to eat, or lecture them about their diet. Be there for them when they want to talk, and try to gently steer them in the right direction. Encourage them to seek professional help, particularly if you're very concerned about their physical health.

Related problems

Bulimia sometimes develops after a bout of anorexia, and in fact there's considerable overlap between the two illnesses, so you may also want to read the undereating entry, too. People with eating disorders often also have problems with **depression**, and **anxiety** (including body dysmorphic disorder, covered in **body image worries**).

Where to go for more information

You'll find lots of excellent information and advice in the following books: *Bulimia Nervosa and Binge Eating* (Robinson, 1993) by Peter Cooper; *Getting Better Bit(e) by Bit(e)* (Psychology Press, 1993) by Ulrike Schmidt and Janet Treasure; *Overcoming Binge Eating* (Guilford, 2005) by Christopher Fairburn

If your child has an eating problem, have a look at *Eating Disorders: Helping Your Child Recover* (Eating Disorders Association, 2006) edited by Steve Bloomfield.

On the Internet, check out:

ⓘ www.anred.com (the website of the US organization Anorexia

Nervosa and Related Eating Disorders)
- ⓘ www.b-eat.co.uk (run by beat, the Eating Disorders Association)
- ⓘ www.nationaleatingdisorders.org (the National Eating Disorders Association is a US charity)

UNDEREATING

Most of us know what it's like to diet. The pressure on everyone, and especially women, to control their weight by eating less is arguably greater now than ever. But our focus here isn't on the temporary restrictions that dieting involves. It's on drastic, sustained and damaging undereating – or anorexia nervosa.

Like binge eating and bulimia, anorexia is much better understood these days, both by the medical profession and by society as a whole. It's no longer trivialized as the 'slimmer's disease', and advances have been made in treatment. But it's still one of the toughest – and most dangerous – psychological problems to tackle.

People with anorexia have an obsessional fear of becoming overweight, even when they're seriously underweight. Their self-image is distorted: how they think they look bears little relation to the way they actually look. And, of course, the distortion isn't a flattering one: the person with anorexia believes they're fat and unattractive (despite all evidence to the contrary). Like bulimia, anorexia seems to build on a belief that what matters most is one's appearance – that self-esteem comes from slimness and self-control.

What all this leads to is a set of extremely strict rules about eating. For example, someone with anorexia will have a long list of forbidden foods, and a very much shorter one of items they allow themselves to eat (usually fruit and vegetables). They may set themselves a (very low) calorie target for the day, or refuse to eat before a certain time (generally late in the day). When they do have a meal, they may eat incredibly slowly or also drink lots of water, so that they feel full as soon as possible.

As you'd expect from what is essentially a programme of self-starvation, anorexia results in significant loss of weight (the official definition is 85 per cent or less of normal weight). Women stop menstruating and very serious health problems can occur, including low blood pressure, anaemia, abdominal pain and increased risk of a variety of infections and illnesses. In extreme cases, major organs such as the heart and liver can be damaged.

Problems with undereating: a personal account

My boyfriend was always making nasty little remarks about my weight, always comparing me to other women. I knew he wasn't right for me, but I was still devastated when we split up. I blamed myself: if I'd been slimmer and more attractive none of this would have happened. So I started this really strict diet – no bread, no potatoes, no dairy, no sugar, no this, no that: pretty much all I ate was fruit and vegetables, plus the odd bowl of breakfast cereal with water. I was so low after the break-up that I didn't have much of an appetite, so it was actually easy to start with. I lost a couple of pounds pretty quickly and my friends said how great I was looking. Which was all I needed: soon I was eating even less than before and also jogging several miles every day. After a few months of that, I was so weak and sick I could barely stand, but I was determined to lose just a couple more pounds …

Kelly, aged 24

What makes anorexia especially difficult to combat is the fact that very often the sufferer doesn't recognize that they have a problem. On the contrary, they see anorexia as the solution to their troubles. Partly, this is a consequence of the depression that starvation inevitably triggers. It locks people even more tightly into the belief that the way to improve their life is by achieving the 'perfect' body.

Anorexia has a lot in common with bulimia, not least in the factors that cause it, so make sure you also read the **binge eating** entry on pp. 199–211. About 50 per cent of people with anorexia also binge eat, then try to compensate by making themselves vomit, taking laxatives or exercising excessively. These strategies bring their own health risks. Regular vomiting, for example, can cause permanent dental problems, swelling of the salivary glands (making the face look puffy), damage to the throat and intestines, and can even upset the chemical balance of the bodily fluids, which can result in serious heart and kidney conditions.

Apart from the devastating effects – both physical and psychological – that anorexia can have on the sufferer, the toll it takes on loved ones is often huge. Few things can be more distressing than watching someone you care about starve themselves, while claiming that they're fine. And the changes in mood that anorexia can cause can make the sufferer very difficult to live with. Anorexia is a problem that needs to be tackled as early as possible, for everyone's benefit.

Food, mind, and body

One of the curious features of anorexia is an obsession with food. Some people hoard vast (and unused) stocks of food. Others develop a passion for cooking, collecting recipes and preparing sumptuous meals for family and friends that they themselves wouldn't dream of tasting. And almost everyone with anorexia spends a large part of every day thinking about food.

This sort of behaviour is a rather extreme example of the effect that any strict diet has on us – an effect perfectly illustrated by a research study carried out during the Second World War, in which thirty-six volunteers existed for six months on half their normal amount of food. Over the following three months, the volunteers' diet was gradually brought back up to normal levels.

Apart from the physical effects of such a restricted diet (the volunteers lost around a quarter of their body weight) there were also dramatic psychological changes, one of the most striking being the volunteers' obsession with food; it dominated their conversations, their thoughts and their dreams (one poor soul even dreamed of cannibalism). Rather like people with anorexia, many of the volunteers began to show a keen – and novel – interest in cooking and started collecting recipes and other food-related items. For some, this preoccupation with food never left them, even after the experiment had ended.

So, it seems that while we can deprive the body of food, the same is not true for the mind. It is determined to get us back to eating. This is partly why dieting doesn't work (at least, on a long-term basis). It also helps to explain why people with anorexia so often become preoccupied with food, and why one of the defining characteristics of the illness is an obsessional struggle to subdue the urge to eat.

How common is anorexia?

Around 0.3 per cent of women have anorexia nervosa, though since most of those affected are young women, the rate is higher for that age group. Like bulimia, anorexia is overwhelmingly a female illness, with 10 times more women affected than men. It can strike at any age, but typically begins between the ages of 16 and 19.

Self-assessment

If you're worried that you might be suffering from anorexia, have a go at the Eating Attitudes Test on p. 202 and the BMI calculator on p. 218.

How to Overcome Undereating

Anorexia is a tough problem to overcome, but it can definitely be done. If you haven't lost much weight, you may be able to manage by following our suggestions or those in one of the self-help books we recommend on p. 217. But you should still start by seeing your GP, who will be able to check your physical health and talk over treatment options with you. They may, for example, recommend that you see a cognitive behaviour therapist (CBT being a standard treatment for anorexia). If you're very underweight, your doctor may recommend hospital care, either as an inpatient or an outpatient.

Reading this means that you may already have taken the most important step towards beating your anorexia: recognizing that you have a problem. Part of the reason why anorexia is so dangerous is that it can feel like a friend or a part of your identity. If you're not sure whether you can cope without your anorexia, have a look at the books listed at the end of this entry (p. 217). They'll help you to understand the damage you're risking to your health, as well as the advantages that life without anorexia will bring.

Read about what other people with anorexia have gone through, and talk over your situation with your loved ones. Imagine what life will be like in, say, five years' time if you carry on as you are, and then what it might be like if you were to overcome your anorexia. Write down the positives and negatives of being underweight, and those of being a normal weight.

Your eating habits have probably developed over a number of months or years, and they're not likely to disappear overnight. It'll take a lot of motivation and perseverance. But remember: you're not alone. Many, many people have lived with anorexia and recovered – and you can too. It'll be easier if you enlist the support of your friends and family, and also if there's someone you're not quite so close to but who you can talk to regularly about your eating (your GP, for example).

Your first priority has to be getting back to a normal weight (if you're not sure what your normal weight is, you can get an idea from the BMI calculator on p. 218). Start by keeping a food diary. Write down what, where and when you eat; whether you binge or vomit; and your feelings at the time. This is the best way both to get an accurate sense of where you are now and to track your progress. Make sure, incidentally, that you don't weigh yourself more than once a week.

Now you need to set clear goals for gaining weight, and plan how you're going to achieve them. Gradually increase the amount you're eating, and cut back on whatever it is you do to stop yourself gaining weight (for example, exercising or making yourself vomit). Take things steadily – you're bound to feel anxious or uncomfortable at first. It's best to go for frequent, small meals. But keep in mind that you'll only gain weight if you're eating more than about 2000 calories a day. To put on half a kilogram a week, you'll need to eat around 2500 calories each day.

The other steps in your recovery programme are the same as for bulimia (see pp. 206–9), so we won't go into detail here. But in particular, you need to:

- get back to a normal eating pattern
- challenge unhelpful attitudes about your body
- make time for fun.

Medication and/or other approaches

Medication isn't generally used to combat anorexia. Cognitive Behaviour Therapy is probably the most commonly used treatment, but there are other effective options:

Cognitive Analytic Therapy (CAT) – explores the early-life experiences and the problematic relationships that may have contributed to the eating disorder.

Interpersonal Therapy (IPT) – focuses on tackling problems in relationships, which often turns out to be the key to improving eating habits.

Family intervention – it can be very helpful to the whole family to take part in therapy, especially when the person suffering from anorexia is a child or teenager.

Some people also find it useful to discuss food issues with a dietitian.

Does your child have an eating disorder?

Here are some common warning signs:

- Losing weight
- Wearing baggy clothes
- Avoiding eating with the rest of the family
- Preferring fruit and vegetables, rather than fats and carbohydrates
- Exercising excessively
- Drinking lots of caffeine drinks
- Mood changes
- Keeping to herself
- Binge eating
- Vomiting
- Taking laxatives
- Visiting the bathroom during meals, or as soon as possible afterwards

What to do if a close friend or family member has an undereating problem

Again, the advice we outline in the binge eating entry (see p. 210) applies here. But because people with anorexia are often unwilling to accept that they have a problem, loved ones can be especially valuable in helping them to make this first crucial step towards recovery.

When dealing with someone who has an eating disorder, it's generally best to adopt the role of facilitator, working with them to achieve their goals, rather than dictating or cajoling. But you'll probably need to take a more hands-on approach if your child or teenager is suffering from anorexia – for example, sitting with them while they eat or helping them question their attitudes to their body. (If you're worried that your child might have anorexia, see the warning signs above.)

And last, but certainly not least, look after yourself. Caring for someone with an eating disorder can be an exhausting and sometimes distressing task. So it's really important that you make time to do things you enjoy. Share your concerns with friends and family, and make use of the specialist support organizations listed on p. 217.

Related problems

As we've mentioned, anorexia and bulimia are so similar in many ways that you should also read the **binge eating** entry.

People with anorexia very often suffer from problems with **anxiety**, particularly body dysmorphic disorder (covered in **body image worries**), **panic, fears and phobias, obsessions and compulsions** and **depression**.

Where to go for more information

Overcoming Anorexia Nervosa (Robinson, 2001) by Christopher Freeman is an excellent self-help guide. People with anorexia (and their loved ones) will find lots of useful advice in *Anorexia Nervosa: A Survival Guide for Families, Friends and Sufferers* (Psychology Press, 1997) by Janet Treasure, and parents should also have a look at *Eating Disorders: Helping Your Child Recover* (Eating Disorders Association, 2006) edited by Steve Bloomfield.

On the Internet, check out:

- ⓘ www.anred.com (the website of the US organization Anorexia Nervosa and Related Eating Disorders)
- ⓘ www.b-eat.co.uk (run by beat, the Eating Disorders Association)
- ⓘ www.nationaleatingdisorders.org (the National Eating Disorders Association is a US charity)

BEING OVERWEIGHT

. . . .

Eddy: Inside of me there's a thin person screaming to get out.
June: Just the one, dear?
Absolutely Fabulous

. . . .

Today, more of us than ever before are overweight. No one can deny the pleasures of munching a pizza in front of the TV after a hard day at work. But takeaways, snacks and ready meals, combined with a decline in the amount of exercise we take, have led to two-thirds of people in the UK being heavier than they ought to be.

Your weight is the product of a combination of factors, from your genes and metabolism to your socio-economic group. Sometimes weight problems can be caused by physical factors, such as thyroid disease or some types of medication (for example, the contraceptive pill). But eating so badly and exercising so rarely are what's led to the recent rapid rise in the number of overweight people.

Most people are just carrying a few extra pounds, but even so there are lots of good reasons to slim down. Losing just a little weight can make you feel happier, healthier and more energetic. And you'll also reduce the risk of developing serious illnesses like cancer, heart disease, diabetes, stroke and arthritis.

The most commonly accepted method of deciding whether someone is overweight or not is the body mass index (BMI), which is calculated using a ratio of weight to height (see below).

How common is it to be overweight?

Adult obesity rates in the UK have doubled over the past 25 years. In 2003 the Department of Health found that 43 per cent of men in England were overweight, with a further 22 per cent being obese (extremely overweight), while 33 per cent of women were overweight and 23 per cent were obese. Roughly a third of children were either overweight or obese. Children are much more likely to be overweight or obese if one of their parents is too, and even more likely if both parents are.

The figures for the US tell a similar story, with 73 per cent of US adults estimated to be either overweight or obese in 2008.

Self-assessment: calculate your body mass index (or BMI)

You may have heard about healthy weight in terms of a healthy body mass index (BMI). Body mass index is calculated as your weight (in kilograms) divided by your height (in metres) squared. For example, the average woman in the UK weighs 70 kilograms (11 stone) and is 1.61 metres (5 feet 3½ inches) tall, which means she has a BMI of 27.

BMI = $\dfrac{\text{weight}}{(\text{height} \times \text{height})}$	BMI = $\dfrac{70}{(1.61 \times 1.61)}$	= 27

Here's how the scores are interpreted for adults:
Below 18.5: underweight
18.5–24.9: healthy weight
25–29.9: overweight
30 and above: obese

Problems with being overweight: a personal account

Until my late 20s I weighed 61 kilograms (9 stone 6lb). Then I had three kids! By the time I reached 40 I was 78.5 kilograms (12 stone 4lb). I'd slipped into a lot of bad habits. I didn't take any exercise – I thought I didn't have time. Plus we were eating a lot of takeaways and ready meals. But my weight was getting me down. I had headaches and back pain and felt tired all the time. I was so miserable though that I didn't have the willpower or self-confidence to think I could really lose weight. But then we were invited to my sister-in-law's wedding. When I went to buy an outfit I found I was a size 18. At first I was so depressed I didn't want to leave the house, but I had a long talk with my husband and we decided to make some changes. We began planning our weekly menus, which made it a lot easier to eat healthier food. We went for a walk every day. And we each kept a weekly record of our weight. Just doing these three things made such a big difference!

Susie, aged 44

Alternatively, you can find lots of BMI calculators on the Internet. You just enter your height and weight and the website does the calculation for you.

Remember though that your BMI is just an indicator, not a cast-iron statement of fact. So if you're not sure whether or not you're overweight, it's best to check with your GP.

HOW TO LOSE WEIGHT

At first glance it all seems so simple. You put on weight when the energy you consume – in the form of food calories – exceeds the energy you use up in your daily life. So, to lose weight, all you have to do is reverse that balance and use more calories than you take in. In other words, eat less and exercise more.

In reality, of course, weight loss turns out to be easier said than done. But you can do it, and here are some steps to help you on the way.

Commit to losing weight

Quick fixes – such as crash diets – don't work. What you need is a long-term change in your eating and exercising habits. But you won't succeed unless you're really committed to it.

So before you do anything else, write down your reasons for losing weight. Are you sure you know why you want to slim down? What are the short- and long-term benefits? What are the costs? Are you sure you feel the benefits are greater than the costs? Can you commit to the long-term effort?

When you're trying to break old, ingrained habits, you can't expect it to happen without a lot of planning and persistence. So, once you're sure you want to lose weight, write down your reasons and try to keep them handy – maybe pin them up in the kitchen or carry them around with you on a card. You're bound to have moments when your resolve slips a bit, and those are the perfect times for a reminder of what you're in it for.

Challenge negative thoughts

'I can't lose weight at the moment – my life is just too stressful; I need my comfort foods!' 'There's no point in trying – I've never had any willpower.' 'I don't have the time to exercise; or the energy.' If you're going to lose weight, you'll need to beat these kinds of negative thoughts.

The weight-loss experts

The National Weight Control Registry in the US comprises 5000 people who've successfully kept their weight down over the long term. These weight-loss experts have some interesting lessons to teach us. What they all have in common is:

- a low-fat diet
- eating breakfast
- weighing themselves weekly
- being physically active for at least an hour a day
- watching much less television than the national average.

If you can adopt these five good habits, the chances are you'll lose weight too – and keep it off.

Is obesity contagious?

You're much more likely to put on weight when your friends are obese.

That was the conclusion of a research study in the US that tracked more than 12,000 people from 1971 to 2003. The researchers knew who was friends with who; they knew who was a spouse, a sibling or a neighbour; and they knew how much each person weighed at various times over those 32 years.

What the researchers found was that your chance of becoming obese rises by 57 per cent if you have a friend who is obese, even if that friend is several hundred miles away. If a sibling is obese, you're 40 per cent more likely to become obese as well. And the risk increases by 37 per cent if your spouse is obese. It's almost as though obesity is contagious, spreading from person to person.

Why does this happen? The researchers explain these figures by arguing that: 'People come to think it's OK to be bigger, because those around them are bigger.' In other words, your view of what a 'normal' body looks like changes. Of course, your weight is the product of a multitude of factors, not just who you know. But the study is a fascinating insight into the workings of one of those factors – your social network.

Try to identify the sort of thinking that's holding you back and see whether there's any evidence to support it. Is there a more positive take on things that you could replace these negative thoughts with? What would you advise a friend in your position?

It's always a good idea to test out negative thoughts to see whether they stack up. For example, people often think they're too tired at the end of the day to exercise. So try exercising after work and see whether you feel any worse or different from when you don't exercise.

Keep a weight-loss diary

Before you begin changing your diet and exercise habits, try to identify what they're like at the moment. This will be the baseline against which you can measure your progress.

Start by writing down what you've had to eat and drink each day for a week. Can you see any patterns emerging? For example, are there times of the day when you're more likely to eat high-fat foods? Are you eating regularly? How balanced is your diet? How many calories do you think you're consuming? (The average man needs about 2500 a day; the average woman needs 2000.)

And how much exercise are you taking? You can get a good sense of how active you are by wearing a pedometer, which will calculate the number of steps you take. Fewer than 5000 steps is considered inactive, between 5000 and 7500 as low active, between 7500 and 9999 as somewhat active, above 10,000 as active and above 12,500 as very active.

Update your diary regularly and you'll have a great record of your progress.

Be more active

Aim for at least 30 minutes of exercise five times a week. It's a lot easier to do this if you build the exercise into your daily routine – that way you'll get your exercise without really noticing it. So instead of driving to work, walk or cycle instead. Try getting off the bus a couple of stops early and walking the rest of the way. Having a dog is a good solution – provided you do actually take it for its walks!

Ideally, your exercise should at least make your heartbeat and breathing a little faster than normal. You'll feel warm and may well work up a sweat. Aerobic activities like swimming, jogging and tennis are particularly good but, whatever you go for, make sure it's something you enjoy. People tend to give up on exercise when they pick an activity they don't really like. Exercising with other people rather than on your own can be more fun, so think about joining an exercise class or walking group, or playing a team sport.

(Incidentally, your 30 minutes of exercise needn't be taken in one go: you could opt for two 15-minute sessions. That said, a full 30-minute session is ideal because you're raising your heart rate for a more substantial time.)

Try to anticipate the sort of things that will stop you exercising and plan ways around them. If you don't want to run in the rain, maybe opt for swimming on those days instead. If you can't face leaving the house again once you've got back from work, plan your exercise for the morning, or think about what you could do at home.

Eat well

One of the major factors behind the 'obesity epidemic' is the fact that so many people are eating so badly. Portions have got larger and people are eating lots more processed food – which tends to be high in fat, sugar and salt. Instead of preparing proper meals from fresh, raw ingredients, they're opting for ready meals, snacks and fast food.

How can this be turned round? What should you be eating and drinking? Well, nutritionists suggest these nine key steps:

- Base your meals around starchy foods.
- Eat lots of fruit and vegetables.
- Eat more fish.
- Cut down on saturated fat, e.g. butter, ghee, lard, cheese and cream.
- Eat less sugar.
- Reduce your salt intake to no more than 6g a day.
- Drink plenty of water.
- Moderate your alcohol intake.
- Don't skip breakfast.

(For more information on this, see pp. 18–21.)

Inevitably, there'll be moments when you're desperate for a chocolate bar or a burger. You might even want to give up trying to lose weight altogether. So try to plan for these difficult times. For instance, if you find yourself craving something sweet, think of the different ways you could beat the craving. You could distract yourself by getting busy with something else. Or perhaps you could have something sweet, but relatively healthy, like fruit. Maybe you could try reminding yourself of the reasons why you're trying to lose weight, and how you'll feel later if you give in to your craving. Try out these various strategies, as well as referring to your reasons for wanting to lose weight (see p. 220), and see what works best for you.

Cut your calorie intake

As we've mentioned, the average man needs around 2500 calories a day and the average woman needs 2000. Aim for 2000 a day if you're a man and 1500 if you're a woman.

The best – and safest – way of doing this is to follow a low-fat diet, watch your portion sizes, and make sure your plate isn't too big. Plan your meals in advance – getting together a healthy meal at the last moment, and when you're hungry can feel very difficult. Eat regular meals and avoid unplanned, unhealthy snacks. And cook only the amount of food you think you'll eat.

You'll find details of some good low-fat diet books on p. 225, but don't get obsessed with calorie counting: if you eat well you'll find the calories take care of themselves.

Be realistic

Once you've decided to lose weight, it's all too easy to get caught up in very noble but completely unrealistic targets. Exercising hard for an hour each day is a lot to ask if you've not been active before. Swearing never to eat another piece of chocolate is, again, setting yourself up to fail. Aim for gradual progress, not overnight change. Build up your exercise levels bit by bit. Tackle one aspect of your diet at a time. Set yourself realistic goals and track your progress using your weight-loss diary.

Be kind to yourself

Remember to reward yourself when things are going well – treat yourself to a trip to the cinema, perhaps, or buy that CD. And don't get discouraged if you have a bad day: everyone has one once in a while. Just put it behind you and get back on track.

Use your support network

Your friends and family can play a big part in helping you lose weight. Let them know what you're trying to achieve and explain how they can help. Maybe they can stop offering you sweets and snacks. Perhaps they'll join you in a walk or a swim. Most importantly, they can offer you encouragement, especially if you're finding things tough. Many people find it helpful to join a slimming group, which can be a great source of mutual support.

Related problems

Weight problems can be caused by physical factors, such as thyroid disease or some types of medication. If you're concerned about your weight, it's always worth seeing your GP. As well as being able to investigate any physical causes, they may be able to refer you to a dietitian or a local exercise scheme.

Weight problems are also sometimes associated with **depression** and low self-esteem (covered in the **depression** entry).

Where to go for more information

Overcoming Weight Problems by Jeremy Gauntlet-Gilbert and Clare Grace (Constable Robinson, 2005) offers lots of sensible advice.

You'll find useful information about diet at www.bdaweightwise.com and www.eatwell.gov.uk.

And there are lots of good low-fat diet books around, including: *Healthy Eating: Low Fat* (ACP, 2000) by Mary Coleman; *101 Low-fat Feasts* (BBC Books, 2003); *Low-fat Meals in Minutes* (BBC Books, 2002) by Ainsley Harriott

A number of free calorie counters are available on the Internet – try www.caloriecounting.co.uk, for example.

Plain old walking is an excellent form of exercise: have a look at www.whi.org.uk for information on walking for fitness and weight loss.

. . . .

I'm not overweight. I'm just nine inches too short.
Shelley Winters

. . . .

Hallucinations

....

*I was four years old then, and I think it must have been the
next summer that I first heard the voices. I was out playing
alone when I heard them. It was like somebody calling me,
and I thought it was my mother, but there was nobody there.*
Black Elk (Sioux medicine man, 1863–1950)

Hallucinations have a bad reputation. After all, when was the last time
someone admitted to you that they'd heard a strange voice? Have you ever
told anyone about a bizarre sensory experience – perhaps when you thought
someone was calling your name, only to discover that you were alone? Or
when you've seen or smelled or felt or tasted something that you couldn't
account for?

Most people think that hallucinations are a sign of mental illness. So
it's not surprising that those of us who experience them usually keep quiet
about it. But although some people with serious mental health problems
do experience hallucinations, that's not even half the story. Hallucinations
are actually very common, and usually they have nothing at all to do with
mental illness. (Many non-Western cultures, such as the American Indian
society into which Black Elk was born, seem to understand this.)

The technical definition of a hallucination is a perception that occurs
without a cause (or at least a cause in the outside world), and over which
we feel we have no control. Scientists are still trying to pin down exactly
what's going on in our brain when we have a hallucination, but basically
we seem to be mistaking our internal thoughts for external events. I may
believe I'm hearing someone tell me what a fantastic day it is, but what
I'm actually listening to is the 'sound' of my own thoughts.

Mostly, hallucinations occur when we're very tired, bored or stressed,
or when we're under the influence of alcohol or drugs. Occasionally they're

Problems with hallucinations: a personal account

I can always tell how tired or stressed I am by the kinds of voices I hear. If I'm happy, if I've had plenty of rest, I might hear nothing at all. Or I might hear what sounds a bit like my dad's voice, but very warm and encouraging. Usually it'll be commenting on something that's happened to me, or something I've done. And often it's really enlightening! It points out stuff I hadn't noticed. If I think about the voice (and usually I don't), I think of it as a friend. Other times, when I'm run-down or feeling out of sorts, I might hear a different voice and this one is more critical. I could do without it, but I usually just tell it to mind its own business, and I get on with what I'm doing. That soon shuts it up! I know hearing voices seems a bit odd, but it really doesn't bother me. It's only a very tiny part of my life, after all.

Chris, aged 33

triggered by psychological problems like severe depression or Post-Traumatic Stress Disorder, or physical conditions like Alzheimer's or Parkinson's disease.

Hallucinations come in all shapes and sizes, right across our five senses. Most people don't find them alarming; in fact, some positively try to bring them on. But in a minority of cases, the hallucinations are upsetting.

The hallucinations that tend to cause problems are nasty, abusive voices. The person affected may be frightened that someone powerful is out to get them. And it's these distressing hallucinations, often quite frequent, that tend to play havoc with people's lives, prompting them to seek professional help.

Sometimes the hallucinations turn out to be a symptom of a serious mental illness (or 'psychosis', to use the medical term), such as schizophrenia. But remember: this is comparatively unusual. For most people, hallucinations are simply harmless 'tricks of the mind', and there's nothing at all to worry about.

How common are hallucinations?

About 13 per cent of us have experienced a hallucination at some point in our lives. Four per cent of people asked about the previous 12 months say they've heard or seen things that other people couldn't, while 1 per cent report that the voices have spoken quite a few words or sentences.

The figures are even higher if we include night-time experiences. Around a third of people sometimes have hallucinations as they fall asleep and just over 10 per cent while waking up.

Self-assessment

Have you ever had a hallucination? If you can answer 'Yes' to any of the following questions, you may well have done.

Do you ever hear voices saying words or sentences when there is no one around to account for it?

Do you ever hear sounds or music that people near you don't hear?

Do you ever hear voices commenting on what you are thinking or doing?

Do you ever experience smells or odours that people next to you seem unaware of?

Do you ever see things that other people cannot?

Do you ever feel that someone is touching you, but when you look nobody is there?

Do you ever experience unusual burning sensations or other strange feelings in or on your body?

Do you ever experience unexplained tastes in your mouth?

Have you ever heard two or more unexplained voices talking with each other?

Items taken from the Cardiff Anomalous Perceptions Scale by Bell et al (2006).

How to Cope with Hallucinations

A hallucination can be an unsettling, even frightening experience, particularly the first time it happens. But don't panic. They are extremely common, although you'd never guess it because so few people admit to them. And you definitely shouldn't assume you're going mad.

People respond to hallucinations in all kinds of ways. Some find them helpful, some find them unpleasant and upsetting, and others don't take them very seriously at all. Research shows that what makes the difference isn't so much what the hallucinations themselves are like, but how people react to them: if they think there's a powerful and evil force behind them, that they're powerless to stop them happening and that they're unable to cope – well, naturally they are going to find their hallucinations distressing.

Here is a series of strategies to help you learn to cope.

Change the way you think about your hallucinations

Don't struggle against them: you'll just feel more distressed and worried. Accept that they are a part of your life – but a part you have control over.

Magic and loss

Few things in life are as devastating as the loss of a long-term partner. It can be extremely difficult for people to cope, especially in the early months. But now a number of studies have revealed the significant role that hallucinations often play in helping people to adjust to their bereavement.

When researchers in Sweden looked, for example, at the experiences of 50 recently widowed people in their 70s, they found that a third of them were still seeing, hearing or talking to the deceased a year after their bereavement. (The numbers were even higher in the first three months.) Not only were hallucinations very common, but they were almost always found to be extremely comforting – so much so, in fact, that many people actually looked forward to them happening.

Not that this seems to make hallucinations any more socially acceptable. Until the researchers explained how widespread they were, only one of the widowers had mentioned theirs; the others had been worried that they were going mad – or that, if they described their experiences, other people would think they were.

But it isn't like this everywhere. In many non-Western countries, such as Japan, hallucinations are seen as a normal part of the grieving process. That's a message we'd do well to take on board in the West.

Remember: lots of people have these kinds of experiences. They're able to ignore them when they want to, and they don't let them interfere with their lives. You can do the same. Share your feelings with someone you trust. Find out as much as you can about hallucinations, and perhaps contact one of the support groups listed below.

Look after yourself

Hallucinations often happen when you are very run-down or tired or when you're stressed and unhappy. So make sure you eat well, get plenty of good-quality sleep, and take regular exercise (for more on these, see pp. 18–24). Make time for things you enjoy. Watch your alcohol or drug intake (both are common triggers for hallucinations). And, if you're struggling with depression, worry or stress, have a look at the entries on those problems in this book.

Stay one step ahead

Like most challenges in life, hallucinations are a lot easier to cope with if you understand what's going on. So, as well as finding out about hallucinations in general, spend some time analysing your own experiences. A great way to do this is to keep a hallucinations diary for a fortnight. See what sort of situations seem to trigger these odd experiences. Once you've done that, it'll be much easier to work out what you can do to avoid them. (For example, perhaps you'll need to reduce your drug use or think of some activities you can turn to when you're bored or anxious.)

Don't let your hallucinations run your life

The more you think about your hallucinations and the more you fret about them, the more they'll dominate your life. So try not to dwell on them. Don't stop doing the things you enjoy. If your hallucinations are very frequent and regular, try only paying them attention for a short, set period each day – maybe half an hour.

Distracting yourself can help. Wear a Walkman or portable MP3 player, just in case. Or focus on an absorbing activity like practising a musical instrument, doing some housework or playing a sport or game. It doesn't matter what you opt for as long as it keeps you busy. Some people find that humming can silence the voices.

These techniques will work for most people. However, you may also want to have a chat with your doctor, and should definitely do so if:

- you're finding the hallucinations distressing
- it feels as if they're dominating your life
- voices are giving you commands you find difficult to resist
- the hallucinations began when you were over 60.

Your doctor may suggest a course of Cognitive Behaviour Therapy or, perhaps, medication. If you're feeling very low, it may be worth trying an antidepressant. Very severe hallucinations are treated with anti-psychotic drugs (known as major tranquillizers or neuroleptics).

Related problems

Hallucinations can be a feature of **paranoia**, **alcohol** and **drug problems**, **schizophrenia**, **trauma** and **Post-Traumatic Stress Disorder**, and **depression**. **Stress**, **bereavement** and **sleep problems** are also common triggers for hallucinations.

Where to go for more information

Very little has been written about hallucinations, except as a symptom of schizophrenia. Among the best of the latter are:

Accepting Voices (Mind, 1993) by Marius Romme and Sandra Escher; *The Complete Family Guide to Schizophrenia* (Guilford, 2006) by Kim Mueser and Susan Gingerich; *Coping with Schizophrenia* (Oneworld, 2004) by Steven Jones and Peter Hayward.

It's the same situation on the Internet. Discussion of hallucinations as normal, everyday experiences is pretty rare, though www.hearing-voices.org is worth checking out. Generally hallucinations are covered in the context of serious mental illness. If you're after that sort of information, try:

- ⓘ www.mind.org.uk, www.rethink.org, and www.sane.org.uk (Mind, Rethink and Sane are all UK mental health charities)
- ⓘ www.nami.org (the website of the US National Alliance on Mental Illness)
- ⓘ www.schizophrenia.com (a US organization providing support and information for people affected by schizophrenia)

Memory Problems

....

If any one faculty of our nature may be called more wonderful than the rest, I do think it is memory. …. The memory is sometimes so retentive, so serviceable, so obedient; at others, so bewildered and so weak; and at others again, so tyrannic, so beyond control! We are, to be sure, a miracle every way; but our powers of recollecting and of forgetting do seem peculiarly past finding out.
Jane Austen, *Mansfield Park*

Jane Austen was right. The human memory is an extraordinarily complex system – so complex, in fact, that we can hope to do no more than skim the surface here.

And when it comes to problems that can affect memory, our task is no easier. They're so varied that we're going to concentrate on just one here, though it is the most common: the tendency for our memories to work less well as we age.

Let's start with a very quick overview of how memory works. Experts have identified two main types:

- **Short-term memory** (also known as 'working' memory) – this lasts only a few seconds: just long enough for us to complete a task. So when you read this sentence, your working memory will retain the beginning of it so that you can understand the end. Short-term memory is precarious; any interruption or distraction and it can easily be lost.
- **Long-term memory** – this is what most of us think of as our memory. Anything we remember for more than about a minute counts as a long-term memory. Sixty seconds may not seem espe-

cially 'long-term', but research has shown that these very recent memories behave much like older memories. The more times we recall long-term memories, the less likely we are to forget them.

There are several different categories of long-term memory. The main ones are:

- **Episodic memory** – these are memories of 'being there', for example attending a party or visiting a friend.
- **Semantic memory** – this is information about the world (for example that the capital of England is London or indeed what the words 'England' and 'London' mean) that we can't remember learning: we just seem to know it.
- **Implicit (or procedural) memory** – a sort of automatic memory for how to perform tasks, for instance riding a bike or making a phone call.

When it comes to accessing these memories, we might deliberately 'recall' them, or we might need a reminder (this is called 'recognition'). For instance, remembering your PIN number when you need it is recall, whereas spotting washing-up liquid in the supermarket and then remembering that you need to buy a bottle is recognition.

So we all have a short-term memory, several types of long-term memory and at least two ways of accessing them. Adding to the complexity is the fact that memories can be visual (involving images), verbal (words) or spatial (the layout of the world around us). So there's plenty of scope for things to go wrong!

People often remark that they have a bad memory, but actually most of us are better at remembering some things than others. You might, for instance, be terrific at recalling your friends' telephone numbers, but always forget their birthdays. Perhaps you have an encyclopaedic memory for films you've seen, but are hopeless at putting a name to a face. And your memory will work better on some days than others (for example, when you've had plenty of sleep).

All sorts of things can go wrong with memory, and for many different reasons. Head injuries, strokes, alcohol and drug abuse, poisoning and vitamin deficiencies can all cause serious problems. But, for most people, the major challenge to memory is likely to come from the ageing process.

It's a sad fact that as you get older, your memory doesn't work as well as it used to. People often find they have particular trouble recalling words or facts, putting a name to a face or remembering things they have to do in the future. But the good news is that there's lots you can do to boost your memory and compensate for the effects of age, as you'll see below.

Incidentally, although memory problems are normal in older people, they can occasionally be an early sign of dementia (the medical term for a gradual deterioration in the way that the brain works). The most widespread form of dementia is Alzheimer's disease, though vascular dementia (caused by strokes) is also relatively common. People suffering from the early stages of dementia typically find it hard to remember the very recent past; older memories are much less affected. As the disease progresses, the memory may disintegrate completely.

At present, there's no cure for Alzheimer's disease. That said, there's evidence that many of the strategies outlined below for generally improving memory may help delay the onset of the illness and allow people to cope better with the symptoms.

Memory problems: a personal account

I think the memory is like a muscle: you have to exercise it if you want it to work properly. A few years back I was getting very forgetful. To tell the truth, I was a bit worried that I might be developing Alzheimer's. But I happened to watch a programme about memory on TV, and that led me to read a couple of books on the subject. I decided to see what I could do to improve my memory. So I began doing the crossword every day (now I'm very fond of sudoku). I practised using different techniques to help remember things – inventing a story, say, or a funny image. And I became a dedicated note-maker! Now the house is full of reminders to myself to do things – lists and Post-it notes and such like. My wall calendar is my lifeline. I was never very organized, but I do find it helps – I know where to find things now!

Geoff, aged 73

How common are memory problems?

Unfortunately, that's an impossible question to answer. Memory problems are so diverse, and research on their frequency so patchy, that the necessary scientific data just isn't available.

What we do know, however, is that around 1 per cent of people aged 65–74 in the UK have dementia. For the 75–84 age group, that figure rises to 4 per cent and it climbs to 10 per cent for people aged 85 or over.

Self-assessment

The only way to get an accurate assessment of your memory is to be tested by a professional. You can get some pointers from the questionnaire below, but don't be disheartened if it seems to show that your memory is poor: self-assessment is a notoriously unreliable method of judging memory. If you're really worried, have a chat with your doctor.

For each of the following questions, give yourself a score of 1 to 9:

1. Not at all in the last six months
2. About once in the last six months
3. More than once a week but less than once a month
4. About once a month
5. More than once a month but less than once a week
6. About once a week
7. More than once a week but less than once a day
8. About once a day
9. More than once a day

1. Do you forget where you have put things? Lose things around the house?	
2. Do you fail to recognize places that you are told you have often been to before?	
3. Do you find television stories difficult to follow?	
4. Have you forgotten a change in your daily routine, such as a change in the place where something is kept, or a change in the time something happens? Have you followed your old routine by mistake?	

5. Have you had to go back to check whether you have done something that you meant to do?	
6. Have you forgotten when something happened? For example, whether something happened yesterday or last week?	
7. Have you completely forgotten to take things with you, or left things behind and had to go back and fetch them?	
8. Have you forgotten that you were told something yesterday or a few days ago, and had to be reminded about it?	
9. Have you started to read something (a book or an article in a newspaper/magazine) without realizing you have read it before?	
10. Have you let yourself ramble on about unimportant or irrelevant things?	
11. Have you failed to recognize, by sight, close relatives or friends that you meet frequently?	
12. Have you had difficulty picking up a new skill? For example, learning a new game or operating a new gadget after you have practised once or twice?	
13. Have you found that a word is 'on the tip of your tongue'? You know what it is but cannot quite find it.	
14. Have you completely forgotten to do things you said you would do, and things you planned to do?	
15. Have you forgotten important details of what you did or what happened to you the day before yesterday?	
16. When talking to someone, have you forgotten what you have just said? Maybe saying, 'What was I talking about?' or 'Where was I?'	
17. When reading a newspaper or magazine, have you been unable to follow the thread of a story or lost track of what it is about?	
18. Have you forgotten to tell somebody something important? Forgotten to pass on a message or remind someone of something?	

19. Have you forgotten important details about yourself? For example, your date of birth or where you live?	
20. Have you got the details of what someone has told you mixed up and confused?	
21. Have you told someone a story or joke that you have told them already?	
22. Have you forgotten details of things you do regularly, whether at home or at work? For example, details of what to do, or at what time to do something?	
23. Have you found that the faces of famous people, seen on television or in photographs, look unfamiliar?	
24. Have you forgotten where things are normally kept or looked for them in the wrong place?	
25. Have you got lost or taken a wrong turning on a journey, a walk or in a building where you have **often** been before?	
26. Have you got lost or taken a wrong turning on a journey, a walk or in a building where you have only been **once or twice** before?	
27. Have you done some routine thing twice by mistake? For example, putting two lots of tea in the teapot, or going to brush/comb your hair when you have just done so?	
28. Have you repeated to someone what you have just told them or asked them the same question twice?	

Everyday Memory Questionnaire from Sunderland, A., Harris, J. E., & Baddeley, A. D. (1983). 'Do laboratory tests predict everyday memory? A neuropsychological study'. *Journal of Verbal Learning and Verbal Behavior*, 22, 341–57.

If your total score is between 27 and 58, you probably have an above-average memory. A score of 58–116 is average and 116–243 is below average. If your score is lower than you'd like, remember that it doesn't necessarily mean you have a problem. It's quite possibly just a sign of how much you have going on in your life.

Context and memory

Why do the police take witnesses back to the scene of the crime? Why do people who appear to have forgotten a foreign language find it comes back to them as soon as they return to the country in question? And why is it we only remember that we're out of milk when we're in the kitchen, and not while we're walking past the grocery shop?

The answer is that memories are 'context dependent', meaning that we're much more likely to remember something when we're back where we first experienced it. This was demonstrated in a classic experiment carried out by psychologists Alan Baddeley and Duncan Godden.

While they were 10 feet under water, 16 divers were played a tape-recorded list of 36 words and asked to memorize them. Once back on land, they were asked to listen to, and memorize, a different set of words.

The researchers then tested the divers, both under water and on land, to see how many of the words they could remember. They found that the divers performed better when they were back where they'd learned the particular lists. So, they were much more likely to remember words heard under water when they were back under water; words learned on land were best recalled on land. Their memories, in other words, were context dependent.

Now, how are you doing for milk?

HOW TO IMPROVE YOUR MEMORY

Interestingly, according to modern astronomers, space is finite. This is a very comforting thought – particularly for people who can never remember where they have left things.
Woody Allen

Once we reach a certain age, it's easy to be worried by lapses in memory. But keep in mind that it's very unlikely that there's anything seriously wrong. Everyone's memory falters as they get older: it's normal and natural. Even so, your memory is probably a lot better than you think.

Although the 'raw materials' may not be quite up to the standard they were in your youth, there are lots of ways to make the most of them. In fact, if you follow the strategies set out below, you may well find that your memory performs better than it has ever done.

Start by keeping a memory diary. For a couple of weeks, jot down details of any memory problems – forgetting to make a phone call, being unable to recall the name of someone you've recently met or not remembering where you've put your glasses, for example. This will help you get a clear sense of which areas of your memory might need some work. And if you carry on with the diary once you've embarked on the steps below, you'll also have a useful record of how far things have improved.

If you're really worried about your memory, talk to your GP. A proper assessment of memory requires a number of tests, which are usually carried out by a neuropsychologist (a psychologist who specializes in the function of the brain) or a neurologist (a doctor trained in treating problems in the nervous system).

Now, here's how to improve your memory:

Look after yourself
People who keep physically fit seem to have fewer memory problems as they get older. So take regular exercise, eat healthily and get plenty of good-quality sleep. Limit your alcohol consumption and give up smoking if you can. (For help with these, see pp. 48–54.)

It's also a good idea to schedule regular check-ups with your doctor. Keeping track of your blood pressure, for example, may help you avoid the cardiovascular problems that can sometimes impair memory.

Keep socially active
A busy social life helps keep our memories sharp – and delays the onset of dementia.

Use it or lose it
If you don't exercise your brain, it's likely to slow down as you get older. Puzzles, crosswords, reading, chess, electronic 'brain trainers' or any activity, in fact, that gives your brain a workout are helpful. Whatever you opt for, you'll be improving your memory and reducing your risk of dementia.

Remembering names and faces

How good are you at remembering faces? What about names? And how do you fare when faced with the ultimate challenge: putting the correct name to a face?

If you struggle with any of these, you're certainly not alone. And for many people things seem to get more difficult as they age. So if your memory for names and faces isn't what you'd like it to be, try the following:

- When you meet someone for the first time, pay close attention to the way they look. Make a mental note of any distinctive feature – the colour of their eyes or the shape of their nose, for instance.
- Listen to the sound of their name. This may seem obvious, but it's easy to be distracted in social situations, especially if you're a bit shy or nervous.
- Ask the person to repeat their name – even if you've heard it perfectly well.
- Use the person's name when you're saying goodbye.
- Remind yourself of the person's name, and check that you can visualize their face. Do this a few minutes after you've met them, a few hours later (on your way home, for instance), and then the following day.
- Use the techniques we mention below – developing an amusing visual reminder or story, for example – to make names and faces as memorable as possible.

Maximize your memory

Trying to remember something can feel like groping for a black sock in a dark and jumbled cupboard. When we complain about our memory, it's this frustrating effort at retrieval that we tend to focus on. But think how much easier it would be to find that sock if the cupboard was neat and tidy and we knew exactly where to look.

Maximizing our memory is all about improving the way we organize and store the material in it – or, to use the psychological term, how we 'encode' our memories. There are lots of ways to do this:

- **Pay attention** – the more we focus on something, the more likely we are to remember it. Cut out distractions and really concentrate on whatever it is you want to memorize.
- **Make it memorable** – our memory can be a pretty overloaded system. If you don't want something to disappear into the mists, you need to make it as memorable as possible.

A great way to do this is to link the thing you want to remember to something you already know, and preferably to yourself (since nothing is more fascinating and memorable!). So if you meet someone at a party, say, you'll have more chance of remembering their name if you also register the fact that their sister knows your brother.

Try associating the item with an image, preferably one as amusing and distinctive as possible. (These images are called 'visual mnemonics'.) Exaggeration often works well. If someone is very tall, for example, you might visualize their head scraping the ceiling. Memorizing a list of items is easier if you weave them into a story. The more entertaining the story, and the more of your senses it involves, the better. So conjure up the way something looks, sounds, feels and even smells.

There are many established visual mnemonic systems – one that goes back to the ancient Greeks is structured around the rooms of a house. You'll find more about these systems in the books listed below.

- **Chunk!** – research shows that we find it easier to remember complicated information if we break it down into manageable chunks (seven items is normally seen as the maximum for each chunk). For example, it's easier to remember the dozen items you need to buy from the supermarket if you break them down into three chunks – say, food, drink and cleaning products. (Actually, making a shopping list is probably the best solution in this case!)
- **Use verbal mnemonics** – this is a tried-and-tested technique in which a memorable rhyme or phrase helps you recall an otherwise unrelated piece of information. 'Richard Of York Gave Battle In Vain', for example, is a traditional device for remembering the colours of the rainbow; and we like 'On Old Olympia's Towering Top A Finn and German Vault and Hop', used by medical students to help them memorize the names of the cranial nerves.
- **Learn it perfectly** – remembering something properly is much easier

if we learn it perfectly in the first place. Once uncertainty or error creep in, they are difficult to shake off. So, if you're trying to memorize a set of directions, for example, take the time to concentrate properly on the information. Make sure you can repeat it back to yourself without mistakes. Check you can still remember the directions perfectly after an hour or so, and then test yourself again on the following days (this is called 'rehearsal').

If you're revising for an exam or have a lot of new information to memorize, it's best to break down your work into short periods of around half an hour, interspersed with regular, brief breaks.

Use cues and context

If you can improve the encoding of your memories, you'll find it much easier to recall information when you need it. But you can also help yourself by using reminders – or 'cues' – such as putting an egg carton on the passenger seat so you remember to buy eggs when you're out, or leaving your pills in an obvious place in the bathroom so you spot them when you're washing in the morning.

As you'll see from the box on p. 238, our memories are hugely context dependent. We're more likely to remember something if we can recreate the situation in which we first experienced it. So if you're struggling to remember what your friend told you at the pub last night, visualize the scene in as much detail as possible.

Write it down

Diaries, calendars, to-do lists, shopping lists, notes to yourself – most of us use at least some of these to help our overburdened memories. And there are many more of these memory aids. The traditional knot in the handkerchief, writing on your hand, a wrist watch or mobile phone alarm, for example, are all great ways of reminding yourself to do something. Developing a routine will help ensure you don't forget regular chores and keeping things in a set place will help you find them easily.

Don't worry!

Forgetting is normal, especially as you get older, so don't get anxious about it. Do what you can to improve your memory, but don't let it get you down. You don't need to remember everything. Besides, the more stressed and anxious you are, the less well your memory will work. Frantically wracking your brain won't help you remember something; relaxing will.

Medication

At present, there is no miracle drug to boost memory. People suffering from Alzheimer's and other types of dementia are sometimes prescribed medication (Aricept is perhaps the best-known), and these can help some people, at least for a while. But the improvement is generally pretty modest, side effects are common and the drugs don't stop the progression of the disease.

Related problems

Severe **depression**, long-term **alcohol and drug problems**, **stress**, **worry**, **anxiety** and **sleep problems** can all affect memory.

Where to go for more information

The 'guru' of memory research is the psychologist Alan Baddeley; his book, *Your Memory: A User's Guide* (Carlton, 2004), provides a fascinating introduction to the topic. Also worth a look are *The Memory Doctor* (New Harbinger, 2005) by Douglas Mason and Spencer Xavier Smith and *Use Your Memory* (BBC Active, 2006) by Tony Buzan.

To find out more about dementia in general and Alzheimer's disease in particular, go to:

ⓘ www.alz.co.uk (the website of Alzheimer's Disease International)
ⓘ www.alzheimers.org.uk (run by the Alzheimer's Society)

Mood Swings

....

There's no doubt that I do have extremes of mood that are greater than just about anybody else I know. It's tormented me all my life with the deepest of depressions while giving me the energy and creativity that perhaps has made my career. I do get a huge buzz out of the manic side. I rely on it to give my life a sense of adventure, and I think most of the good about me has developed as a result of my mood swings.
Stephen Fry

Most of us know a moody person. In fact, you may be that person yourself and like the character from the famous nursery rhyme, when you're up you're really up, and when you're down you're desperately so.

In this section, we concentrate on the up part of mood swings (for down, see **Depression**, pp. 186–98). This is more than happiness; it's a sensation of intense excitement and joy that makes people believe they can take on – and beat – the world. Psychologists call this feeling hypomania.

Hypomania takes a variety of forms. Usually it's relatively mild and isn't a big problem for people. At the more extreme end, the 'up' can be quite dramatic (but even then, there's a lot that can be done to control it, as we'll see below). Sleep seems a waste of time, and instead people are filled with optimism and energy, constantly conjuring up new ideas and grand plans, totally convinced of their own abilities.

In fact, people going through a particularly intense hypomanic episode sometimes seem almost overwhelmed by their dynamic creativity. There's just so much going on. Their mind will flit from one exciting thought to the next; their speech is so fast that it can be difficult for others to follow; and it can be hard for them to stay in one place for long.

This can sometimes lead to odd, uncharacteristic and even risky behaviour. Inhibitions vanish. There's a tendency to become overfamiliar with other people, chatting away happily to strangers in the street or phoning long-lost friends in the middle of the night. Important – and often unfortunate – decisions may be taken on the spur of the moment, such as spending huge amounts of cash, getting involved in reckless drug or alcohol use or casual sexual encounters.

Which isn't to say that these feelings are always unpleasant. In fact, many people enjoy their hypomania and try to keep it going as long as they can, especially if it's at the relatively mild end of the spectrum. But not everyone finds it so appealing. Together with the excitement and euphoria can come intense irritation, anger and frustration – usually directed at anyone who expresses reservations about the person's behaviour or ideas. And restlessness, agitation and anxiety can all mean that these highs begin to feel like real lows.

And that's the thing about mood swings. The lows can be as extreme as the highs. It's not inevitable, but the adrenaline rush of the up can often be followed by a crash down into depression. The extreme form of this

Problems with mood swings: a personal account

I always know when I'm about to get a bit manic; I've learned to see these episodes coming. They always begin after I've been particularly stressed or down on my sleep. The last one came after a crazy couple of months at work, followed by moving house. I start drinking every night – sometimes quite a lot – but I still feel fantastic the next morning. I feel incredibly affectionate towards my friends and family and begin thinking how great it would be if we all lived close to one another. And I buy myself lots of little treats. As the treats get more expensive, I know I'm getting more manic! I've had some wild rides in the past thanks to my moods, but these days I know how to cope. Basically, I just make my life as calm and relaxing as possible, stay off the booze, and get plenty of sleep. That generally does the trick within a couple of weeks.

Will, aged 36

moodiness, where clinical depression alternates with an exaggerated and damaging form of hypomania (termed 'mania'), is called bipolar disorder, which is what used to be known as manic depression. A less severe, but still distressing form of the illness is called cyclothymic disorder.

How common are mood swings?

Around 1 per cent of adults have bipolar disorder. (It's difficult to put a figure on less severe mood swings since people are less likely to mention them to their doctor.)

Bipolar disorder typically first shows itself in the late teens and early 20s. It seems to affect men and women more or less equally.

Self-assessment

Everyone is prone to mood swings, so it can be hard to know whether what you're experiencing is normal or something that you should have a chat about with your GP. The following questionnaire has been designed to pick up the signs of bipolar disorder.

Section 1

Think back to your experiences over the past 12 months when you answer the following questions. Circle 'Yes' or 'No' as appropriate.

Has there ever been a period of time when you were not your usual self and (while not on drugs or alcohol) …

1. You felt so good or hyper that other people thought you were not your normal self or you were so hyper that you got into trouble?   Yes   No

2. You were so irritable that you shouted at people or started fights or arguments?   Yes   No

3. You felt much more self-confident than usual?   Yes   No

4. You got much less sleep than usual and found you didn't really miss it?   Yes   No

5. You were much more talkative or spoke faster than usual?   Yes   No

6. Thoughts raced through your head or you couldn't slow your mind down?   Yes   No

7. You were so easily distracted by things around you
that you had trouble concentrating or staying on track? Yes No

8. You had much more energy than usual? Yes No

9. You were much more active or did many more things
than usual? Yes No

10. You were much more social or outgoing than usual;
for example, you telephoned friends in the middle of
the night? Yes No

11. You were much more interested in sex than usual? Yes No

12. You did things that were unusual for you or that other
people might have thought excessive, foolish, or risky? Yes No

13. Spending money got you or your family into trouble? Yes No

Section 2
If you selected Yes for more than one of the above,
have several of these ever happened during the same
period of time? Yes No

Section 3
How much of a problem did any of these cause you – like being unable
to work; having family, money or legal troubles; getting into arguments
or fights?

No problem	Yes	No
Minor problem	Yes	No
Moderate problem	Yes	No
Major problem	Yes	No

© 2000. Dr Robert M.A. Hirschfeld licensed by Compact Clinics Kansas City, MO.

You may be suffering from bipolar disorder if:

- you've answered 'Yes' to seven or more questions in Section 1; and
- you've answered 'Yes' to the question in Section 2; and
- you've indicated in Section 3 that the behaviour has caused you
  problems.

Jet lag and mood swings

It's been known for some time that disruptions to our normal routine can trigger mood swings. This probably isn't surprising, given that most of us prefer to get a regular amount of sleep, and ideally in our own bed. We like to eat at roughly the same times each day. And if we don't, we soon feel cross or grumpy or miserable. But researchers studying the psychological effects of flying across time zones have discovered that the picture is more complicated than that.

Predictably, the researchers found that long-haul air travel often sparked severe mood swings in people with a history of these problems. But they also discovered that people travelling west were especially prone to depression, while those flying east were more likely to develop hypomania.

No one knows for sure exactly why this should be the case, but the explanation is likely to lie in the specific – and differing – biochemical disruptions to our body clock caused by flying east or west.

The therapeutic potential of these findings has yet to be explored, though perhaps if you're feeling a little down you could try a long flight eastwards!

How to Cope with Mood Swings

First of all, you need to decide whether you really have a problem you want to tackle. Lots of people (Stephen Fry, for instance) find their 'up' moods both enjoyable and productive. And mood swings are normal; it's only when they get out of hand that they're a problem. If you're managing them well, you may prefer to leave things as they are.

But making this assessment isn't as straightforward as it may seem, because it's often difficult to judge accurately your own moods. (During a hypomanic or manic period, people generally think they're behaving perfectly normally.) So talk to your friends and family and see how they view things.

Jot down a list of the pros and cons of your mood swings. And, if you decide you do have a problem, work out exactly what it is you want to change. For some people, it may simply be cutting out the riskier parts of their behaviour; for others it may be preventing the up mood from taking hold in the first place.

Assuming that you do want to improve the way in which you handle your mood swings, here are some tried-and-tested strategies for doing just that.

Develop a routine

Research has shown that a major trigger for mood swings is a chaotic lifestyle. On the other hand, a routine that involves regular mealtimes and bedtimes can help both to prevent mood swings occurring and, if they do happen, to nip them in the bud.

Your routine doesn't have to be as precise and inflexible as a railway timetable (or at least as a railway timetable used to be!) – just giving your day a basic structure can work wonders. And it doesn't mean your life need be unremittingly dull. If you're into excitement and thrill-seeking, that's fine, but channel it into safe activities, like hiking, travel or computer games.

Look after yourself

We all know the effects that tiredness and hunger can have on our mood. So, although regular meal- and bedtimes are important, you also need to make sure you're eating healthily and getting enough good-quality sleep (for more on these, see pp. 18–21 and 23–24). Regular exercise, relaxation and not overdoing your alcohol or drug intake will also help you to manage your moods.

Get to know your mood swings

The more you understand your mood changes, the better equipped you'll be to control them. Try drawing up a chart that traces your emotional ups and downs over the past few years, and see whether you can recall any major life events and stresses that may have preceded them. What do you think triggers your mood swings? Is it stress or sleep problems or relationship hassles, for example? What could you do to cope better with these triggers? (Stress is very often a factor, so check out that entry on pp. 353–60.)

Have a think too about the early warning signs (maybe you're sleeping less than normal, drinking more or feeling full of energy).

Take early action

The sooner you recognize the signs of an impending hypomanic or manic episode, the easier it is to deal with it. Make a list of the things you'll do if these early symptoms occur. Generally, it's best to cut down your activities and focus instead on being as relaxed as possible. Keep to a routine, get plenty of rest, and steer clear of people, situations, and substances (like alcohol or caffeine) that get you buzzing. Opt instead for calming activities like reading or listening to restful music.

Promise yourself that you won't make any major decisions while your mood is up. Write down what you have in mind and save it for at least 48 hours. After all, if it's such a great idea now, it'll still be a great idea in a couple of days' time! If your hypomania can be particularly intense, you may want to give your credit cards to a trusted friend until you feel that you are back to normal. In fact, it's a good idea to have a couple of people in mind who you can turn to for general advice and help if you need it.

Challenge unhelpful thoughts and beliefs

Your moods are often fuelled by your view of yourself and the world around you. Sometimes these thoughts are deep-rooted; often they're triggered or intensified by the moods they help keep going.

It's common, for example, for people experiencing hypomania to feel extremely self-confident. They might think to themselves: 'I don't need to sleep; I must make the most of my energy.' They may attach huge importance to achieving goals: 'I'm worthless unless I get these things done. All I need to do is keep going.' And they're often not good at taking advice: 'I know what I'm doing; I don't need to listen to negative people.'

These kinds of beliefs are generally pretty unhelpful; they certainly do nothing to calm someone down. Try to identify the thoughts you have when you're feeling really elated. Remember that your attitudes aren't always reliable: you're likely to see the world through rose-tinted spectacles when you're up (and dark glasses when you're down). Practise challenging these thoughts. Write down the evidence for and against. What other ways are there to think about the situation? Could you take a more moderate approach? What would you tell a friend in a similar situation?

Medication and other approaches

The advice given here is based on Cognitive Behaviour Therapy, which is the most popular and most scientifically validated form of psychological therapy for severe mood swings and particularly bipolar disorder.

That said, the main treatment for bipolar disorder is medication. Lithium is the most commonly used 'mood stabilizer', although carbamazepine and valproate are also often prescribed. Antidepressants may be useful if the person is depressed.

Mood stabilizers are often successful at controlling the illness, but they can't cure it. And they don't work for everyone – it's reckoned that between 20 and 40 per cent of patients don't find them helpful. And, as with all drugs, there can be side effects, some of them quite unpleasant.

This is partly why psychological therapy is now increasingly offered to people with bipolar disorder, generally in tandem with medication. Happily, the results have been very encouraging.

Related problems

As we've mentioned, people experiencing the sort of highs associated with major mood swings usually also have to cope, sooner or later, with **depression**. They may also suffer from **insomnia, paranoia, alcohol, drug** and **gambling problems, anxiety** and **hallucinations**.

Where to go for more information

Two useful self-help books are Jan Scott's *Overcoming Mood Swings* (Robinson, 2001) and *Coping with Bipolar Disorder* (Oneworld, 2002) by Steven Jones, Peter Hayward and Dominic Lam.

A fascinating autobiographical perspective on these issues is offered in Kay Redfield Jamison's *An Unquiet Mind* (Picador, 1997). Jamison is an eminent clinical psychologist, as well as having had bipolar disorder for many years.

On the Internet, look at:

- ⓘ www.mdf.org.uk (the website of the BiPolar Organization)
- ⓘ www.mind.org.uk (run by the UK's leading mental health charity)
- ⓘ www.nami.org (the website of the US National Alliance on Mental Illness)
- ⓘ www.ndmda.org (advice and information from the US Depression and Bipolar Support Alliance)
- ⓘ www.rethink.org. and www.sane.org.uk (SANE and Rethink are both UK mental health charities)

Pain

The mind is its own place, and in itself, can make heaven of Hell ...
John Milton, *Paradise Lost*

We all know what pain feels like. Fortunately, it usually doesn't last long. Pain is an early warning system, letting you know that you're likely to be in serious trouble if you don't take urgent action. So, when you pick up a hot plate, you soon realize that you should put it down. When you develop a stabbing pain in your chest, you know you must call the emergency services.

At least, that's how it's supposed to work. The kind of pain we've just described is called 'acute pain'. It's no fun, but it is temporary (rarely more than a couple of weeks at the most), and it's very useful. In some cases though, pain goes on for much longer than expected – for months or even years. And it persists, no matter what you do to try to stop it.

Sometimes this ongoing pain is the result of a medical condition (arthritis, for example), but often its cause is a mystery. It doesn't seem to be a warning. In fact, it doesn't appear to have much of a purpose at all. This kind of pain is known as 'chronic pain', and it's what we focus on in this entry. (Incidentally, chronic pain doesn't include persistent pain caused by serious illnesses such as cancer.)

Chronic pain can turn your life upside down. All kinds of activities you used to take for granted are suddenly impossible – or at least painful and difficult. You may have to give up work. Your social life suffers. You can become preoccupied with your pain and put all your energies into a desperate (and futile) search for a cure.

Not surprisingly, chronic pain often causes depression, frustration and anxiety, and these bring with them even more problems: it's hard to maintain happy relationships with loved ones, for example, when you're feeling so wretched.

Chronic pain, then, is serious stuff. There's no cure, but the picture isn't as bleak as it sounds. Huge advances have been made recently in pain management. As we'll show over the next few pages, you may not be able to get rid of your pain, but you can certainly learn to cope with it – and to get your life back on track.

How common is pain?

Pain is one of the most common reasons why people visit a doctor. In many cases, the pain soon disappears, either with or without treatment (it's the acute type). But chronic pain is also a big problem – and one that you're increasingly likely to face as you get older.

It's estimated that 12 per cent of people suffer from significant chronic pain – defined as pain that's lasted for at least three months and for which the person has often and recently taken painkillers and sought medical treatment. For half of these people, the pain severely limits their day-to-day activities.

Problems with chronic pain: a personal account

Three years ago I injured my back playing five-a-side football. After a month, I was given the all-clear by my doctor. I went back to work, but the pain didn't disappear. In fact, it got worse. I could just about cope at the office, but playing sport was too much for me. Before I hurt my back, my social life had revolved around golf and football. Now I was at a complete loss. I hardly ever went out, I didn't see my mates and I missed the fun and sense of achievement I got from sport. Life seemed miserable and empty. I had all kinds of tests and scans, but the doctors couldn't find anything wrong. I felt like a fool, or a fraud. I was at a really low ebb when my consultant referred me to a pain-management clinic. Three years later, I still don't play football, but I can manage a round of golf and I swim and cycle. The pain hasn't disappeared; what's changed is that I know how to cope with it.
Mark, aged 30

Back problems and arthritis are the most common triggers for chronic pain, while injuries, angina and menstrual pain and gynaecological problems also figure prominently.

Self-assessment

Most of us suffer from aches and pains from time to time. But how do you know whether what you're experiencing is normal or a problem that needs tackling? Well, a good starting place is the Chronic Pain Grade Questionnaire below.

	Rating
1. How would you rate your pain on a 0–10 scale at the present time, that is right now, where 0 is 'no pain' and 10 is 'pain as bad as could be'?	
2. In the past six months, how intense was your worst pain rated on a 0–10 scale where 0 is 'no pain' and 10 is 'pain as bad as could be'?	
3. In the past six months, on average, how intense was your pain rated on a 0–10 scale, where 0 is 'no pain' and 10 is 'pain as bad as could be'? (That is, your usual pain at times you were experiencing pain.)	
4. About how many days in the last six months have you been kept from your usual activities (work, school, or housework) because of this pain? 0–6 days 7–14 days 15–30 days 31 or more days	
5. In the past six months, how much has this pain interfered with your daily activities rated on a 0–10 scale where 0 is 'no interference' and 10 is 'unable to carry on activities'?	
6. In the past six months, how much has this pain changed your ability to take part in recreational, social, and family activities rated on a 0–10 scale where 0 is 'no change' and 10 is 'extreme change'?	

	Rating
7. In the past six months, how much has this pain changed your ability to work (including housework) rated on a 0–10 scale where 0 is 'no change' and 10 is 'extreme change'?	

Now comes the scoring for the Chronic Pain Grade, which can be a bit of a headache in itself.

First, you need to work out your 'pain intensity'. To do this, calculate your average score for questions 1–3 and then multiply by 10.

Next is your 'disability' score:

1. Calculate your average score for questions 5–7 and multiply by 10.
2. If the total is over 70, give yourself 3 points. A total of 50–69 gets 2 points; 30–49, 1 point; and 0–29 no points.
3. Now look at your response to question 4. If you've selected 31 or more days, give yourself 3 points; 15–30 days gets 2 points; 7–14 days, 1 point; and 0–6 days, no points.
4. To produce your disability score, add up your points from steps 2 and 3. It should be somewhere between 0 and 6!

Now you can discover your Chronic Pain Grade:

Score	Grade	Definition
Pain intensity and disability points = 0	0	Pain-free
Pain intensity 50 or less and disability points 3 or less	1	Low intensity and low disability
Pain intensity greater than 50 and disability points 3 or less	2	High intensity, but low disability
Disability points 3 or 4 (regardless of pain intensity)	3	High disability, moderately limiting your activity
Disability points 5 or 6 (regardless of pain intensity)	4	High disability, severely limiting your activity

Reprinted from *Pain*, 50, Von Korff, M., Ormel, J., Keefe, F. J. & Dworkin, S.F., Grading the severity of chronic pain, 133–49, 1992, with permission from Elsevier.

How to Overcome Chronic Pain

If you haven't already done so, talk to your doctor. They'll be able to investigate the possible causes of your pain and may refer you on to a pain-management clinic or physiotherapist.

Usually, there's no magical cure for chronic pain. But it can still be beaten. Although you may not be able to make it disappear, you can control the effect your pain has on you. That may seem flippant; it may sound as though we're not taking your pain seriously. But people's experience of pain varies enormously. Two people with similar levels of pain may react in completely different ways. Because it's not the physical sensations that count; it's how you respond to them.

So how do you go about changing your reaction to pain?

Increase your activity levels

People with chronic pain generally end up doing less than they used to, mainly because it hurts so much. Often they overdo things on their 'good' days, when the pain is relatively manageable, and then feel worse than ever. Gradually, they come to associate activity with pain – and that's not a good route to go down, for at least a couple of reasons.

Psychologically, it leads to a host of negative feelings – depression, frustration, boredom and anger. Physically, the consequences are just as bad, because the less you do, the less you're able to do. Your body loses condition as soon as you stop using it. Then when you go to do something, you find that you get tired sooner and feel more pain. All of which makes you even more reluctant to try things.

In fact, all the evidence suggests that people who keep busy, who don't let their pain run their lives, cope much better. So try to increase your activity levels. Make a list of the things you'd like to be able to do and prioritize two or three of them. (It's best if these activities are varied, so you might, for example, choose one that's work-related, one to do with housework and another that's just about having fun.)

With the activities you've prioritized in mind, set yourself a few long-term goals and break those down into shorter-term ones. If, for example, your long-term goal is to redesign your garden, your short-term goals might involve gradually increasing the amount of time you spend working on it each day.

Take things gently. Start at a level you're comfortable with and gradually increase the amount you do (this is known as 'pacing'). It's better to keep going slowly but steadily, despite the pain, rather than have your pain levels dictate how much you do each day. Make sure you schedule in regular, short breaks. Keep a record of your progress, and reward yourself when things go well.

People with chronic pain often worry that they'll make things worse by being active. You won't. You will probably feel a little more pain in the short term, but this is perfectly normal. And remember: pain doesn't always mean that there's a problem.

Take regular exercise

The more positive activities you can build into your life, the easier you'll find it to cope with your pain – and nothing is more positive than regular exercise. It won't make your pain go away, but it will strengthen your body and make you feel much better about yourself.

When you start exercising, follow exactly the same guidelines as you use for increasing your other activities.

Close the 'gate'

It may not feel like it, but pain is the result of a complex process in which your nerves send messages along the spinal cord to your brain. But not every message makes it as far as the brain – there's a 'gate' in the spinal cord that it's possible to close, and if the gate is closed, you don't feel the pain (or at least not so intensely).

So, how do you close the gate? Well, you do it instinctively when you rub a sore part of your body. But you can also make it happen by focusing your attention away from the pain – for example, by doing something enjoyable or trying a relaxation exercise. It doesn't matter what you do, as long as it takes your mind off your pain.

Challenge negative thinking

The way in which you respond to pain is coloured by your thoughts, experiences, memories and expectations. All too often, chronic pain can lead you into a pattern of negative thinking. This is completely understandable, but it doesn't help you to deal with the pain.

So you need to challenge your negative thoughts. For example, if you find yourself thinking, 'This pain is the worst it's ever been – I can't cope', write down all the evidence you can come up with both for and against that statement. Remember how you've managed in the past. Imagine what you'd tell a friend in a similar position. What positive ways are there of looking at the situation?

People often spend a lot of time worrying about their chronic pain, and tend to assume the worst (psychologists call this 'catastrophizing'); have a look at the entry on worry, pp. 109–12, to help you deal with this.

You might also find it helpful to develop a 'mindful' attitude towards your pain. Don't try to shut out the pain – that never works. Instead, remember that it's nothing new; there's no need to panic. Calmly observe the pain, as if you were a scientist engaged in an experiment, and be as detached as you possibly can. For more information about mindfulness, look at *The Mindful Way through Depression* (see opposite).

Learn to accept your pain. Constantly denying or fighting it is exhausting and pointless: the pain will always outlast you. Pain management is all about changing your relationship with your pain, not getting rid of it completely (if that were possible, you'd have done it long ago). And a major step towards achieving that change is accepting the reality of your pain.

Try relaxation exercises
Knowing how to relax properly is a really important skill, and not just for dealing with pain; see p. 359 for more information.

Make time for fun
Living with chronic pain is tough, but you'll find it much easier if you can keep the enjoyable aspects of life going. Keep in touch with friends and family, and try to schedule in regular social or fun activities.

Prepare for setbacks
You're bound to have times when you can't keep to your activity or exercise plans, or when your pain gets too much for you. This doesn't mean you've failed; it simply means you're human. Don't dwell on these setbacks – see if you can work out what causes them and how you might cope with them in the future. Then move on.

Medication and other approaches
Four main types of medication are used to treat pain:

Painkillers – also known as analgesics, these range all the way from paracetamol to morphine
Anti-convulsants – originally developed to combat epilepsy

Antidepressants – usually the older type called 'tricyclics'
Anti-inflammatories – for example, steroids

All these drugs can be effective, but none of them can cure chronic pain, and some people experience unpleasant side effects. Unless you're sure that your medication is really helping, it's worth talking to your doctor about stopping it.

Physiotherapy can play an important part in pain management, while acupuncture and TENS machines (which send a low-level electrical charge to the body) are only really helpful for short periods.

Related problems
Chronic pain can trigger **depression, anxiety, worry, stress, sleep problems, anger** and **relationship problems.**

Where to go for more information
Manage Your Pain (Souvenir, 2003) by Michael Nicholas, Allan Molloy, Lois Tonkin and Lee Beeston is a terrific self-help guide.

Also worth checking out are *Overcoming Chronic Pain* (Robinson, 2005) by Frances Cole, Helen Macdonald, Catherine Carus and Hazel Howden-Leach and, for specific advice on mindfulness techniques, *The Mindful Way through Depression* (Guilford Press, 2007) by Mark Williams, John Teasdale, Zindel Segal and Jon Kabat-Zinn.

Useful websites include:

ⓘ www.painconcern.org.uk
ⓘ www.painsupport.co.uk
ⓘ www.action-on-pain.co.uk
ⓘ www.arthritiscare.org.uk
ⓘ www.backcare.org.uk

Paranoia

....

*You go into a strange diner in the South and everything goes
quiet, and you realize all the other customers are looking at
you as if they are sizing up the risk involved in murdering you
and leaving your body in a shallow grave somewhere out in
the swamps.*
Bill Bryson

Paranoia is a term that's used so often that its meaning has become a little
blurred. So let's start with a definition: paranoia is the unrealistic thought
that other people want to harm us.

Paranoia takes a huge variety of forms, from the occasional worry that
our friends are deliberately neglecting us or are complaining about us
behind our backs, to the anguished belief that someone is out to kill us.

Now, just because you have a suspicious thought from time to time
doesn't mean that you're going to end up fearing that the secret service
wants to do away with you. Even people who have quite frequent paranoid
thoughts generally don't find them a big problem, although they can still
cause distress or anxiety.

But psychologists have recently discovered that, despite the big varia-
tion in experiences of paranoia, there are also certain similarities (for
example in the factors that help trigger paranoid thoughts). It's what is
known as the spectrum of paranoia, with mild suspicions at one end and,
at the other, the sort of severe delusions characteristic of serious mental
illnesses like schizophrenia.

Paranoia is much more common than previously suspected (until
recently, doctors only looked at the very severe end of the scale). In fact,
it's almost as widespread as depression or anxiety.

How can I tell whether my suspicious thoughts are justified or not?

It's often very difficult to decide whether suspicions are valid, but asking yourself the following questions will help:
1. Would other people think my suspicions are realistic?
2. What would my best friend say?
3. Have I talked to others about my worries? (Research has indicated that people who share their anxieties are less likely to become paranoid.)
4. Is it possible that I have exaggerated the threat?
5. Is there any indisputable evidence for my suspicions?
6. Are my worries based on ambiguous events (i.e. events that are difficult to interpret)?
7. Are my worries based on my feelings rather than indisputable evidence?
8. Is it very likely that I would be singled out above anyone else?
9. Is there any evidence that runs contrary to my suspicions?
10. Is it possible that I'm being at all oversensitive?
11. Do my suspicions persist despite reassurance from others that they are unfounded?

This isn't surprising. In almost every aspect of life, you have to decide whether to trust or mistrust. But these are often difficult decisions. After all, how can you know whether the look someone gives you on the train is menacing or not? How can you be sure that a colleague is trustworthy, or that your friends aren't gossiping about you? And, of course, sometimes it's only sensible to be cautious (most people would cross the road if they spotted a group of drunken men up ahead late at night). But when you get the judgement wrong, paranoia – with all the worry and unhappiness that it can sometimes bring – is the result.

How common is paranoia?
Around 15 to 20 per cent of people have frequent paranoid thoughts. Generally, they're not a big problem, but about 3–5 per cent of people will have quite severe paranoia (what psychologists call persecutory delusions)

Problems with paranoia: some personal accounts

I sometimes find bus journeys and train trips difficult. If someone looks at me it can feel as though they're weighing me up. I don't know why. Once I was on the train and the guy next to me was coughing every five seconds. It felt like he was doing it on purpose to annoy me even though I knew he wasn't.
Melissa, aged 23

There are times when, for some reason, I see all sorts of things as suspicious: someone sitting on a bench, someone talking on a mobile phone, someone wearing sunglasses when it isn't very sunny.
Sharon, aged 41

When I'm low, I feel as though people hate me – especially colleagues at work – and that they're constantly trying to put me down.
Keith, aged 53

The other day I was with a friend when his mobile rang. My mate said he was with me and the caller (I didn't know who it was) replied and then my friend laughed. I was sure they were laughing at me.
Cameron, aged 19

at some point in their lives. And in around 1 per cent, paranoia is a symptom of serious mental illness (for instance, schizophrenia).

Trust, paranoia, and the healthy society

Paranoia, like all psychological problems, is caused by the complex interaction of several factors. Some of these relate to a person's personality and life experiences, but others stem from broader social and cultural influences.

One such social influence is inequality of wealth. The more unequal people in a society are, the less they see themselves as part of a single, unified community, and the less they trust each other. One study of 39 US states by Ichiro Kawachi and colleagues, for instance, found that the states with the biggest inequalities of wealth also had the lowest levels of voluntary group membership and the highest levels of distrust.

But it doesn't end there, because societies with the highest levels of distrust also seem to have higher mortality rates. Although we don't yet have a clear sense of the causes, the figures are startling. For example, Kawachi found that as levels of trust rise by 10 per cent, the death rate declines by 8 per cent. Or, to put it another way, for every 1 per cent increase in the number of individuals believing that other people want to take advantage of them, there are 6.7 more deaths per 100,000 of the population.

The stakes involved in beating paranoia may be higher than anyone suspected…

Self-assessment

How paranoid are you? Have a look at the 16 statements below. Use the scale from 1 (not at all) to 5 (totally) to rate how strongly you agree with each of the statements in the light of your thoughts and feelings during the last month.

	Not at all		Somewhat		Totally
1. Certain individuals have had it in for me.	1	2	3	4	5
2. I have definitely been persecuted.	1	2	3	4	5
3. People have intended me harm.	1	2	3	4	5
4. People wanted me to feel threatened, so they stared at me.	1	2	3	4	5
5. I was sure certain people did things in order to annoy me.	1	2	3	4	5
6. I was convinced there was a conspiracy against me.	1	2	3	4	5

	Not at all		Somewhat		Totally
7. I was sure someone wanted to hurt me.	1	2	3	4	5
8. I was distressed by people wanting to harm me in some way.	1	2	3	4	5
9. I was preoccupied with thoughts of people trying to upset me deliberately.	1	2	3	4	5
10. I couldn't stop thinking about people wanting to confuse me.	1	2	3	4	5
11. I was distressed by being persecuted.	1	2	3	4	5
12. I was annoyed because others wanted to deliberately upset me.	1	2	3	4	5
13. The thought that people were persecuting me played on my mind.	1	2	3	4	5
14. It was difficult to stop thinking about people wanting to make me feel bad.	1	2	3	4	5
15. People have been hostile towards me on purpose.	1	2	3	4	5
16. I was angry that someone wanted to hurt me.	1	2	3	4	5

Once you've completed the questionnaire, add up your score. Most people (85 per cent) will score between 16 and 31, while more than 31 suggests an above-average level of paranoia. People with severe paranoia generally score between 40 and 70.

How to Overcome Paranoia

Having paranoid thoughts doesn't mean that you're going crazy, so don't panic! Although people don't tend to talk about these kinds of feelings, they're actually very common. The strategies outlined below will help you deal with any problems of paranoia.

Look after yourself

You're more likely to be troubled by paranoia if you are tired, run-down or very stressed. So make sure you eat healthily, get plenty of good-quality sleep and exercise regularly (see pp. 18–24 for more information.) Make time too for things you enjoy: the more positive activities you have in your life, the less scope there'll be for paranoia to take hold.

Drinking too much and using illicit drugs can sometimes trigger paranoid thoughts. If you think they may be a factor in your paranoia, cut back or stop completely.

Consider the pros and cons

As we've seen, underlying paranoia is a fundamental decision about whether or not to trust other people. As a device to help you explore your own approach to this issue, make a list of the pros and cons of both trusting and mistrusting people. Have you got the balance right, do you think? Would you like to be less mistrustful? Are there experiences from your past that might be having too great an influence on how you see people now?

Share your fears

We know that people who don't talk about their paranoid thoughts generally find them more upsetting, so confide in someone you trust. Getting another person's perspective on your worries can be really helpful.

Get to know your paranoia

Like all problems, it's much easier to cope with paranoid thoughts if you have a clear picture of them. So for the next seven days keep a diary of your paranoid thoughts – what they are, when they occur and what seems to trigger them.

You may well find that particular situations tend to spark your paranoia (perhaps being very anxious or angry or bored, for example), and that will give you the chance to think about how you can prevent these situations from occurring, or at least how to deal with them better.

Incidentally, one of the great benefits of keeping a diary is that it gets your paranoid thoughts out of your head and on to paper. For many people, that can be a huge relief, and a terrific way of putting some distance between themselves and their paranoia.

Manage your worry

Worry is a very common reaction to paranoid thoughts. People fret about the harm they think other people intend towards them, and sometimes they also worry about what having these thoughts might mean (for example, that they're going mad). But the more we worry, the more anxious and fearful we become. Worry feeds on worry.

So we need to learn to manage our worry. One very useful technique is to save up all your worrying for one half-hour session every day: your 'worry period'. And instead of worrying, try focusing your energy on solving the problem that's troubling you. (For more about coping with worry, have a look at pp. 109–12.)

Challenge your paranoid thoughts

Choose a suspicious thought from your paranoia diary, and weigh up the evidence for and against it. Ask yourself these questions:

- Is there anything that might suggest the thought is wrong?
- What would my family or friends say if I talked to them about the thought?
- What would I say to a friend who came to me with a similar problem?
- Are there any alternative explanations for what seems to have happened?
- Are my thoughts based more on the way I feel than on solid evidence?
- Have I been jumping to conclusions?
- If I were feeling happier or less anxious or less tired, would I still see things in the same way?

Test out your thoughts

Paranoia can make people so anxious and afraid that they change their behaviour, avoiding the situations that trigger their fears. But this only reinforces their paranoia, because it robs them of the chance to discover whether or not their fears are justified.

Testing out your paranoid thoughts involves actively seeking out the situations you're afraid of. That can be pretty nerve-wracking, so you need to go carefully. Draw up a list of tasks you find difficult and start with the relatively easy ones; once you're comfortable with those, gradually work your way up to the more difficult ones.

Incidentally, don't put yourself in situations where you're likely to be at real risk. You may be worried about going out alone, for instance, but don't test this by going into a dangerous neighbourhood at night. Concentrate on activities that most people would find reasonable, and where you think your suspicious thoughts are probably exaggerated.

Let go of your paranoid thoughts
We're bound to have suspicious thoughts from time to time. It's unrealistic to think we can put a complete stop to them, but we can improve the way we deal with these thoughts when they do occur.

The trick is not to focus on them, to develop what's known as a 'mindful' attitude. Don't fight your thoughts and don't spend time thinking about them. Try to be detached. Watch a thought come to you, remind yourself that it doesn't matter, and let it go off into the distance. Concentrate on what you're doing, rather than what you're thinking.

Many people find it helps to repeat an encouraging phrase to themselves – for example: 'They're only thoughts – they don't matter'; 'Keep going – you're doing really well'; 'These thoughts don't scare me. I can cope.'

Medication
Medication is often prescribed for people who experience very severe paranoid thoughts, and many of them find it helps – although, as with all drugs, there can be unpleasant side effects.

The main type of medication for severe paranoia is neuroleptics, also called 'anti-psychotics' or 'major tranquillizers', such as risperidone, amisulpride, olanzepine and clozapine. Antidepressants are sometimes prescribed – generally one of the newer SSRIs (selective serotonin reuptake inhibitors) like fluoxetine, paroxetine, citalopram and sertraline.

Increasingly, however, Cognitive Behaviour Therapy (CBT – the approach drawn on in this book) is used in tandem with medication.

Related problems

Paranoia is normal, but we're more likely to have problems with it if we're also struggling with **worry, anxiety, trauma, depression, hallucinations** (especially as a symptom of schizophrenia) or **mood swings**.

Where to go for more information

The only self-help book for people struggling with paranoia is *Overcoming Paranoid and Suspicious Thoughts* (Robinson, 2006), which we wrote with Philippa Garety. In *Paranoia: The Twenty-first Century Fear* (Oxford, 2008), we offer a concise and accessible look at how widespread paranoia is and what may be causing it to grow. Have a look at our website, www. paranoidthoughts.com, too.

If your paranoia is triggered by schizophrenia, you may also want to check out *The Complete Family Guide to Schizophrenia* (Guilford, 2006) by Kim Mueser and Susan Gingerich.

The following mental health websites may also be worth a visit:

- ⓘ www.mind.org.uk
- ⓘ www.nami.org
- ⓘ www.rethink.org.uk
- ⓘ www.sane.org.uk
- ⓘ www.schizophrenia.com

Relationship Problems

The course of true love never did run smooth.
William Shakespeare, *A Midsummer Night's Dream*

How right Shakespeare was! Doubtless we can all think of relationships that appear to consist entirely of bickering and petty disputes. But even for the rest, the occasional – or not so occasional – argument is generally an inescapable element of any long-term romantic relationship. And that's the focus of this entry: arguments and disagreements between couples.

This isn't to say that arguments are necessarily a problem. Quite the contrary, in fact: they're often a very healthy way to air differences and reach an agreement about how to go forward. They're particularly inevitable – and useful – once the ecstatic glow of new love has dimmed a fraction and people are getting to know each other properly. Indeed, a relationship without arguments is probably one in which the partners aren't voicing their needs and desires – and this is clearly not a good thing.

On the other hand, if disagreements aren't handled properly, the relationship can really suffer. Partners can end up feeling hurt, resentful, angry and upset. Frequent or especially nasty arguments suck the life blood from a relationship, leaving misery in its place.

What are the bad habits that put strain on a relationship? The main culprits are:

- mistrusting your partner
- mind-reading – assuming you know what your partner is thinking
- focusing on the aspects of your partner's behaviour that you don't like, rather than those that brought you together in the first place
- criticizing and blaming your partner

- being hostile or disrespectful
- having unrealistic expectations of your partner.

Stress is often a big factor in relationship problems, whether it's the struggle to make ends meet or bring up children, the demands of work or the challenges posed by retirement. Things can get especially bad if either partner is drinking too much or taking illegal drugs. Most damaging of all for many relationships are the after-effects of an affair.

But just as certain behaviours can jeopardize a relationship, others can strengthen it, including:

- shared decision-making
- trust
- intimacy – physical, emotional and psychological
- sexual attraction

Relationship problems: a personal account

Tony and I had been together for a couple of years when the cracks began to develop: lots of unpleasant arguments over trivial things like the way he did the dishes (not enough washing-up liquid) or the state of the car (too much of my clutter). We got stuck in this pattern of behaviour: each of us driving the other one crazy but neither of us knowing how to stop it. One day I was moaning to my best friend and she asked me very directly whether I wanted to continue in the relationship. I knew that I did. 'Right,' she said, 'then you've got to do something about it.' That night, I sat down with Tony and we discussed – for the first time in months – how things were between us. We realized that we just weren't spending enough fun time together. We were both out all day at work and were exhausted in the evening. We never talked – not properly. We hardly went out. We weren't a couple; we were housemates. When we started to put those things right, the arguments soon stopped.
Amy, aged 29

'Not that again!' – the top 20 topics for arguments

1. Partner's friends
2. Partner's family
3. Partner's friends of opposite sex
4. Partner's job
5. Partner's mood or temper
6. Partner's honesty
7. Partner's behaviour at social events
8. Partner's support in a crisis
9. Religious beliefs
10. Church attendance
11. Charitable donations
12. Love and affection
13. Sexual activities
14. Frequency of sex
15. Infidelity
16. Savings and investments
17. Paying bills
18. Spending on clothes/hobbies
19. Use of credit cards
20. Long-term goals and priorities

- investing time and energy in working at the relationship
- agreement about who does which household chores
- emotional support for each other
- positive actions, whether this is giving your partner a hug, bringing them a cup of tea in bed or being ready to listen when they need to talk
- clear communication
- tolerance, flexibility and patience
- negotiation skills.

We'll explore these vital ingredients for a successful relationship in more detail below.

How common are relationship problems?

All long-term relationships go through rocky patches: it's normal. When it comes to divorce, rates in the UK are declining. Indeed, the divorce rate in England and Wales in 2007 was the lowest since 1981, with 11.9 divorcing people per thousand married people. Good news, for sure, though there were still around 140,000 divorces in the UK in 2007.

The reasons for the decline in the divorce rate aren't known, though a reduction in the number of people getting married is surely a factor. Sadly, there's no evidence to suggest we're handling our relationship problems any better.

Self-assessment

Every couple rows from time to time, so how do you know whether what you're experiencing is normal or a sign that your relationship isn't working as well as it might? The following questionnaire will give you some pointers:

1. Please indicate the degree of happiness, all things considered, of your relationship.

Extremely unhappy	Fairly unhappy	A little unhappy	Happy	Very happy	Extremely happy	Perfect
0	1	2	3	4	5	6

2. In general, how often do you think that things between you and your partner are going well?

All of the time	Most of the time	More often than not	Occasionally	Rarely	Never
5	4	3	2	1	0

3. Our relationship is strong.

Not at all true	A little true	Somewhat true	Mostly true	Almost completely true	Completely true
0	1	2	3	4	5

4. My relationship with my partner makes me happy.

Not at all true	A little true	Somewhat true	Mostly true	Almost completely true	Completely true
0	1	2	3	4	5

5. I have a warm and comfortable relationship with my partner.

Not at all true	A little true	Somewhat true	Mostly true	Almost completely true	Completely true
0	1	2	3	4	5

6. I really feel like part of a team with my partner.

Not at all true	A little true	Somewhat true	Mostly true	Almost completely true	Completely true
0	1	2	3	4	5

7. How rewarding is your relationship with your partner?

Not at all	A little	Somewhat	Mostly	Almost completely	Completely
0	1	2	3	4	5

8. How well does your partner meet your needs?

Not at all	A little	Somewhat	Mostly	Almost completely	Completely
0	1	2	3	4	5

9. To what extent has your relationship met your original expectations?

Not at all	A little	Somewhat	Mostly	Almost completely	Completely
0	1	2	3	4	5

10. In general, how satisfied are you with your relationship?

Not at all	A little	Somewhat	Mostly	Almost completely	Completely
0	1	2	3	4	5

For each of the following items, select the answer that best describes how you feel about your relationship. Base your responses on your first impressions and immediate feelings about the item.

11.	Interesting	5	4	3	2	1	0	Boring
12.	Bad	0	1	2	3	4	5	Good
13.	Full	5	4	3	2	1	0	Empty
14.	Sturdy	5	4	3	2	1	0	Fragile
15.	Discouraging	0	1	2	3	4	5	Hopeful
16.	Enjoyable	5	4	3	2	1	0	Miserable

© 2007 by the American Psychological Association. Couples Satisfaction Index (CSI-16) from Funk, Janette L. and Rogge, Ronald D. 'Testing the ruler with item response theory: Increasing precision of measurement for relationship satisfaction with the Couples Satisfaction Index'. *Journal of Family Psychology* vol. 21 (4), Dec 2007, 572–83.

Now add up your total score for the 16 questions. If it's more than 51, your relationship looks to be in good shape. A score of between 47 and 51 indicates mild dissatisfaction, and a total of 46 or less suggests that your relationship is causing you distress.

The secret of a successful relationship

What's the secret of a successful relationship? Well, part of the answer to that $64,000 question seems to be the way we handle conflict.

This was demonstrated in a study carried out by the US psychologists Sybil Carrère and John Gottman. They recruited 124 newly married couples in Washington State and observed each of them having a 15-minute discussion about an issue causing ongoing tension in the marriage. The fortunes of the couples were then followed over a six-year period.

At the end of those six years, 17 of the 124 couples had divorced. But what was so striking was that it was possible for the researchers to predict accurately the success or failure of those marriages based solely on analysis of that initial 15-minute discussion.

Domestic abuse

Arguments between partners are normal; domestic abuse is a crime. Legally, it encompasses any threatening, violent or abusive behaviour between partners, whether psychological, physical, sexual, emotional or financial (for example, withholding money or interrogating aggressively about spending).

The official figures for domestic abuse are probably the tip of the iceberg because it's believed that most victims remain silent. Even so, 16 million incidents are reported each year in the UK, at a cost to health and social services of around £3 billion.

Annually, 4 per cent of women and 2 per cent of men in the UK go public about their experience of domestic violence. Every week, two women are killed by a current or previous male partner. Men are often victims of domestic abuse, but when it comes to domestic violence it's women who are more likely to be injured or killed.

Domestic abuse can have a brutal effect on its victims, shattering self-confidence and breeding fear, shame, guilt, isolation and depression. It's these kinds of very low feelings that partly explain why women often find it so difficult to leave an abusive partner, though concern for their children and a continuing love for the abuser frequently figure too.

What are the warning signs that your partner may become abusive? By far the most reliable indicator is a past history of such behaviour. If they've done it before, they're likely to do it again. But being aggressive, hypercritical, possessive, extremely moody or consistently disrespectful towards you are also potential red flags.

Alcohol is frequently a trigger for domestic abuse, but deeper factors are also often at work. For example, men who were beaten as children, or who saw their mothers being beaten, are more likely to become abusers themselves. Women who suffered abuse as children are prone to become victims as adults. Pregnancy and the initial period after giving birth seem to be times when women are at most risk of domestic violence.

If you are a victim of domestic abuse, don't brush it under the carpet. Remember: you are *not* to blame. Things won't improve unless you take action, so tell a trusted friend or family member what's been going on and decide on a plan for tackling the situation. You may be able to work with your partner to ensure the abuse doesn't happen again, but if that isn't successful you will need to separate.

Whatever your situation, we recommend you get more information and advice from the following websites and 24-hour phone helplines:

English National Domestic Violence Helpline: 0808 2000 247

Northern Ireland Women's Aid Domestic Violence Helpline: 028 9033 1818

Scottish Domestic Abuse Helpline: 0800 027 1234

ⓘ www.womensaid.org.uk or 0808 2000 247

ⓘ www.mankind.org.uk

In fact, they didn't even need the full 15 minutes: the first three were enough. The more positive the interaction – for example, in the tone of voice the couples used towards each other, the things they said and the expression on their faces – the more likely it was that the couple would still be together six years later. It was the couples who communicated most negatively who subsequently ended up in the divorce courts.

So, if you needed a reminder of the value of communication, here it is! And remember, how you start a discussion is key. Once you set the agenda for how you're going to talk to one another, it's hard to shift gears; begin in the wrong one, and you're likely simply to dig yourself deeper …

DEALING WITH RELATIONSHIP PROBLEMS

There's no point in trying to avoid arguments with your partner. They're a vital part of any healthy relationship. The objective is not to remove conflict from your relationship, but rather to manage it effectively. Here's how:

Don't mind-read

Imagine that when your partner comes in from work they barely look at you and merely mutter a cool greeting. Do you think they're angry with you or upset – or even that they're perhaps no longer committed to the relationship? Do you feel fed up with their apparent rudeness and retreat to the living room to flick angrily through the newspaper on your own? Or do you conclude that they're probably tired and stressed, and ask them lovingly whether they're OK?

Many of the conflicts that occur in relationships do so because one partner assumes they know what the other is thinking. And it can be a vicious circle. Mind-reading causes arguments, which in turn can poison the atmosphere between partners and prompt them to think the worst of each other, leading to even more disputes. When a relationship is faltering, misunderstandings tend to be rife.

So, don't jump to conclusions. If your partner is behaving in a way that troubles you, think through all the possible explanations.

And don't take things personally. Your partner's emotions or actions probably have nothing at all to do with you. When you're calm, let your partner know how you interpreted their behaviour and find out from them what was really going on.

Talk through your mutual expectations

We all bring a lot of 'baggage' to a relationship. People have strong views about everything from how the household should run to the kind of sex life they expect. Lots of this baggage comes from upbringing and previous relationships. Some of it may stem from gender: men and women often have very different approaches to the various issues that crop up in a relationship (not least of which, how to handle arguments).

It's crucial that you have an honest discussion with your partner about your expectations for the relationship. Who's going to clean the house? Who is responsible for childcare? How will you handle the finances? How much 'personal' time should you each have? How often should you expect to have sex? What are your respective views on fidelity, commitment and trust?

Remember: it's not a question of 'winning' an argument. The aim is to understand and respect where each of you is coming from, and to reach an agreement on how you'll proceed in the future. If you're very lucky, you'll agree on most things; more likely, you'll both need to compromise.

Work at your communication skills

No relationship can thrive unless the communication within it is up to scratch. So if you take nothing else away from these pages, remember these guidelines:

Be clear and specific about what's troubling you

Resist the temptation to make sweeping, general complaints – 'You never lift a finger around the house', for example. Instead, focus on the particular: 'We need to work out a rota for the washing up and the hoovering.'

Let your partner talk

No matter how badly you need to get things off your chest, don't simply rant on. Be as calm and measured as you can, and keep it short, sweet and to the point. Leave gaps for your partner to speak.

Be positive

No one likes being criticized, so don't focus on the negative aspects of your partner's behaviour. Instead, present your requests in terms of positive actions you'd like them to take. For example, instead of 'You're always undermining me', try: 'I'd like you to back me up even if you don't always agree.'

Remember that the best way of changing someone's behaviour isn't to criticize what you don't like; it's to praise and encourage what you do like.

Use 'I' and 'We' – not 'You'

Don't point the finger at your partner – 'You're always ...', 'You never ...'; be up front about your own wishes: 'I'd like ...', 'I think we need to ...'. It's a way of signalling that you're willing to take your share of the responsibility for solving the problem, rather than simply blaming your partner. Using 'We' will work wonders too; it's a subtle but eloquent sign that you want to work together to sort things out.

Remember: communication is not simply about the things you say

It's also about the hugs and kisses, the smiles and caresses and the willingness to make eye contact – in other words, the full range of non-verbal signals that we're constantly sending out to our partner.

Show your partner that you understand and empathize

We all know the middle-aged man's chat-up line: 'My wife doesn't understand me.' But although this phrase has become a joke, it does contain the seeds of a useful reminder for us all: it's critical that you make every effort to understand your partner's views and feelings.

Even more important, you need to *show* your partner you understand, by your facial expression, the nod of your head, the words you use and the actions you take. Simply reiterating what your partner has told you will help enormously: 'I understand that you're exhausted after your day at work and that you don't want to cook every night.'

And it is equally important to work at empathizing with your partner. This means not only understanding intellectually what they're telling you, but being able to think yourself into their position and share their feelings.

Set aside a regular time to talk together

Let your partner know how you're feeling, discuss how you think the relationship is going, whether your needs and expectations have changed and work together to solve problems (for more on problem-solving techniques, see p. 110).

Call a truce

When things are really difficult between you, it can help to call a truce. Both partners agree to discuss their differences at a set time, in a comfortable, quiet and private place, without being rude, aggressive or hostile. One partner talks for five minutes while the other listens carefully and respectfully. Then the other partner has their turn.

Generally 10 minutes is enough to begin with, though you may want to build up to 20. Hold these discussions regularly, but don't discuss your problems in the meantime. Putting thoughts down in a letter is another technique that people find useful.

Listen!

This might be the most important communication skill of all. Give your partner the space and time to tell you what's on their mind. Don't interrupt, don't mind-read and don't let your attention wander. Try not to dismiss what they say – be open-minded and flexible. Make listening your priority.

Negotiate

Winning an argument with your partner may feel like a victory, but in reality it's anything but. All you're doing is breeding frustration, anger and resentment, thereby priming the pumps for further conflict. So make agreement and compromise the end point of your arguments – and the best way to achieve that is by polishing up your negotiation skills:

- **Don't complain: request.** Moaning may feel good, but it's unlikely to help bring about the kind of change you're looking for. So don't complain that your partner doesn't help out with the childcare, request that they bathe the kids three times a week. Make the request as specific as possible. And ensure that it's realistic; it's better to set modest targets that can be met than wildly optimistic ones that can only end in failure.
- **Be clear about what you want.** It can be difficult to say what's really on your mind, but if you don't the problems are likely to continue. Don't make it a test of your partner's sensitivity: help them out by explaining calmly and clearly how you feel.
- **Focus on the future, not on the past.** Raking over past issues isn't going to create the sense of positive, co-operative problem-solving that strong relationships need. So let go of what you can't change and concentrate on what you can: the future.
- **Give and take.** If you're asking your partner to do something they might rather avoid (washing the car, hoovering the house, visiting your family), it'll help if you can offer something positive in return. It's the essence of negotiation: finding a mutually acceptable balance between your respective needs and desires. In other words, give and take.
- **Timetable.** This can be a great way of ensuring everyone's require- ments are met. For example, if you're concerned that your partner spends all their free time on the Internet instead of with you, schedule a night out together every week and, in return, agree that your partner can surf the Internet for a couple of hours two evenings a week.

If all this feels rather too formal and lacking in spontaneity, remember that there's no need to timetable your every waking moment – just focus on those activities that matter to you both. And once you've both got used to the new way of doing things, you probably won't need the timetable any longer.

Make time for fun together

Many relationships suffer through sheer neglect, through simply not spend- ing enough quality time together. As a result, the partners become distanced from one another and the relationship seems devoid of the positives that brought them together in the first place, filled instead with dreary routine and familiar disagreements.

Think back to the things you used to enjoy as a couple – going out to the cinema, staying in bed till noon, buying each other little gifts – and start doing them again. Or schedule in other activities you both think you might enjoy. Plan ahead and make a date: just as you did when you first got together.

Lead by example

It's hard to change someone else's behaviour, though the strategies we set out here will certainly help. Much easier (though not simple) is to focus on your own actions. Have a think about your attitudes to the relationship and to handling conflict. Where did they come from? Are you perhaps merely following the example your parents gave you? Could you do things differently? If you can change your own behaviour for the better, you'll probably find your partner will make a similar adjustment.

Defuse arguments before they get out of hand

If tempers do begin to flare, there's still a lot that you can do to prevent things from developing into a full-blown row:

- **Don't be hostile or aggressive and stay clear of sarcasm.** The 'sting in the tail' – a negative comment at the end of a positive message – can be particularly damaging.
- **Be sensitive to the fact that the argument is escalating.** Learn to recognize the signs, perhaps in the way that you're feeling or how you and your partner are interacting. Step outside the conflict and ask your partner whether they've noticed what's happening.
- **Speak more quietly and slowly.**
- **Relax.** Count to ten, or practise deep breathing (see p. 359).
- **Reach out to your partner.** Shift the mood by smiling or giving your partner a hug. Humour can be effective – as long as you're sure your partner will find your comment funny.
- **Be prepared to apologize** – provided you really mean it.
- **If things are getting really heated, call a time out.** Separate for at least 20 minutes, then come back together to discuss things calmly.

Jealousy

. . . .

'We can't build our dreams on suspicious minds.'
Elvis Presley

. . . .

One very common cause of trouble in a relationship is jealousy, or the 'green-eyed monster' as Shakespeare described it in *Othello*; the seemingly irresistible, and often intensely painful fear that we're losing our partner to someone else.

Sometimes jealousy is understandable; if your partner has been unfaithful in the past, naturally you'll worry that they might stray again in future. And certain situations can be a powerful trigger – for instance, if your partner is working away from home or spending a lot of time with a colleague of the opposite sex. On the other hand, jealousy can take root without any provocation, even in relationships where both partners are devoted to each other and almost always together.

Jealousy isn't necessarily a problem. For some people, a mildly jealous partner is a partner that cares. And a degree of jealousy can serve as a useful reminder that you mustn't take your loved one for granted; that you need to work at keeping them happy.

More often, though, jealousy is a distressing and destructive emotion. Trust is critical to a successful relationship, but jealousy breeds suspicion, doubt and mistrust. A person who is jealous becomes preoccupied with the fear of betrayal, constantly checking up on their partner's movements, rummaging through their possessions, trying to catch them out. They may become extremely possessive, putting pressure on their partner to stop seeing friends or going out without them. What began as a partnership of romantic equals can degenerate into the unhappy relationship of guard and prisoner.

But jealousy can be overcome:

Weigh up the evidence
Is your partner really the sort of person who'd go off with someone else? What evidence is there for your fears? What evidence might contradict your suspicions? Talk things over with a trusted friend:

how likely do they think it is that your partner might be deceiving you?

Talk to your partner

All relationships benefit from mutually agreed ground rules on issues like trust and faithfulness; if you haven't talked these things over with your partner yet, we recommend you do so. It can also be helpful to let your partner know about your jealousy, but don't go overboard: if you are continually seeking reassurance it is likely to irritate them.

Instead, explain why you're prone to jealousy (perhaps a previous partner was unfaithful) and what sort of things trigger it (maybe your partner staying out late with friends). Get their perspective on the issue and decide how you'll both handle it in future.

Think through the pros and cons of your jealousy

For all the distress jealousy can cause us, it can sometimes seem like a necessary burden. After all, if we don't keep an eye on our partner's movements, it'll be easy for them to meet someone else – won't it?

So, it's a good idea to ask yourself whether your jealousy really is advantageous. Write down all the pros and cons of being jealous, then list those for trusting your partner. When you weigh it all up, which looks the best bet? Ultimately, you may never know for sure whether your partner has been unfaithful, but you'll save yourself (and your relationship) a huge amount of anxiety, stress and misery if you opt for trust.

Uncover your fears

At the root of everyone's jealousy is fear: fear that their partner will abandon them, fear that they'll never find someone else, fear that they'll become a laughing stock ... What fear lies behind your jealousy? And what strategies could you use to deal with this nightmare if it did occur? If you can feel confident about your ability to handle the situation you dread, your jealousy will exert far less of a hold on you.

Set yourself some ground rules

It's ironic. The more time you spend at the service of your jealousy

– checking and fretting and questioning your partner – the less reassured you feel. Far from assuaging your fears, this kind of behaviour only reinforces them.

So you need to put some practical limits on your jealousy. For example: resolve not to look through your partner's diary; don't call them to find out what they're up to; and only let yourself think jealous thoughts in a daily 'worry period' – if they pop into your head at any other time, jot them down and save them for later. (For more on worry periods, see p. 110.)

Embrace the situations that fuel your jealousy

As with any other fear, one very effective way of tackling jealousy is deliberately to expose yourself to the circumstances that trigger it. So, for example, if your partner wants to meet a friend for a drink, let them; if they like chatting to new people at parties, don't object. Resist the jealous behaviours you normally use in these situations (for example, pressurizing your partner not to go out, or interrogating them when they come back).

If you find yourself thinking jealous thoughts, either save them for your worry period (see p. 110) or adopt a 'mindfulness' approach. Mindfulness focuses on living in the present moment, cultivating a way of seeing negative thoughts as passing mental events, rather than always as reflections of truth or reality. Notice your jealous thoughts, but don't attach any importance to them; instead, just let them go. (For more on mindfulness, see p. 293.)

If you can do all this, you'll soon discover that what you fear (for example, your partner meeting someone they prefer to you at a party) simply hasn't happened. And in time you'll realize that it probably won't ever happen. Of course, we can never know for certain what's up around the bend, but you'll find you can cope with this uncertainty too.

Focus on the positive

Don't go looking for the negative in your relationship – the behaviour that sparks your jealousy. Instead, make an effort to notice the pleasing aspects of your relationship and those things about your partner that drew you to them in the first place. Channel your energy into planning enjoyable activities for the two of you. The more fun you can have together, the less powerful your jealousy will be.

Boost your self-esteem

Jealous fears about a partner often have their roots in negative views about oneself. 'Of course she's going to be interested in other men. The world is full of guys who are more intelligent/better looking/ richer/better in bed than me.' Our sense of self-worth can rest entirely on how we believe our partner feels about us.

If your self-esteem is low, you need to give it a boost:

- Make sure you have interests and activities outside your relationship.
- Don't neglect your social life.
- Make a list of your positive qualities, and spend a little time each day thinking about them.

For detailed advice on these strategies and other tips on building self-esteem, check out the 'How to Overcome Depression' section on pp. 192–8.

Don't be afraid to ask for help

Chances are, you'll make huge progress by following the suggestions given here. But if you're still finding your jealousy a problem, do get in touch with a therapist. Cognitive Behaviour Therapy in particular has an excellent track record in helping people overcome their jealousy.

Be clear about whether you want to remain in the relationship

If things are really difficult between you and your partner, you may need to decide whether it's worth staying together. Talk to trusted friends. Weigh up the pros and cons, both of remaining in the relationship and splitting up. Don't base your decision on how you feel right now; imagine how things might be in three, six or twelve months' time.

Get help

Don't be afraid to seek professional advice on your relationship – after all, what could be more important? You may want to see a counsellor on your own or, if you're both in agreement, attend couple therapy together. Mediation, which involves a neutral third party helping you to come to an agreement on practical issues, is also a worthwhile option.

HOW TO COPE WHEN A RELATIONSHIP ENDS

The end of a relationship can sometimes come as a big relief. But generally emotions are much more mixed. Often, it can feel as if a huge and very empty hole has suddenly opened up in the centre of your life.

In fact, a break-up can be as traumatic as a bereavement. Like bereavement, it can amount to what psychologists call a 'life event' – an experience so unsettling that we can be totally knocked for six. Life events can wreck your self-esteem and trigger depression, anxiety, and even Post-Traumatic Stress Disorder. A break-up is no different, especially if the relationship was a long one, children are involved or if you're not the person who is doing the leaving.

If you're struggling to cope with the end of a relationship, make sure that you:

- seek the advice of friends and people whose opinions you respect
- make time in your week for fun and relaxation
- do those things you've been meaning to for ages, whether it's getting on top of the garden, seeing friends or joining a language class
- eat and sleep properly and take regular exercise
- think about how the relationship began, why it failed and what you'll look for in the future.

Related problems

Sexual problems are a common cause of difficulties between partners, as is **stress**. A relationship is also likely to come under pressure if one or both partners is suffering from a psychological problem such as **depression**, struggling with **alcohol** or **drug** use or finding it hard to control their **anger**.

Where to go for more information

Bookshop shelves are groaning with guides to better relationships, and it can be hard to know which is worth your time and money. Here's a selection of titles we've found especially helpful:

Love is Never Enough (Harper, 1989) by Aaron T. Beck; *Overcoming Relationship Problems* (Robinson, 2005) by Michael Crowe; *Stop Arguing, Start Talking* (Vermilion, 2001) by Susan Quilliam; *Reconcilable Differences* (Guilford, 2002) by Andrew Christensen and Neil Jacobson; *Everyone Can Win* (Simon & Schuster, 2006) by Helena Cornelius and Shoshana Faire; *Surviving Infidelity* (Adams, 2005) by Rona Subotnik and Gloria Harris; *Moving On* (Vermilion, 2001) by Suzie Hayman.

Also, check out the following websites:

- ⓘ www.relate.org.uk (the website of 'the UK's largest provider of relationship counselling and sex therapy')
- ⓘ www.instituteoffamilytherapy.org.uk
- ⓘ www.aamft.org (run by the American Association for Marriage and Family Therapy)

Self-injury

··

*I'd locked myself in the bathroom and turned on the taps so
nobody could hear me crying. That's when I saw a pair of
scissors. I picked them up and started to cut my left arm. I
made one cut for every day I'd been injured. With each one I
felt I was punishing myself, but at the same time I felt a sense
of release that drove me to do it again and again. I felt such a
hatred for everything that was going wrong. I had never felt
so desperate.*
Kelly Holmes

The revelation by Olympic champion Dame Kelly Holmes that she had self-
harmed for a period in 2003 came as a distressing reminder of just how
powerful the urge to injure oneself can be. Holmes joined the lengthening
list of celebrities who have spoken about their self-injury including Princess
Diana, Christina Ricci and Richey Edwards of Manic Street Preachers.

When we talk about self-injury, we mean the deliberate inflicting of
physical wounds on the body. Cutting is the most usual form of self-injury,
but burning and hitting are also common.

That said, self-injury can encompass a bewildering range of behaviour
including scratching, poisoning, skin picking, hair pulling, reopening
wounds to stop them healing, biting, asphyxiation and even, in very rare
cases, bone breaking and amputation. Typically people target their arms
and legs, though pretty much any part of the body can be harmed.

People who self-injure generally view it as a coping mechanism. For
some, it can seem like the only way they can deal with unpleasant and
uncontrollable emotions, such as anger, shame, guilt, sadness or emptiness. For people who are prone to feelings of numbness, injuring them-

Problems with self-injury: a personal account

I've never had a great opinion of myself – not clever enough, not pretty enough, not thin enough: the usual stuff. But I never imagined hurting myself until I had a huge falling-out with my best friend. I was lonely, miserable, and most of all angry – at my friend and, particularly, myself. One evening I drank a bottle of wine and cut my arms with a razor. It was entirely unplanned, but it felt incredible. All those negative emotions seemed to flow out of me with the blood. Except, of course, that they didn't. I woke up the next day, took a look at my arm, and felt lower than I'd ever felt in my entire life. The bandage I wore seemed like a badge of disgrace – the ultimate public declaration of my inadequacies. I began to think that I deserved this punishment, and that the only way to make up for all my mistakes was to cut myself again ...

Jackie, aged 24

selves can make them feel alive. It can also be a form of self-punishment, and a way of communicating distress to others – or, more usually (since self-injury tends to be a secret activity), expressing it to themselves.

Many people who self-injure report feeling a lot better immediately after an episode. They describe the experience as bringing relief, a sense of control and even euphoria. But it doesn't last. Shame and self-loathing soon kick in, the negative feelings that lie behind the self-injury are reinforced, and the cycle begins again.

This is destructive behaviour to be sure, but it isn't suicidal. It's an attempt to keep going, not to end life. That said, people who self-injure are also more likely to attempt suicide. For advice on coping with suicidal thoughts – either your own or those of a friend or family member – see the **depression** entry (pp. 186–98).

For a minority of people, self-injury can be a sign of what's known as borderline personality disorder. To make a diagnosis, a doctor will look for at least five of the following:

- intense fear of being abandoned
- very unstable personal relationships
- fragile and changeable sense of identity
- impulsiveness (for example, reckless spending, binge eating, or drug or alcohol use)
- suicidal behaviour
- self-injury
- severe mood swings
- feelings of emptiness
- anger problems
- paranoia
- feeling numb or disconnected from the world.

Other names for self-injury include: self-harm, self-mutilation, self-wounding, self-inflicted violence, self-injurious behaviour, self-destructive behaviour, self-abuse, parasuicide, cutting and self-cutting.

How common is self-injury?

Putting an exact figure to the number of people who self-harm is difficult, not least because many (perhaps most) cases are never reported. Self-injury is often a secretive activity and people go to great lengths to prevent friends and family from finding out.

Nevertheless, the best estimates indicate that around 5 to 10 per cent of adolescents have harmed themselves at some point. For adults, that figure is around 4 per cent, though it's thought that fewer than 1 per cent self-injure on a regular basis.

Self-injury is often regarded as a typically teenage activity. In fact, though it does tend to be more of a problem in young people, and usually first occurs between the ages of 14 and 24, younger children and older adults also self-harm.

Similarly, although the media usually portrays self-injury as a female problem, the research data are mixed, with some studies suggesting that females are more at risk and others arguing that it's just as common in males.

For borderline personality disorder, around 1 per cent of the population are believed to be affected.

How to Overcome Self-injury

It can be difficult to stop self-injuring, partly because it often seems like an effective coping strategy – in the short term at least. But you can stop. Give yourself time; if you've been self-injuring for a while, it's unrealistic to think you'll be able to stop overnight. And keep trying, even if you have the occasional setback. You'll get there in the end. Here's how we recommend you go about it:

Improve your mood

Easier said than done? Actually, just getting the basics in place can make a huge difference to how you feel. That means keeping to a good sleep routine, eating well, taking regular exercise and making sure your week includes at least some enjoyable activities. For more on how to improve your mood in this way, check out the Introduction on pp. 6–24.

Boost your self-esteem

People who self-injure usually have a pretty low opinion of themselves. But you need to start valuing yourself. One way of doing this is by playing

Resisting the urge to self-injure

How do you fight the all-too-powerful desire to harm yourself? That was the question posed to a group of young, self-injuring adults by the psychologists E. David Klonsky and Catherine Glenn. Here are the group's top 10 strategies (in descending order):

1. Doing recreational sports or exercise.
2. Removing whatever is generally used to self-injure.
3. Finding someone who is understanding.
4. Turning to religion or spirituality.
5. Being around friends.
6. Writing about how you feel.
7. Thinking of someone who cares about you.
8. Talking to someone about how you feel.
9. Anticipating how other people will react to your self-injury.
10. Keeping busy.

to your strengths: do stuff that gives you a sense of achievement, whether it's working in the garden, cooking a meal or writing a poem.

Another useful strategy is to write down five positive qualities you have. Then, for a few minutes every day, close your eyes and think back to situations in which you've shown those qualities. And for a week – or longer if you can – make a note of every time you do something you're pleased with or when something positive happens.

Use your support network

Letting your loved ones know that you've self-injured can be a daunting prospect. But it's worth it. Your feelings of isolation and guilt will begin to recede. You'll feel the relief that comes when you express your feelings rather than keeping them secret. And you'll be starting to build a support network.

It can also be really useful to be in touch with others who've gone through the same experiences. So, as well as friends and family, think about contacting one of the organizations listed below.

Keep a self-injury diary

In order for you to be able to stop self-injuring, it's crucial to work out exactly why you're doing it. Is it, for example, a way of coping with your emotions? Are you trying to punish yourself or to feel alive? Whatever your motivations, keeping a diary is a great way of discovering them. Write down when and where the urge to self-injure arises, and what you are doing, thinking and feeling when it does. What are the triggers for your behaviour? Get into the habit of updating your diary every time you want to self-injure.

Keep going with your diary even when you've understood the function of your self-injury. It's an excellent way of expressing your thoughts and feelings – getting them out of your head and on to paper. And, as you work to stop self-injuring, you'll have a morale-boosting record of just how far you've come.

Replace self-injury with other ways of dealing with your feelings

Once you've identified why you're self-injuring, you can start to think of more positive ways of achieving the results you're after – for example, coping with your sadness or boredom or traumatic memories. What would be a better way of reacting to your self-injury triggers?

How you do this is a personal thing, but a general guideline is to develop ways of accepting your emotions, and reacting to them differently. For example, if you cut yourself after rows with your family, you might decide not to be alone after an argument and instead to talk to a friend about your anger and unhappiness. If you self-injure when your feelings of emptiness and despair get too much to bear, try expressing your emotions by writing them down in your diary.

One strategy that many people find helpful is developing a mindful approach to unpleasant thoughts. Mindfulness is about living in the present moment and learning to see negative thoughts as passing mental events, rather than as reflections of truth or reality. Notice your unpleasant thoughts, but don't attach any importance to them. Don't fight or dwell on them; instead, simply let them go.

Another tip is to focus on pleasurable sensations, rather than the distressing feelings that make you want to harm yourself. Some people make themselves a 'sensory box', filled with pleasant objects to smell and touch (perhaps feathers or dried flowers or a scent-infused piece of fabric). You could try lighting an aromatherapy candle or taking a long, relaxing bath. Experiment, and see what works best for you.

Be ready for the situations that trigger your urge to self-injure and plan how you'll deal with them. You may need to experiment to see which tactic is right for you: perhaps write down five alternatives and test each of them out. Have a look at the box on p.291 to see what one group of people who self-injure found worked best.

Challenge unhelpful thoughts

Have a look at your diary and try to identify the thoughts that give you 'permission' to self-injure. For example, 'I really need to do this', 'It's the only way to get rid of these feelings' or 'I deserve this'.

These negative thoughts need to be challenged. Write down the evidence for and against. What other ways are there to think about the situation? Imagine what you'd advise a friend in a similar situation. Are you being too hard on yourself? What could you tell yourself that will help to combat these thoughts when they occur?

Write a journal

As well as your self-injury diary, try writing a more general journal: it's a tried-and-tested way of dealing with difficult emotions. Aim for about

20–30 minutes several times a week. What you write about is, of course, up to you, but people often find it helps to describe their life, their past and recent experiences and their thoughts and feelings.

In fact, all forms of creative expression are helpful. If you prefer to paint or play music or sing, for example, by all means do so.

Manage your anger

The impulse to self-injure can be sparked by all types of emotions, but anger is often in the mix somewhere. If anger is a problem for you, check out the entry on pp. 55–64.

Learn to cope with stress

As with almost all of the problems in this book, stress can play a big role in self-injury. You'll find lots of stress-management tips on pp. 355–60.

Don't be afraid to ask for professional help

It's not essential for everyone, but many people find that working with a therapist is really helpful. Excellent results have been achieved with Cognitive Behaviour Therapy (CBT) and especially with Dialectical Behaviour Therapy (DBT).

DBT (which we draw on here) includes elements of CBT, mindfulness and individual and group work, with an emphasis on helping people to understand and cope with their emotions, develop their communication skills and problem-solving abilities and deal with past traumatic events that may be fuelling the urge to self-injure. DBT is very often used to treat people with borderline personality disorder.

Medication, for example antidepressants, is sometimes prescribed to help people deal with the emotional problems (such as depression) that generally accompany self-injury.

Related problems

People who self-injure are often battling with a number of other issues including **anxiety**, **depression**, low self-esteem, and suicidal thoughts (for more information on the last two, see the **depression** entry). **Eating problems**, drug and alcohol **addictions** and the lasting **trauma** caused by **child abuse** are also common.

Where to go for more information

Healing the Hurt Within (How To Books, 2007) by Jan Sutton makes extensive use of personal accounts from people who self-injure. As such, it gives a particularly compelling insight into the nature of the problem and what can be done to overcome it.

Bodily Harm (Little, Brown, 1999) by Karen Conterio and Wendy Lader provides a self-help version of the approach used by the S.A.F.E. (Self Abuse Finally Ends) programme (www.selfinjury.com).

Useful websites include:

- ⓘ www.nshn.co.uk (The National Self-harm Network)
- ⓘ www.selfharm.org.uk is aimed particularly at young people who self-injure, together with their friends and family
- ⓘ www.selfharm.org (not to be confused with the very similarly named selfharm.org.uk site) is the website of UK voluntary organization FirstSigns (Self-Injury Guidance & Network Support)
- ⓘ www.siari.co.uk (Self-Injury and Related Issues) is run by Jan Sutton, author of the excellent *Healing the Hurt Within*
- ⓘ www.selfinjury.org (American Self-Harm Information Clearinghouse)
- ⓘ www.palace.net/~llama/psych/injury.html (Secret Shame) hasn't been updated for a few years, but none the less contains a lot of helpful material.

Sexual Problems

Give me chastity and continency – but not yet!
St Augustine

We've divided this entry on common sexual problems into separate sections for men and women. But you may well want to read through the whole entry. Some of the problems that affect women are also experienced by men (though less often). Many of the strategies to deal with these issues are relevant to both men and women, whatever their specific problem. And if you're in a relationship, it's best to tackle any sexual difficulty together.

Women's Sexual Problems

I blame my mother for my poor sex life. All she told me was, 'The man goes on top and the woman underneath.' For three years my husband and I slept in bunk beds.
Joan Rivers

Self-assessment
This questionnaire covers all the sexual problems affecting women that we discuss in the following pages.

Before you get started, here are a couple of definitions:

Sexual activity: anything that is sexually stimulating or pleasurable, with or without a partner, for example intercourse, caressing, foreplay, masturbation and oral sex.

Sexual life: both the physical sexual activities and the emotional sexual relationship you have with your partner.

When you answer the questions, think back to your experiences over the last four weeks.

As you'll have noticed, many of the questions include a not applicable (n/a) response, usually if you haven't had sex in the four-week period that the questionnaire covers. There are two ways to deal with this. *Either*:

- think back to the last time you were sexually active, even if it was longer than four weeks ago; *or*
- provided you've answered at least half of the questions in a section, work out your average score for these and then give that score to the n/a questions too.

1. How often have you had pleasurable thoughts and feelings about sexual activity?	
Not at all	1
Rarely	2
Sometimes	3
Often	4
Very often	5
2. How often have you wanted to be sensually touched and caressed by your partner?	
Not at all	1
Rarely	2
Sometimes	3
Often	4
Very often	5
3. How often have you wanted to take part in sexual activity?	
Not at all	1

Rarely	2
Sometimes	3
Often	4
Very often	5

4. How often have you initiated sexual activity with your partner?

Not at all	1
Rarely	2
Sometimes	3
Often	4
Very often	5

5. How often did you take part in sexual activity with penetration (i.e. vaginal penetration and intercourse)?

Never	n/a
Once/twice	1
3–4 times	2
5–8 times	3
9–12 times	4
13–16 times	5
More than 16 times	6

6. How often did you look forward to sexual activity?

Not at all	1
Rarely	2
Sometimes	3
Often	4

7. How often did you have a feeling of 'warmth' in your vagina/ genital area when you took part in sexual activity?

I did not take part in sexual activity	n/a
Not at all	1
Sometimes	2
Often	3
Very often	4
Every time	5

8. In general, how much 'warmth' did you feel in your vagina/genital area when you took part in sexual activity?

I did not take part in sexual activity	n/a
None	1
Slightly 'warm'	2
Moderately 'warm'	3
Very 'warm'	4
Extremely 'warm'	5

9. How often did you have a sensation of 'pulsating' ('tingling') in your vagina/genital area when you took part in sexual activity?

I did not take part in sexual activity	n/a
Not at all	1
Sometimes	2
Often	3
Very often	4
Every time	5

10. In general, how much 'pulsating' ('tingling') in your vagina/genital area did you notice when you took part in sexual activity?

I did not take part in sexual activity	n/a
No sensation	1
A mild sensation	2
A moderate sensation	3
A strong sensation	4
A very strong sensation	5

11. How often did you notice vaginal wetness/lubrication when you took part in sexual activity?

I did not take part in sexual activity	n/a
Not at all	1
Sometimes	2
Often	3
Very often	4
Every time	5

12. In general, how much vaginal wetness/lubrication did you notice when you took part in sexual activity?

I did not take part in sexual activity	n/a
No wetness/lubrication	1
Slightly wet/lubricated	2
Moderately wet/lubricated	3
Very wet/lubricated	4
Extremely wet/lubricated	5

13. In general, how often did you have an orgasm when you took part in sexual activity (with or without a partner)?

I did not take part in sexual activity	n/a
Not at all	1
Sometimes	2
Often	3
Very often	4
Every time	5

14. In general, how pleasurable were the orgasms that you had?

I did not take part in sexual activity	n/a
Not pleasurable	1
Slightly pleasurable	2
Moderately pleasurable	3
Very pleasurable	4
Extremely pleasurable	5

15. In general, how easy was it for you to reach orgasm?

I did not have any orgasms	n/a
Very difficult	1
Quite difficult	2
Neither easy nor difficult	3
Quite easy	4
Very easy	5

16. How often did you experience pain in your vagina/genital area during or after sexual activity (e.g. penetration, intercourse)?

I did not take part in sexual activity	n/a
Not at all	5
Sometimes	4
Often	3
Very often	5
Every time	1

17. In general, how much pain did you experience in your vagina/ genital area during or after sexual activity (e.g. penetration, intercourse)

I did not take part in sexual activity	n/a
No pain	5
Slightly painful	4
Moderately painful	3
Very painful	5
Extremely painful	1

18. How often have you been worried or anxious about pain during sexual activity?

I did not take part in sexual activity	n/a
I did not take part in sexual activity because of being worried or anxious about pain	0
Not at all	5
Sometimes	4
Often	3
Very often	5
Every time	1

19. In general, how enjoyable has it been to be sensually touched and caressed by your partner?

I have not been touched or caressed	n/a
Not enjoyable	1
Slightly enjoyable	2
Moderately enjoyable	3
Very enjoyable	4
Extremely enjoyable	5

20. In general, how much did you enjoy penetration and intercourse?

I have not been touched or caressed	n/a
Not enjoyable	1
Slightly enjoyable	2
Moderately enjoyable	3
Very enjoyable	4
Extremely enjoyable	5

21. In general, how much did you enjoy sexual activity without penetration (e.g. masturbation, oral sex)?

I have not been touched or caressed	n/a
Not enjoyable	1
Slightly enjoyable	2
Moderately enjoyable	3
Very enjoyable	4
Extremely enjoyable	5

22. How often did you feel emotionally close to your partner when you took part in sexual activity?

I did not take part in sexual activity	n/a
Not at all	1
Sometimes	2
Often	3
Very often	4
Every time	5

23. Did you feel good about yourself when you were sexually active?

I did not take part in sexual activity	n/a
Not at all	1
Slightly	2
Moderately	3
Very	4
Extremely	5

24. How confident have you felt about yourself as a sexual partner?

Not at all	1
Slightly	2

Moderately	3
Very	4
Extremely	5

Female Sexual Function Questionnaire © Pfizer (1997).

The questions are grouped to assess particular sexual problems:

Questions 1–6 focus on desire:
- A score of 23–31 indicates no problems.
- A score of 17–22 suggests there may be a problem.
- A score of 5–16 means a problem is very likely.

Questions 7–12 focus on arousal:
- A score of 22–30 indicates no problems.
- A score of 21–16 suggests there may be a problem.
- A score of 6–15 means a problem is very likely.

Questions 13–15 focus on orgasm:
- A score of 12–15 indicates no problems.
- A score of 9–11 suggests there may be a problem.
- A score of 3–8 means a problem is very likely.

Questions 16–18 focus on pain:
- A score of 12–15 indicates no problems.
- A score of 9–11 suggests there may be a problem.
- A score of 2–8 means a problem is very likely.

Questions 19–24 focus on general enjoyment of sex:
- A score of 23–30 indicates no problems.
- A score of 17–22 suggests there may be a problem.
- A score of 6–16 means a problem is very likely.

LOSS OF SEXUAL DESIRE

Surprising though it may seem for such an intensely physical experience, sex begins in the brain. We think about sex; we fantasize about sex; we're acutely receptive to sexual feelings and possibilities: we have, in other words, sexual desire.

But everyone (men as well as women) goes through periods during which they're less interested than usual in sex, whether it be fantasies or masturbation or sex with a partner. The urge simply seems to vanish.

Any number of factors can lie behind this loss of desire – common ones are stress, illness, depression and relationship difficulties. But it's not necessarily a problem. If you're OK with it, and so is your partner, that's fine. Bear in mind that there's no 'normal' level of desire. It varies from person to person, and everyone will experience changes in desire according to where they happen to be in their life. The chances are that things will be back to how they were pretty soon.

But loss of desire can cause real distress, depriving a person of a vital part of their life – even of their identity – and, quite possibly, generating tension in their relationship. Things aren't helped by the omnipresence of sexual images in our culture, and the apparent message that we should all be turned on all the time.

Loss of desire varies from the mild to the severe, and from the temporary to the persistent. A doctor will make a diagnosis of hypoactive sexual desire disorder if the situation has been going on for a while and is causing significant unhappiness or relationship problems. If even the thought of sex fills someone with fear, panic or disgust, they may be suffering from what's known as sexual aversion disorder.

Problems with loss of sexual desire: a personal account

Andy and I have been married for 14 years and we have three children. Sex was brilliant for us in the first few months, as it is for most people, but it was still pretty good until a couple of years ago. Basically, I went off it – not overnight, but gradually. I'm not sure how to explain it except to say that sex just didn't interest me. Andy would try to get me in the mood, but all that did was make me feel pressured. Naturally, he got incredibly frustrated and very down. He felt I'd gone off him, which I suppose I had a bit. But I loved him, and I didn't want to lose him, and we ended up seeing a sex therapist. That first session was so embarrassing! But it also felt great to discuss these things in a structured way, without it ending up in a row. The therapist taught us how to be more intimate, and to make our sex life a priority, and since then things have been much better.
Maggie, aged 40

Sex and alcohol

Alcohol is often a major factor in sex, and especially in helping people to get together in the first place. In fact, it can sometimes seem as if no one would ever start a relationship without the aid of a few drinks!

What is it about alcohol that enables it to play such a role? Partly, it's the powerful effect it exerts on our inhibitions: alcohol gives us licence to behave in ways we wouldn't dare when sober. It can also make us feel more confident, witty and attractive. And, crucially, alcohol can make other people seem more attractive too.

This last point was perfectly illustrated by a study carried out by a team of psychologists at the universities of Glasgow and St Andrews. They showed more than 100 photographs of faces to 80 heterosexual students, some of whom had been drinking and some of whom had not. The students were asked to rate the attractiveness of the faces.

Those who'd been drinking gave a consistently higher rating than those who hadn't – though only for faces of people of the opposite sex. It wasn't that alcohol made the world in general look more appealing – faces of people of the same sex didn't seem any more attractive to students who'd been drinking, and neither did a range of objects they were also shown.

Besides shedding light on the mysteries of courtship, these findings have important implications for public sexual health. Because if alcohol has this effect, it's likely to be a major factor in one-night stands and other casual, potentially risky sexual encounters.

How common is a loss of sexual desire?

In any year, 40 per cent of women experience a loss of sexual desire that lasts at least a month. For 10 per cent of women, that loss of desire continues for six months or longer.

AROUSAL PROBLEMS

Sex begins with desire; the next stage is arousal. If we're getting the sort of stimulation we like, our body undergoes a series of changes. We become sexually excited or, in other words, aroused.

Problems with arousal: a personal account

I've always had quite a complicated, conflicted experience of sex. Essentially, I want it but my body doesn't! I find my boyfriend sexy and I desire him, but that doesn't seem to be enough to get me properly wet – or as wet as I feel in my mind, if you see what I mean. He's really good about it, but it's a problem I'm desperate to sort out. I think it may be because of my upbringing. My parents are devoutly religious and their view of sex is that it's something that should happen solely between married men and women and really only to conceive children. I am not married! And I seem to have inherited an embarrassment and awkwardness about sex, even though rationally I know that's crazy. I have fantasies, and I masturbate, but I feel so guilty afterwards!

Lucy, aged 25

For women, these changes include: faster breathing and heart rate, lips becoming pinker, pupils dilating, skin reddening, breasts swelling and nipples becoming erect. The vagina becomes wet and, if arousal goes on long enough, alters its shape ready for penetration. The clitoris grows larger and becomes erect.

Women and men experience arousal in different ways. For example, women often need more time and stimulation before they're ready for intercourse, but they stay aroused for longer and, after sex, can become excited again more quickly than men. Men can be very aroused by a visual turn-on (a glimpse of a sexy, scantily clad woman, for instance, will do it for most), whereas women generally need physical touch.

Sometimes, however, people aren't able to move from desire to arousal. Their body just doesn't respond, no matter how much they may want sex. For men, that generally means they can't get or maintain an erection. For women, it's usually a failure to become sufficiently lubricated. For some people, arousal problems aren't a big deal, especially if they don't last long. For others, though, they can lead to real distress and serious relationship difficulties.

Arousal difficulties vary in their severity. A doctor may diagnose female sexual arousal disorder if the problem is a long-lasting one and is causing a lot of unhappiness or relationship problems.

How common are arousal problems?

Over the course of a year, 9 per cent of women experience lubrication difficulties lasting for a month or more and 3 per cent for at least six months.

Difficulties having an orgasm

An orgasm a day keeps the doctor away.
Mae West

Orgasm is generally seen as the pinnacle of sexual experience, the overwhelming and fantastically pleasurable culmination of intense arousal.

Heart rate, blood pressure and breathing peak, and women experience a series of exquisite contractions of the vagina, uterus, pelvic floor muscles and anus. Tension seems suddenly, and wonderfully, released. (For men, something very similar happens, though of course the contractions primarily affect the penis and urethra and are generally accompanied by ejaculation.) After orgasm, the muscles relax and the blood that surged to the genital areas during arousal flows away again.

Women's orgasms are brought on either by stimulation of the clitoris or of the vagina (and in particular the especially sensitive part known as the 'G' spot). Because of the location of the clitoris, intercourse isn't always enough to bring on an orgasm and stimulation with fingers or mouth may be necessary too.

Men and women vary in their experience of orgasms. Women, for example, are much more likely to have multiple orgasms. But their orgasms are more easily derailed – once men reach the 'point of inevitability', an orgasm will happen, while women can lose the feeling of arousal right up until the moment of orgasm.

Everyone's orgasms are different – for instance, in the quantity of contractions, how long they last, how strong they feel, how easy orgasms are to achieve and how numerous. Not only that, our orgasms vary depending on how we're feeling at any particular moment, for example, stressed or relaxed, tired or energetic, in love or having second thoughts about a partner.

Because there's no 'normal' experience of orgasm, deciding whether

Difficulties having an orgasm: a personal account

I was 29 before I had an orgasm during sex. I had masturbated occasionally as a teenager, but after I got married I stopped (I thought it was disloyal to my husband). We had a lot of sex, but he had all the orgasms. Initially, I blamed myself. But then I began to wonder whether it was his fault. Other women had orgasms during intercourse, didn't they? Why couldn't my husband make me come? I bought a sex tips book and read it while he wasn't around. What an eye-opener that turned out to be! I'd had no idea that most women didn't climax in intercourse. I'd thought men and women were supposed to come at the same time. And it hadn't even occurred to me that I could have an orgasm through foreplay (we'd never done much of that: we were always rushing to get to the 'real' sex). It's embarrassing to admit how naive I was – how naive we both were back then …

Jane, aged 50

there's a problem is likely to be a very personal matter. Only you will know what's right for you. Things aren't helped by the importance placed on orgasm by our culture. It's easy to feel that you should be having multiple orgasms during every sexual encounter, when in reality sex can be perfecting fulfilling without orgasm.

Female orgasmic disorder is the term doctors use for long-running failure to have an orgasm or if orgasm usually takes a very long time to achieve. But difficulty reaching orgasm isn't enough to warrant this diagnosis: it must also be causing significant distress or relationship problems. The causes are generally very similar to those for arousal problems (see p. 305).

How common are difficulties having an orgasm?

Each year 14 per cent of women are unable to achieve an orgasm for at least a month. For 4 per cent, the problem lasts for six months or longer. It's the most common reason for women to seek sex therapy.

Pain During Intercourse

Pain during intercourse can be caused by many medical conditions, but where there isn't a clear physical cause doctors are likely to look for the following problems:

- dyspareunia
- vaginismus.

Dyspareunia is the term used to describe recurrent pain in the genital area, generally during intercourse, but sometimes immediately before or afterwards. It can range from mild discomfort to quite intense pain, and it isn't caused simply by a lack of lubrication.

Vaginismus describes unpleasant and sometimes painful spasms in the muscles in the outer third of the vagina. These spasms can occur during attempted intercourse – often they're so bad that intercourse is impossible – or in any situation that involves something being inserted into the vagina, whether a tampon or a doctor's fingers during a gynaecological examination. For some women, even the thought of sex is enough to bring on the spasms.

Dyspareunia and vaginismus often go together; if you have one, you may well have the other. In fact, some experts have suggested that they aren't separate conditions at all, but rather different aspects of the same problem. What we know for certain is that they can be hugely distressing for women, wrecking their sex life and putting severe strain on relationships.

What causes pain during sex? Infections and other medical problems are often responsible. But for dyspareunia and vaginismus, psychological factors (for example, fear or anxiety about sex), personal history (having been sexually abused, for instance, or being brought up in a culture that sees sex as dangerous or sinful) and relationship difficulties are thought to play a central role, sometimes in combination with physical problems.

How common is pain during intercourse?
Pain during intercourse is a persistent problem for around 12 per cent of women each year. For 3 per cent of women, the problem continues for six months or longer.

Problems with pain during intercourse: a personal account

After my daughter was born, I remember the midwife telling me to avoid intercourse for six weeks, but six weeks came and went and I still couldn't face the thought of my husband inside me. When we did eventually try, I had to stop before he was even halfway in. It was just really painful. The same thing happened a couple of weeks later and (largely because my husband asked me to) I went to my GP. She examined me and said she couldn't find any physical explanation. I told her I knew she'd say that! We had a wonderful talk about my feelings towards sex and I admitted that I was now terrified of intercourse, though I didn't really know why. She put me in touch with a terrific counsellor who recommended some exercises for me and my husband. We started off with lots of kisses and cuddles and massages, and over several weeks gradually worked our way up to intercourse. To cut a long story short, it worked!
Felicity, aged 36

HOW TO OVERCOME WOMEN'S SEXUAL PROBLEMS

Our culture is so saturated with sexual images and references that it's easy to believe there's something wrong with you if you're not constantly either having wonderful, fulfilling, multi-orgasmic sex or thinking about it. But remember: whatever the state of your love life, it's only a problem if you – or your partner if you're in a relationship – feel it is.

What causes sexual problems? Despite a lot of excellent research in this area, there's still a lot we don't know. Usually it's a combination of factors, for example:

- relationship difficulties (arguments, boredom, affairs)
- stress
- lack of time or energy (if you're busy bringing up kids, for example,

sex can drift pretty low on the list of priorities)
- depression
- tiredness
- worries about your sexual performance or body image
- alcohol or drug use
- negative views about sex
- having suffered rape or sexual abuse
- getting older (though this is by no means inevitable or true for everyone)
- illness (for example, yeast infections can cause genital pain and cardiovascular problems can hamper arousal)
- certain medications (antidepressants, for instance, or drugs to control high blood pressure)

But of course the exact reasons will vary from person to person. It's worth having a think about what might lie behind your difficulties and talking things over with your partner. What you do about the problem may well depend on what you decide is causing it, but here's what we recommend:

Talk to your doctor

Sometimes sexual problems can have a clear physical or medical cause and it's best to rule these out early on. It's especially important to see your doctor if you're suffering with pain or discomfort during sex.

One very common physical cause of sexual problems is the menopause. Contrary to received wisdom, the menopause need not signal the end of sexual desire or activity (though women do frequently feel 'off' sex while they're adjusting to this life change). But menopause means a loss of oestrogen and one of the consequences is a reduction in blood flow to the vagina and clitoris and, as a result, much less lubrication.

Happily, there are a number of ways in which to counteract this loss of oestrogen, ranging from Hormone Replacement Therapy (HRT) to vaginal creams, tablets and rings, so talk through the options with your GP. While you're waiting for your oestrogen levels to get back up, it's a good idea to use a vaginal lubricant.

Look after yourself

How you feel physically can make a big difference to your sexual life. So get the basics in place. That means sleeping and eating well, cutting back on alcohol, stopping smoking and taking regular exercise. (You'll find more about all of these on pp. 6–24.)

Exercise your pelvic floor muscles

Getting your pelvic floor muscles into shape can increase feelings of arousal and make sex much more pleasurable; it's also helpful if you're suffering from vaginismus (see p. 309). (If you're not sure how to find your pelvic floor muscles, they're the ones you'd use to stop urinating mid-stream.)

You only need a few minutes each day for these exercises. Start by tightening the muscles and then letting go. Do this 10 times. When you can comfortably manage 15, tighten and then hold the muscles for 3 seconds. Start by doing this 10 times, then work your way up to 40 or 50 or however many you can manage.

Make sure you don't overdo things; you can strain your pelvic floor muscles just like any others. But stick with it and you should notice an improvement in a month or so.

Deal with any external issues

As we've mentioned, problems in bed often have their origins in issues far removed from sex. Common ones are stress, depression, relationship difficulties and traumatic past sexual experiences (such as abuse). If you can sort these out, your sexual hassles will probably disappear along with them. Start by having a look at the entries on these topics in this book.

Involve your partner

'Sex is a conversation carried out by other means. If you get on well out of bed, half the problems of bed are solved,' wrote the actor Peter Ustinov. He was right. But not only are sexual problems often a product of struggling relationships, a healthy partnership – based on open, honest, and constructive communication – is crucial to solving any issues that do crop up.

It doesn't matter 'whose' problem it appears to be – his premature ejaculation, your inability to have an orgasm during sex. You need to think of it as a joint problem. No blame; no guilt. Instead, the two of you working together as a team to make things better.

On the subject of healthy relationships, one important tip is to make sure your expectations are realistic. Sometimes you're going to experience wonderful, earth-moving sex; most of the time it's unlikely to reach those heights. Occasionally sex may be downright disappointing. It's no one's fault; it's natural. None of us is a sexual machine.

If you're in a long-term relationship, don't compare the sex you had when you first got together with the sex you have now. You're not comparing like with like! The kind of passionate, intense sex that most people have at the start of a relationship can't last. But that doesn't mean that sex based on deep and lasting love and true intimacy is inferior; quite the contrary in fact.

Focus on pleasure, not performance

A successful sex life shouldn't be defined by the number of orgasms you have, by how often you have intercourse or by how long it lasts. What's truly important is the depth of intimacy between you and your partner, the pleasure you can experience in each other's arms, and the freshness and inventiveness of your erotic life together.

Let's look now at how you can develop and strengthen these crucial elements of your relationship.

Touch, kiss, and caress

For some couples, pretty much the only time they touch each other is during sex, or when one partner tries to initiate it. But intimacy is best built on regular hugs, cuddles, kisses and caresses – in fact, any loving touch, even a playful pat on the bottom.

This contact can be erotic and it might sometimes lead to sex, but it isn't a request for intercourse. Instead, it's a way of acknowledging and strengthening both the bond between you and your partner and your comfort and confidence with each other's bodies. Experts call this kind of touching 'non-demand pleasuring' and you should attempt to do as much of it as possible!

Practise sensate focus

This exercise is a fantastic way to build intimacy – it's so effective, in fact, that it's become a mainstay of sex therapy for a whole range of problems. A programme of sensate focus can take several weeks, and you and your partner should avoid sex at other times (including masturbation). That may sound daunting, but you're likely to find the exercises very pleasurable once you get used to them. They won't seem a chore, we promise!

Aim for three sessions a week, though not on consecutive days. And always start by having a relaxing bath and getting your bedroom just how you want it.

Week 1 Caress your partner's naked body from head to toe, though avoid the genital areas and breasts. Concentrate on what gives *you* pleasure, not your partner, though don't do anything they really don't like. Spend about 30 minutes on this. Then it's your partner's turn to touch you.

Try not to talk during the sessions – but you should let your partner know if something they do feels uncomfortable. Afterwards (and you need to do this throughout the following weeks) discuss how it went: what you liked and didn't like, your thoughts, feelings and emotions.

Week 2 Repeat week 1's activities, but as well as caressing your partner with your hands you can use lotions, creams, massage oils, feathers or silk – in fact, anything you like. (And remember, when you're the active partner, your focus should be on what pleases you.)

Week 3 The exercise is the same as the previous week, but now genitals and breasts aren't off limits.

Week 4 Massage each other as you've done in previous weeks, but afterwards take turns in focusing on each other's genitals and breasts. Look, and gently touch, but no more than that. And, unlike previous weeks, concentrate on discovering what gives your partner pleasure.

Week 5 Repeat everything you've done so far, but while you're doing so, let your partner know how it feels and what you particularly like.

As you may have noticed, intercourse doesn't feature in these exercises. That's because the emphasis is on becoming comfortable with your own body and then with your partner's. But there are slightly shorter versions of sensate focus that do incorporate intercourse in the later stages. For example:

Week 1 This week's exercise is the same as the one above.

Week 2 Now the focus is on what the person being massaged likes (tell and show your partner what feels good).

Week 3 This week, include the breasts and genitals.

Week 4 Now you can touch each other to the point of orgasm. If that goes well, and you both want to, you can move on to intercourse.

Get to know your body – and what turns you on
Many of us aren't at ease with our bodies. We don't much like the way we look, and we're especially uncomfortable when it comes to the sexual parts of our body. These are attitudes that can make it difficult for us to really enjoy sex.

So it's important that we accept our bodies for what they are and learn to enjoy them. The sensate focus exercises will help enormously, but it's also worth spending time alone building your awareness and understanding of your body, and in particular what feels good sexually.

Start by having a long, luxurious bath. Gently towel yourself dry and take the time to study your body in the mirror – even the bits you normally try to pretend aren't there! Then lie down and gently explore your body with your fingers. Don't rush; pay close attention to how each touch feels and, especially, what gives you pleasure. Use oils, lotions or anything else you fancy.

When you're ready, choose a favourite fantasy and begin to masturbate. See whether you can identify any triggers that lead you into orgasm. One technique that works for many women is to take a deep breath when close to climax, then tip the head right back and push down with the diaphragm without letting any air escape.

Experiment with vibrators, especially if you find it difficult to have an orgasm. Ask your partner to show you how they like to be stimulated to orgasm and then show them how they should touch you.

Embrace fantasy

Sex, you may remember us commenting, begins in the brain. And there's no better way of enhancing desire and arousal than by developing a rich repertoire of sexual fantasies. Spend time thinking about what turns you on. Read or watch erotica, if that's right for you. And, provided you're comfortable doing so, share your fantasies with your partner: it can be a very sexy experience for you both!

Incidentally, as you can see from the box on the following page, men and women's sexual fantasies can sometimes be pretty wild. And that's absolutely fine: thinking about something is not the same as actually doing it. But if you're worried about your fantasies – if they involve children, for example, or other inappropriate behaviour – it's best not to actively engage with them, for example during sex or masturbation or by looking for related material on the Internet.

Be an erotic explorer

Sex is like any other activity: the more time and effort you devote to it, the better it'll be.

Read as much you can on the subject. You'll pick up lots of tips on how to strengthen and reinvigorate your sex life, plus you'll have the satisfying

Fantasies: his and hers

All men and women have sexual fantasies, but there's often a big difference between the content of those fantasies.

The most common fantasies for women according to Miriam Stoppard are:

- making love to their partner
- having sex with someone other than their partner (perhaps a former lover or a complete stranger)
- making love somewhere exotic
- being forced to have sex
- having sex in public while people watch
- taking part in group sex
- making love to someone of a different colour
- having sex with a woman
- being taken from behind by a stranger whose face they never see
- stripping in public.

And for men:

- taking part in group sex
- watching other people have sex
- having sex in public
- making love to someone other than their partner
- watching two women they know have sex
- being forced to make love
- forcing a woman to have sex
- forcing a woman to have oral sex
- making love somewhere unusual
- being part of a threesome, either with two women or with another man and a woman.

experience of watching several sexual myths explode – for example, the notion that most women climax through intercourse or that 'proper' sex means orgasms (preferably lots of them and with both partners coming simultaneously).

You'll also learn more about the differences between male and female sexuality that, if not well understood, can cause such tension in a relationship (we give a quick summary of these in the box on p. 319).

Reading is all very well, of course, but putting what you've learned into practice is what really counts. So work with your partner to make sex a priority, rather than something you fit in on the rare occasions when work and chores have been done and you both still have a modicum of energy.

Spontaneous sex can be great, but for many couples that's not very practical. So make a date: plan an evening together or a weekend without the kids. (Even a regular chat over a glass of wine will help keep intimacy alive.) Take turns to suggest new erotic techniques or scenarios. Tell your partner what turns you on – and specifically what you'd like them to do. And don't let things become stale; innovation is sexy!

Don't be afraid to ask for help
Simply following the advice we provide here will probably be enough to get your sex life back on track. But if things don't improve, do contact a sex therapist or relationship counsellor. Ask your GP for a recommendation.

If you're suffering from pain or discomfort during sex, let your doctor advise on treatment. For vaginismus, women are usually taught to insert dilators of gradually increasing size into their vagina. For pain, it's generally sensible to use lubrication and experiment with different positions and styles of intercourse (for example, with the woman on top or with the man thrusting less deeply). It's critical that you let your partner know how you feel and what they should and shouldn't do.

Related problems
Sexual problems rarely occur in isolation; in fact, they tend to be interrelated. It's not simply that women often have more than one sexual problem; they are also likely to be affected by any difficulties their partner is experiencing. Because of this, you may well find it helpful to read the whole of this entry.

Problems in other areas of life are also frequently a factor, especially **relationship difficulties**, **stress**, **depression**, and **trauma** (for example, **child abuse**).

Where to go for more information
These recommended books mostly focus on women's sexuality and sexual problems, but the title by McCarthy and Stoppard covers men's issues too:

For Yourself: The Fulfillment of Female Sexuality (Signet, 2000) by Lonnie Barbach; *Reclaiming Desire* (Rodale, 2004) by Andrew Goldstein and Marianne Brandon; *Rekindling Desire* (Taylor & Francis, 2003) by Barry and Emily McCarthy; *Women on Top* (Arrow, 2003) by Nancy Friday; *The V Book: A Doctor's Guide to Complete Vulvovaginal Health* (Bantam, 2002) by Elizabeth Stewart.

For sex tips – for women, men and couples – try:
Healthy Sex (Dorling Kindersley, 1998) by Miriam Stoppard; *Sensual Sex: A Lover's Manual* (Lorenz, 2007) by Judy Bastyra; *The Best Sex You'll Ever Have!* (Carlton, 2002) by Richard Emerson.

Also, check out the following websites:

- ⓘ www.sexualhealth.com (aimed at men as well as women)
- ⓘ www.hisandherhealth.com (a mass of sexual health information for men and women, together with links to other more specialized websites, for example on the menopause or gynaecological issues)
- ⓘ www.nva.org (the website of the US National Vulvodynia Association)

For sex aids, visit:
- ⓘ www.sh-womenstore.com
- ⓘ www.beecourse.com
- ⓘ www.touchofawomen.com

Men's Sexual Problems

Men want sex. If men ruled the world, they could get sex anywhere, any time. Restaurants would give you sex instead of breath mints on the way out. Gas stations would give sex with every fill-up. Banks would give sex to anyone who opened a checking account.
Scott Adams

In the following pages, we look at two of the most common male sexual problems: difficulties with erections and premature ejaculation.

However, we urge men to read through the discussion of women's sexual

Male and female sexuality: the differences

The news that there seem to be significant differences between men and women's attitudes to sex will come as a surprise to no one. But what exactly are those differences?

This was the question that psychologist Letitia Anne Peplau sought to answer when she reviewed the mass of scientific research on the subject. Bearing in mind that these are only general observations, and that many men and women won't fit these categorizations, here's what she concluded:

- **Men show greater sexual desire than women.** Men think about sex more often than women, report more sexual fantasies, and have more frequent feelings of sexual desire. Men tend to want sex more often than women, and are more likely to masturbate.
- **Women are more likely to view sex in the context of a committed relationship.** Women see sex as a way of building intimacy with their partner – as a romantic activity, in other words. For men, on the other hand, sex is more a matter of physical pleasure.
- **There's more of a link between sexuality and aggression for men than women.** Unlike women, sex for men is often an important way of asserting feelings of power, domination and even aggression. In heterosexual relationships, men are more likely to initiate sex and to play the lead role.
- **Women's sexuality is more flexible and changeable.** Women's sexual attitudes are more influenced by social and cultural factors and by their immediate life situation. For instance, a woman who's not in a relationship may have no sex at all, including masturbation; a man is less likely to alter his sexual behaviour. Peplau also reports increasing evidence to suggest that women are more likely than men to change their sexual orientation.

problems too. Why? Well, for a start, the division into male and female problems is a little artificial. Loss of sexual desire, arousal problems and pain during sex are more common in women, but they are far from unknown in men. (For example, each year 17 per cent of men will experience a loss of desire lasting a month or more. For 2 per cent of men, it will go on for at least six months.)

Difficulties with getting and maintaining an erection:
a personal account

I'd been having problems for a couple of years and my confidence was at rock bottom. I dreaded sex. My girlfriend and I never discussed it: we were both too embarrassed. But when we decided to start a family, we knew we couldn't keep muddling along as we were.

We ended up seeing a sex therapist. She thought my impotence was probably due to anxiety, and suggested that we start by not even attempting penetration for a few weeks. Instead we should spend time caressing, exploring each other's bodies and generally relaxing with each other. I think we were both a little nervous at first. But gradually, I began really looking forward to our sessions together. I stopped worrying about whether I'd have a strong enough erection to have proper intercourse. And I began to have erections while we were kissing and cuddling and touching one another. After about eight weeks, the therapist suggested that we try full inter-course and I discovered that, after all that time, I was actually able to perform like I wanted to.

Mike, aged 38

Because many of the problems affect both men and women, many of the strategies to overcome them are relevant to both. (Have a look in particular at our discussion above of sensate focus, masturbation, sexual fantasy, intimacy and non-demand pleasuring, and how to boost your enjoyment of sex.)

Then there's the fact that, if you're in a relationship, sexual problems are often interrelated. A man whose partner is finding it difficult to have an orgasm, for example, may feel intense pressure to perform and conse-quently struggle to achieve a strong erection. Women's sexuality shouldn't be off limits to men; on the contrary, the more you learn about it the better. Whatever the issue, if you're part of a couple, any sexual problems are best tackled as a couple.

Difficulties with Getting and Maintaining an Erection

There can be few problems that cause men as much shame, distress and embarrassment as difficulties with getting and keeping an erection. And this is one of the reasons why it can seem so tricky to talk about.

If you're having problems with erections, you'll know how depressing it can be. Not only is the pleasure and fulfilment of sex taken away, but it can feel as if your manhood has disappeared too. It doesn't help your relationship with your partner either – they can often feel rejected or hurt, and you lose the special intimacy that sex brings.

At a basic, physiological level, erections happen when blood flows faster into the penis than it does out. Signals from the brain and from the genitals relax the microscopic muscles surrounding the arteries into the penis. This makes the arteries expand, blood rushes in and the penis enlarges.

Well, that's how it's supposed to work. But a lot of factors can interfere with this delicate process, including:

- stress, anxiety, and depression
- bad sexual experiences in the past
- relationship problems
- alcohol
- medical problems, especially diabetes, cardiovascular disease (problems with the heart and blood vessels), hypertension (high blood pressure) and atherosclerosis (hardening of the arteries)
- medicines such as antidepressants and antihypertensives (drugs for high blood pressure).

Other names: these problems are often called impotence or erectile dysfunction (ED).

How common are difficulties with getting and maintaining an erection?

Short-term difficulties with getting or keeping an erection are very common, but for around 15–20 per cent of men it's a persistent, significant problem. The risk increases with age:

Age range	Percentage affected
20–39	5
40–59	15
60–69	44
70 and above	70

If you're concerned about this aspect of your sex life, try the self-assessment exercise below. But it's worth bearing in mind that even in healthy men the way this part of our body works changes with age. The older we get, the longer it takes to achieve an erection – and the more physical stimulation is needed. Erections are generally weaker, ejaculations are less powerful and the amount of ejaculate decreases. It also takes longer until we're ready for another erection.

Self-assessment

When you answer the following five questions think back to your experience over the past six months.

How do you rate your confidence that you could get and keep an erection?

Very low	Low	Moderate	High	Very high
1	2	3	4	5

When you had erections with sexual stimulation, how often were your erections hard enough for penetration?

Never or almost never	Much less than half the time	About half the time	Most times	Always or almost always
1	2	3	4	5

During sexual intercourse, how often were you able to maintain your erection after you entered your partner?

Never or almost never	Much less than half the time	About half the time	Most times	Always or almost always
1	2	3	4	5

During sexual intercourse, how difficult was it to maintain your erection until intercourse was complete?

Extremely difficult	Very difficult	Difficult	Slightly difficult	Not difficult
1	2	3	4	5

When you attempted intercourse, how often was it satisfactory for you?

Never or almost never	Much less than half the time	About half the time	Most times	Always or almost always
1	2	3	4	5

© Rosen, R. C., Cappelleri, J. C., Smith, M.D., Lipsky, J. & Peña, B. M. (1999). Development and evaluation of an abridged, 5-item version of the International Index of Erectile Function (IIEF-5) as a diagnostic tool for erectile dysfunction. *International Journal of Impotence Research*, 11, 319–26

Now add up the scores for your answers. A score of 22–25 indicates no problems. A score of 17–21 suggests you might be mildly affected. If you scored 12–16, you might have mild to moderate problems. A score of 8–11 indicates moderate problems and 5–7 suggests you might be severely affected.

How to Overcome Difficulties with Getting and Maintaining an Erection

The good news is that there are now a number of very effective treatments, ranging from medication to the sorts of ideas we list here.

Talk things over with your GP

If you think you might have a problem, your first step should be to see your GP so that any clear physical causes can be ruled out.

Men often have erections when they wake up or as they fall asleep. If you don't, or if you can't achieve an erection through masturbation, there may be a very clear physical cause.

If you can manage an erection sometimes, it's probably not a simple physical issue – though you should still start with your GP. The techniques we recommend here usually help whatever the cause.

Of course talking about this sort of intimate issue with someone else can be difficult, so you might want to rehearse what you want to say beforehand.

Over the past few years a number of very effective drug treatments have come on to the market: sildenafil (better known by the trade names Viagra and Revatio), tadalafil (Cialis), verdenafil (Levitra) and apomorphine (Uprima).

They work by helping the normal sexual process – so they won't give you erections when you're not aroused. There can be side effects, such as headaches, and it's best to combine medication with the techniques below. In fact, these other techniques can often sort out the problem without you needing to take medication.

Incidentally, hormone treatment isn't generally recommended for difficulties with erections unless you have a hormone deficiency, which isn't a common cause of this sort of problem. In most cases, taking hormones will increase your sexual desire but won't improve your ability to have an erection.

Look after yourself

Being in good physical shape can make a big difference. Eat well, cut out smoking, get plenty of sleep and take regular exercise.

Try to reduce your stress levels and make time for your sex life, whether it's masturbation, sexual thoughts or intercourse. And limit your alcohol intake: as Shakespeare wrote, 'It provokes the desire, but it takes away the performance.'

Focus on pleasure, not performance

Being anxious can have a really negative effect on your ability to have an erection. And sex is an area that provokes a lot of anxiety. Will I please my partner? What if the contraception doesn't work? Am I going to catch a sexually transmitted disease?

On your bike?

Cycling is undergoing a renaissance, with more and more of us getting on our bikes for pleasure, exercise or to beat the traffic jams on the way to work. Cycling is fun, environmentally friendly and has lots of positive effects on our health.

But recent research has shown that riding a bike can lead to difficulties with erections – in fact, if you cycle for more than three hours a week you're twice as likely to have problems.

The reason is simple: the saddle. Sitting on most regular saddles temporarily reduces blood flow to the penis and can damage or even block some of the blood vessels.

Fortunately, you can minimize the chances of developing these problems by making a few changes to your bike:

- Switch to a 'noseless' saddle.
- Try not to lean forwards when you cycle. The more upright you are, the better.
- Use a saddle that has gel padding.
- Tilt the saddle downwards.

Particularly problematic is 'performance anxiety' in which people become so worried about whether they're good in bed that they become totally focused on their erection and sexual technique. Instead of getting lost in the pleasure of the moment, they seem to hover above it, constantly assessing their own performance.

If you're prone to this kind of anxiety, you need to switch your focus. Concentrate on pleasure, not performance. Even if you don't manage an erection, there is still plenty of enjoyment to be had from a sexual experience.

Relax and shift your attention from your penis to the rest of your body. And go easy on yourself: remember that your body isn't going to be as responsive as it was when you were a teenager. It might take longer to get an erection, but that's normal. Good sex is all about taking the time.

Try the following exercise to improve your erections and build up your confidence:

1. Find somewhere comfortable and spend a few minutes getting really relaxed – have a shower if that helps or try a relaxation

exercise. Take the phone off the hook and make sure you give yourself all the time you need.

2. Start by stroking and gently touching your penis and scrotum.

3. As you begin to feel your erection grow, focus your thoughts on what it feels like.

4. Once you're fully erect, allow your erection to go away. Use whatever form of distraction works for you until you're completely soft.

5. Repeat twice more. You can get quite close to ejaculation before you let your erection soften.

6. Repeat once more, but on this occasion continuing stroking yourself until you ejaculate.

Once you've done this exercise successfully a few times, try using a lubricant. This will make it feel a little more as if you were with a partner.

Exercise your pelvic floor

This is a great way to strengthen the muscles around the penis and increase the blood flow – making for stronger erections. The pelvic floor consists of a number of muscles running beneath the pelvis. You can feel these muscles by imagining you're urinating and then trying to stop the flow, or by trying to stop yourself passing wind.

1. Sit, stand, or lie with your knees slightly apart. Slowly squeeze your pelvic floor muscles, hold for five seconds, and then release. Do this 15 times.

2. Repeat, but this time don't hold for five seconds: let go immediately.

3. Once you've got the hang of the fast and slow exercises, try mixing them up.

4. Practise the exercises every day. You don't need to take time out – you can do your exercises while you're waiting for the bus, doing the ironing or watching TV.

It may take a few months to feel the difference, but stick with these exercises; it'll be worth it in the end.

Involve your partner

Relationship problems can really affect your sexual performance. You need to feel completely comfortable with your partner, so make sure you address any issues in your relationship that you think might be damaging your sex life.

If your relationship is strong, but you're having problems with your erections, make sure you involve your partner. It's not an easy issue to discuss, of course – you may feel embarrassed and ashamed. All too often, men close up emotionally when they can't get an erection.

But if you can share your thoughts and feelings with your partner, you'll deepen the intimacy and trust between you. Decide together how the two of you will deal with the situation if you can't manage an erection. Talk through the ways you can both still enjoy sex.

Plan sexual encounters where intercourse is forbidden – try sensual touching and non-genital pleasuring, genital touching, oral sex and talking in a sexual way. You could begin with 15–30 minutes of gentle sensual touching, and then let your partner gently touch your genitals and penis. Give yourself at least 5 to 10 minutes for an erection to begin. Try letting your partner do the masturbation exercise for you. And you can return the favour.

Related problems

Men often find it difficult to have strong erections when they're suffering with **depression**, **stress** or **anxiety**, or experiencing **relationship problems**. Not surprisingly, with a **loss of sexual desire** there are also problems with getting erections.

Where to go for more information

Coping with Erectile Dysfunction: How to Regain Confidence and Enjoy Great Sex by Michael Metz and Barry McCarthy (New Harbinger, 2004) is an excellent source of thorough, professional advice.

Also recommended is Philip Kell and Wallace Dinsmore's clear and sensible *Impotence: A Guide for Men of All Ages* (Royal Society of Medicine Press, 2001).

ⓘ www.impotence.org.uk and
ⓘ www.informed.org.uk are useful sources of information.

PREMATURE EJACULATION

Premature ejaculation is the most common sexual problem faced by men and it can cause real misery. Apart from the damage to men's self-esteem, and the anxiety and depression that can follow, premature ejaculation can put significant strain on relationships. Assuming a man is in a relationship,

Problems with premature ejaculation: a personal account

I always suspected that I was coming too soon, but I didn't really know what was normal. How long was I supposed to last? I never dared discuss it with any of my girlfriends (beyond the occasional mumbled apology), and they didn't mention it either (except for sometimes telling me kindly that 'it didn't matter' – which of course only made me feel that it did). I was pretty miserable about the whole thing, to be honest. And it used to make me very nervous about going to bed with people. Thankfully, the person I ended up marrying was much braver than me! She helped me to talk about our sex life and very cleverly suggested we each think of one change that might improve it. Of course, I said that I'd like to last longer. The next day she came home with a couple of books and we started practising there and then!

Chris, aged 32

that is; the shame of premature ejaculation can be enough to put men off looking for a partner.

But what is premature ejaculation? Coming too soon, for sure. But what's too soon? There's no easy answer to this question; ultimately, it's a personal judgement. Here's how premature ejaculation is defined in the textbooks: 'Persistent or recurrent ejaculation with minimal sexual stimulation before, on, or after penetration and before the person wishes it.'

Essentially, if you're consistently ejaculating quicker than you'd like, and if it's causing you and/or your partner distress, you probably have a problem.

But you need to have realistic expectations; performing for hours on end like some porn star isn't normal (or even, in most cases, much fun). In fact, research has shown that the average time from the start of intercourse to ejaculation is five and a half minutes. So you may not be coming particularly quickly after all!

The causes of premature ejaculation aren't well understood, but a number of factors can certainly exacerbate it. Anxiety about sexual performance is often involved, and of course this can easily set up a vicious circle: you're worried about coming too quickly, which makes it more likely that you will, which only increases your anxiety, and so on. Men are also more likely to ejaculate prematurely if they're young, in a new relationship, highly sexually aroused or haven't had sex for a long time.

At the opposite end of the spectrum, some men find it difficult to ejaculate at all. This relatively rare problem is known as 'male orgasmic disorder', EjD, or retarded/inhibited ejaculation. Generally men with the disorder are able to ejaculate through masturbation; it's orgasm in intercourse that is either very delayed or totally absent – and you can imagine the frustration, anxiety and relationship difficulties that can result.

How common is premature ejaculation?

Around a third of men say that they ejaculate too quickly at least half the time. Twelve per cent report problems lasting at least a month in the past year and 3 per cent have suffered from premature ejaculation for at least six of the previous 12 months. Tellingly, only 9 per cent of men with this extremely common problem talk to their doctor about it.

Self-assessment

All men sometimes ejaculate sooner than they'd like, so when you answer the following questions think about your general experience: it's what sex is normally like for you that's important, not occasional problems.

1. How difficult is it for you to delay ejaculation?

Not difficult at all	Somewhat difficult	Moderately difficult	Very difficult	Extremely difficult
0	1	2	3	4

2. Do you ejaculate before you want to?

Almost never or never	Less than half the time	About half the time	More than half the time	Almost always or always
0	1	2	3	4

3. Do you ejaculate with very little stimulation?

Almost never or never	Less than half the time	About half the time	More than half the time	Almost always or always
0	1	2	3	4

4. Do you feel frustrated because of ejaculating before you want to?

Not at all	Slightly	Moderately	Very	Extremely
0	1	2	3	4

5. How concerned are you that your time to ejaculation leaves your partner sexually unfulfilled?

Not at all	Slightly	Moderately	Very	Extremely
0	1	2	3	4

© Pfizer (2007)

A total score of 8 or less suggests all is well. If you've scored 9 or 10, you probably suffer from premature ejaculation, and a total of 11 or more indicates that it's very likely.

How to Overcome Problems with Premature Ejaculation

Most men never seek help with premature ejaculation, which is a real shame since there are many effective ways of treating the problem, as we'll see now.

Talk to your doctor

This should be your first step. Premature ejaculation isn't usually caused by physiological problems, but it can be (lower urinary tract infections or the side effects of some medications, for example, are occasionally to blame).

Get to know your 'point of inevitability'

As all men know, once a certain level of excitement is reached there's no way back! (It's very different for women, whose orgasms can stall at the very last moment.) That irresistible level of excitement is known as the point of inevitability; if you can learn to identify this, along with the feelings leading up to it, you'll also be able to delay it – and, with it, ejaculation.

Many of the strategies we outline below – and especially the next one – are designed to help you understand your point of inevitability.

Practise the stop–start masturbation exercise

(This is similar to the exercise we recommend for erection problems on p. 325.)

1. Find somewhere comfortable and spend a few minutes getting really relaxed – have a shower if that helps, or try a relaxation exercise. Take the phone off the hook and make sure you give yourself all the time you need.
2. Start by stroking and gently touching your penis and scrotum.
3. As you begin to feel your erection grow and your arousal build, focus your thoughts on what it feels like.
4. Before you ejaculate, stop stroking. The idea is to reduce your excitement but not so much that you lose your erection.
5. Start stroking yourself again, and again stop before ejaculation.
6. Do this one more time and then allow yourself to ejaculate.

When you're confident doing the exercise, try to prevent your orgasm not by stopping stroking, but by changing the way you touch yourself. Perhaps slow down, or use less pressure; try a different style of stroking, or focus on another part of your penis.

Don't be discouraged if it takes a while to master this exercise; it's definitely worth persisting. When you feel ready to move on, try doing the exercise using a lubricant. This will make it feel a little more like being with a partner.

Once you've got that sorted, it's time for the real thing. All sexual problems are best tackled as a couple, and premature ejaculation is no exception. Begin with the stop–start exercise, but this time let your partner masturbate you.

Finally, and only when you're confident with the previous stages, try the exercise while having intercourse. It's best if your partner is on top, or if you're side by side (controlling ejaculation is especially difficult in the 'missionary' position). Get close to the point of inevitability and then slow down. Breathing deeply, making your thrusts shallower or moving your pelvis in a circular motion can also help.

If the desire to come is really overwhelming, try squeezing your penis just below the head (or glans). It can take a bit of practice to get this right, but eventually you'll find that squeezing for several seconds will be enough for the urge to ejaculate to pass.

Aim for the mid-range of arousal

If we think of arousal as a scale from 0 to 10, then the point of inevitability is 9. What you need to practise is spending as much time as you can in the mid-range (5–7) of the scale.

Some men find it helps to reduce sexual stimulation if they use certain types of condoms, or anaesthetic creams, gels and sprays. But these aren't long-term solutions. The best way to prolong the mid-range of arousal is to become really familiar with your feelings of arousal, and to learn to slow down when things are moving too fast. The stop–start exercise above will go a long way to helping you achieve this.

Focus on pleasure, not performance

Worrying about your sexual performance is almost guaranteed to cause problems. There's such enormous pressure on men to live up to mythical performance standards that taking an alternative view requires a conscious effort – and a good deal of courage. But your sex life will be all the better if you can shift your focus from performance to pleasure.

To this end, explore the possibilities of sensate focus (see p. 313). Despite the impression we may receive from films and books, sex is definitely not all about penetration and orgasm. And remember that your partner is almost certain to welcome an emphasis on foreplay and non-penetrative sex. After all, most women don't reach orgasm through intercourse; erotic use of your fingers or mouth is much more likely to bring her to climax.

Exercise your pelvic floor muscles

The more relaxed you can keep your pelvic floor muscles during sex, the more control you'll have over ejaculation. For details of how to exercise these muscles, see p. 326.

Medication and other approaches

The newer SSRI antidepressants (most famously Prozac) are often helpful in combating premature ejaculation. But they have side effects, and they don't work for everyone. Perhaps most importantly, they aren't a cure: once men stop taking the drug, their premature ejaculation usually returns.

If the strategies we describe above aren't working for you, do think about visiting a sex therapist, alone if you prefer, but ideally with your partner.

Related problems

Like the other issues we cover in this entry, premature ejaculation is often linked to other sexual problems, including those experienced by a female partner. For this reason, it's worth reading through the whole of this entry.

Premature ejaculation is also often associated with **depression**, **stress** and **anxiety**.

Where to go for more information

Premature ejaculation is discussed in several of the books we recommend in this entry, but if you're looking for a volume that focuses entirely on the issue try *Coping with Premature Ejaculation* (New Harbinger, 2003) by Michael Metz and Barry McCarthy.

Sleep Problems

> *Blessed be whoever invented sleep, the mantle that covers all*
> *human thought, the food that satisfies hunger, the water that*
> *quenches thirst, the fire that warms the cold, the cold that*
> *cools down ardour, and, finally, the general coin with which*
> *all things are bought, the scale and the balance that make the*
> *shepherd equal to the king, and the simple man equal to the*
> *wise.*
> Cervantes, *Don Quixote*

Anyone who has ever had to suffer a sleepless night (in other words every-one!) will know just how disruptive it can be. The following day you're tired, irritable and generally out of sorts. And the longer sleep problems go on, the more wretched you feel. Unfortunately, increasing numbers of people aren't getting the sleep they need – indeed, some experts argue that most of us are running a 'sleep debt'.

In this entry we look at the most common sleep problems, focusing on insomnia but also taking in nightmares, sleepwalking, snoring and sleep apnoea (a breathing disorder), narcolepsy and restless legs syndrome.

The advice we provide here will be enough for many readers to over-come their sleep problems. But if you need more help, don't hesitate to speak to your GP. If necessary, they'll be able to refer you to a specialist sleep clinic. In some cases, the only way to get a clear picture of the prob-lem is to watch you sleep overnight, and these clinics are equipped to do this. And because sleep problems can be the result of physical or psycho-logical issues (and often a combination of both), sleep clinics often include professionals from a range of backgrounds, for example: neurologists (brain and nervous system specialists), pulmonologists (respiratory experts) and psychologists (often specialist behavioural sleep medicine therapists).

Because sleep problems tend to be interrelated, you'll find suggestions on where to look for more information in one section at the very end of the entry. If you're concerned about your child's sleep, check out the section on pp. 157–64. But let's start with a general self-assessment questionnaire.

Self-assessment

It's normal to have times when you don't sleep as well as you'd like, but how can you tell whether you have a real sleep problem? The following questionnaire is a good place to start.

Part A	Not at all	Some-what	Quite a lot	Very much
Insomnia				
1. I find it difficult to fall asleep.	1	2	3	4
2. Thoughts go through my head and keep me awake.	1	2	3	4
3. I worry and find it hard to relax.	1	2	3	4
4. I wake up during the night.	1	2	3	4
5. After waking up during the night, I fall asleep slowly.	1	2	3	4
6. I wake up early and cannot get back to sleep.	1	2	3	4
7. I sleep lightly.	1	2	3	4
8. I sleep too little.	1	2	3	4
9. Generally, I sleep badly.	1	2	3	4
Total score for insomnia section:				
Nightmares				
1. I have frightening dreams.	1	2	3	4
2. I wake up from these dreams.	1	2	3	4

3. I remember the content of these dreams.	1	2	3	4
4. I can orientate quickly after these dreams.	1	2	3	4
Total score for nightmares section:				

Sleepwalking	Not at all	Some-what	Quite a lot	Very much
1. I sometimes walk when I am sleeping.	1	2	3	4
2. I sometimes wake up in a different place than where I fell asleep.	1	2	3	4
3. I sometimes find evidence of having performed an action during the night I do not remember.	1	2	3	4
Total score for sleepwalking section:				

Sleep apnoea

1. I am told that I snore.	1	2	3	4
2. I sweat during the night.	1	2	3	4
3. I am told that I hold my breath when sleeping.	1	2	3	4
4. I am told that I wake up gasping for air.	1	2	3	4
5. I wake up with a dry mouth.	1	2	3	4
6. I wake up during the night while coughing or being short of breath.	1	2	3	4
7. I wake up with a sour taste in my mouth.	1	2	3	4
8. I wake up with a headache.	1	2	3	4

Total score for sleep apnoea section:				
Narcolepsy	Not at all	Some-what	Quite a lot	Very much
1. I see dreamlike images when falling asleep or waking up.	1	2	3	4
2. I sometimes fall asleep at a social occasion.	1	2	3	4
3. I have sleep attacks during the day.	1	2	3	4
4. With intense emotions, my muscles sometimes collapse during the day.	1	2	3	4
5. I sometimes cannot move when falling asleep or waking up.	1	2	3	4
Total score for narcolepsy section:				

Restless legs and periodic limb movements

	Not at all	Some-what	Quite a lot	Very much
1. I am told that I kick my legs when I am asleep.	1	2	3	4
2. I have cramps or pain in my legs during the night.	1	2	3	4
3. I feel little shocks in my legs during the night.	1	2	3	4
4. I cannot keep my legs at rest when falling asleep.	1	2	3	4
Total score for restless legs and periodic limb movements section:				
Part B	Not at all	Some-what	Quite a lot	Very much
1. I feel tired when I get up.	1	2	3	4
2. I feel sleepy during the day and struggle to remain alert.	1	2	3	4

3. I would like to have more energy during the day.	1	2	3	4
4. People tell me I'm easily irritated.	1	2	3	4
5. I have difficulty concentrating at work or school.	1	2	3	4
6. I worry whether I sleep enough.	1	2	3	4
7. I have sleep attacks (i.e. suddenly feeling very sleepy) during the day.	1	2	3	4
Total score for Part B:				

Reprinted by permission of the publisher (Taylor & Francis Ltd). Spoormaker, V. I., Verbeek, I., van den Bout, J., & Klip, E. C. (2005). Initial validation of the SLEEP-50 questionnaire. *Behavioural Sleep Medicine*, 3, 227–46.

Now add up your scores for Parts A and B. For both parts, the lower your score, the less severe your sleep problems.

Part A focuses on specific problems; Part B is designed to gauge their impact on you.

Insomnia
You may be suffering from insomnia if you've scored:

19 or more on Part A and

15 or more on Part B.

Nightmares
A serious problem is likely if you've scored:

3 or 4 on question 1 or a total of 9 or more on questions 2–4 of Part A and

15 or more on Part B.

Sleepwalking, narcolepsy, and restless legs and periodic limb movements
A serious problem is likely if you've scored:

7 or more on Part A and

15 or more on Part B.

Sleep apnoea
A serious problem is likely if you've scored:

15 or more on Part A and

15 or more on Part B.

INSOMNIA

....

The worst thing in the world is to try to sleep and not be able to.
F. Scott Fitzgerald

....

Insomnia is a general term for a number of sleep problems that include:

- finding it difficult to fall asleep
- finding it hard to stay asleep
- not having enough sleep
- not having enough good-quality sleep.

As well as making your nights a misery, insomnia can mean that it's harder to function properly during the day. Sufferers often feel exhausted. They find it hard to concentrate and have low energy levels. Not surprisingly, people with insomnia often feel miserable, depressed and irritable.

If your sleeplessness has been going on for a long time, and if it's causing significant problems for you, you may be suffering from what doctors call clinical insomnia.

The signs of clinical insomnia are:

- taking longer than half an hour to fall asleep
- experiencing these problems several nights a week
- experiencing these problems for more than a month
- finding it really difficult to function during the day.

People with clinical insomnia often find they are lying awake worrying instead of sleeping. They might worry about their health, their work or their relationships, for example. But they also worry about their insomnia – how long they've been awake; how tired or awake they feel; how they'll feel the next day.

Clinical insomnia doesn't do much for people's relationships either. Even assuming your partner isn't kept awake by your tossing and turning, things are bound to be difficult when you're so tired and stressed.

Other names for insomnia: people often describe their experiences of insomnia as sleeplessness, or talk about problems sleeping.

How common is insomnia?

Insomnia is extremely common and most of us, at some point in our lives, will experience it. Studies have shown that, on any given night, one in three people will be struggling with it. And women are twice as likely to be affected as men. Ten per cent of people have clinical insomnia.

If you find yourself sleeping less than you did in the past, one factor to bear in mind is that your sleep requirements do change as you age. The older you get, the less sleep – and the less really deep sleep – you need.

Age	Average amount of sleep needed
Birth–2 months	10.5–18 hours
2–12 months	14–15 hours
12–18 months	13–15 hours
18 months–3 years	12–14 hours
3–5 years	11–13 hours
5–12 years	9–11 hours
Teenagers	8–10 hours
Adults (18–65)	7–9 hours
Older adults (65 and above)	6–7 hours

How to Overcome Insomnia

Insomnia is like hiccups. Everybody has a cure but none of them work.
Bob Dylan

Right in so many things, we're happy to say that Bob is wrong in this case. Here are several, tried-and-tested ways to overcome your insomnia, no matter how severe it is.

Exercise every day

We all know that exercise is good for our health, but all too often we forget the great effect it has on our sleep. Exercise tires you out. And if you're tired, you're likely to sleep better. (Don't exercise late in the evening though:

you'll just feel more awake.)

Avoid caffeine, alcohol, and nicotine in the evening

Caffeine and nicotine are stimulants, which means they'll keep you awake. Alcohol will probably make it easier to fall asleep, but it interferes with the natural stages of sleep. If you've drunk a lot, you're also likely to wake up feeling thirsty or unwell. All in all, you won't sleep as deeply or as long as you will if you haven't been drinking alcohol.

Develop a relaxing evening routine

If you go straight to bed after being busy with something, your mind will be buzzing with whatever it was you were doing. So at least half an hour before bedtime, begin winding down. Avoid the temptation to check your email one last time, or surf the Internet – and stay clear of computer games. Instead, do something calm and relaxing: maybe have a warm bath or spend some time reading. Try listening to gentle music or doing a relaxation exercise.

Have a bedtime snack

This one might seem a bit surprising, but a little bit of food about half an hour before bed can help with sleep. Make it something healthy and relatively plain: a glass of milk, a banana or maybe a piece of wholemeal toast. Don't eat too much: your body won't be able to rest if it has to digest a four-course meal.

Make your sleeping environment a good one

You've probably discovered how difficult it is to sleep well if your bed's uncomfortable or if there's a lot of noise outside or if it's too light. So make sure your bedroom is set up with whatever you need for a good night's sleep.

Follow basic sleep rules

Stick with the above techniques and chances are you'll soon see a big improvement in your sleep patterns. But if things aren't getting better, add in these sleep rules – they should make a positive difference within a few days:

Cut out daytime naps

Naps during the day will only make you feel less tired at night. But be careful if you need to be especially alert during the day – for example if you're driving or operating machinery. In these instances, it's best to grab whatever sleep you need to stay safe.

Learn to associate your bed with sleep

We're creatures of habit. If you use your bed for all kinds of non-sleep related activities – reading, eating, watching TV, writing a diary – your body will expect to be awake and alert when you go to bed. Instead, you need to train your body to start winding down for sleep the moment you get into bed. So do all those other things beforehand, and use your bed only for sleep and sex.

Only go to bed when you're tired

You need to minimize the time you spend in bed before falling asleep. It's part of the process of teaching your body that bed means sleep.

If you aren't asleep within 20 minutes, get up and do something else

Try to do something relaxing – listening to calming music or reading a book. It's the same if you wake up in the night: if you haven't fallen back to sleep after 20 minutes, get up and only go back to bed when you're feeling tired.

Don't lie in

This doesn't sound much fun, but it's important to get up at the same time each morning rather than trying to 'catch up' on sleep. Stick to this rule even at weekends.

Don't make bedtime 'worry time'

Many people find they're kept awake by worrying. If this happens to you, try using 'worry periods'. Save up all your worrying for a daily 30-minute worry period – and don't pick bedtime! Let go of your worries for now and deal with them in your next worry period.

When you start your new regime of only going to bed when you're tired and getting up at the same time every morning, you may find that you feel sleepy during the day. That's normal: it's a sign that your body is adjusting to the changes.

Don't give in to the temptation to have a nap in the day or go to bed really early. If you're tired at your normal bedtime, that's great: it'll help you get to sleep. Within a few days, you'll find that your body has got used to your new sleep pattern – and your sleeping will be all the better for it.

Problems with insomnia: a personal account

I t used to take me at least an hour, and usually more, to get to sleep at night. As soon as I closed my eyes, my brain seemed to go into overdrive. I'd find myself thinking about all kinds of nonsense, but mostly it was worries – really trivial stuff, on the whole, but it seemed crucial at the time. It got so bad that I dreaded going to bed. I even tried sleeping on the sofa and on a mattress on the floor but it made no difference. It took me so long to get to sleep that I found it almost impossible to wake up in the morning. I used two alarm clocks and the alarm on my mobile phone but often I'd sleep through them all. I was late to work so frequently I was convinced I'd be sacked. And I was tired all the time, not to mention grumpy and forgetful. I was so exhausted that the slightest setback would have me nearly in tears.

Carrie, aged 28

Sleeping pills and other remedies

The prospect of being able to get a good night's sleep just by taking a pill is a tempting one for many people. Sleeping pills (for example, zopicline or temazepam) can be useful for very short periods, but we don't recommend them as a long-term solution. Your body will get used to the pills, and you'll find them less effective as a result. Sleeping pills also tend to be addictive, which means that stopping them can be difficult.

Your doctor may suggest that you take an antidepressant drug. If you're feeling particularly down, depression may be contributing to your insomnia. But some antidepressants (for example, amitriptyline and trazodone) are sometimes prescribed because they make people sleepy.

Be aware though that prescribing antidepressants to people who aren't depressed is a controversial approach – we don't yet have the research to prove whether it's effective or not.

Incidentally, a number of physical problems and illnesses can make it hard to sleep and you should talk to your doctor about these. Angina, asthma, indigestion and bladder problems all often cause insomnia. Women can suffer disturbed sleep during pregnancy or with the menopause, and sometimes before or during their period.

Instead of sleeping pills, people often try over-the-counter remedies like Nytol or Sleep-Eze from the chemist. Most of these contain antihistamines and, though they can be helpful for a few nights, they can make you feel drowsy the next day. You'll also find that they don't work so well if you take them for an extended time; just like sleeping pills, your body will get used to them.

Health shops stock a variety of natural remedies (such as valerian, chamomile, and lavender). Unfortunately, there's no conclusive evidence that these work.

Many people believe drinking warm milk helps combat insomnia. Again, the hard scientific evidence to back this up isn't yet there. But we do know

---

Which animal needs the least sleep? – and other curious facts about sleep and sleeplessness ...

- If you're having problems sleeping, spare a thought for the giraffe. Always on the lookout for predators, giraffes sleep deeply for only about 30 minutes a day, usually broken up into five-minute naps. Giraffes get the least sleep of any mammal. At the other end of the spectrum, bats sleep for 20 hours a day, and pythons get a solid 18 hours. Interestingly, dolphins sleep with one half of their brain awake so they can carry on swimming.
- How long could you go without sleep? The world record is 11 days (264 hours), set in 1964 by Randy Gardner, a 17-year-old schoolboy from California, whose friends worked in shifts to keep him awake. Having set the record, Gardner slept for 15 hours.
- Twenty per cent of car accidents are caused by sleepiness – more than those caused by alcohol.
- In 1963 artist Andy Warhol made *Sleep*, a five-hour film showing John Giorno sleeping – and nothing else. Its usefulness in combating insomnia has not yet been tested ...

---

that warm milk contains high levels of tryptophan, which is a natural sedative. Adding honey to the milk is said to help the body absorb the tryptophan more quickly.

NIGHTMARES

Why nightmares occur is a question that still baffles experts. A theory that can probably be ruled out, however, is the one that gave these troubling dreams their name: that nightmares are caused by a demon crouching on you while you sleep ('mare' being the Old English word for demon).

These highly visual, and often very frightening or upsetting, dreams are a product of REM sleep (a relatively light form of sleep characterized by rapid eye movements – hence the name). As such, they tend to occur more often in the second half of the night. People can frequently recall their nightmares in great detail. Certainly, the unpleasant emotions they trigger – typically fear and anxiety, but sometimes anger, grief or sadness – can linger long after the individual has woken. (Strictly speaking, to qualify as a nightmare a bad dream must wake you up.)

If you're experiencing frequent nightmares, and they're causing you a lot of distress or interfering with your day-to-day life, you may be suffering from nightmare disorder.

Sometimes people may scream or struggle or yell, and wake up with their heart pounding, their body drenched in sweat and gripped by a vague but extremely powerful sense of panic. This can seem like a nightmare, but it may actually be a night or sleep terror.

Sleep terrors usually occur during deep, non-REM sleep (so it's unlikely that they're caused by nightmares). And if the person wakes up because of the terror – and they often don't, even if a partner tries to rouse them – they can't remember it, though they're generally confused and disorientated. The most severe form of night terrors is known as sleep terror disorder.

How common are nightmares?

Just about everyone has experienced a nightmare at some point of their lives, especially during childhood. Three per cent of adults have them at least weekly, and 10 per cent every month.

Night terrors are rare, affecting fewer than 1 per cent of adults.

How to Cope with Nightmares

If you're struggling with nightmares, the good news is that a treatment has been developed specifically to help people cope with this problem. It's called imagery rehearsal and you can do it yourself, without the aid of a therapist.

Essentially, you need to retell the story of your nightmare. But this time you're in charge and you can change the story any way you like. So you might remove a particularly unpleasant event or a threatening person, or introduce a friendly face or a happy ending. Then spend a few minutes every day running through this new version in your mind. Gradually, you'll find that the events of your nightmare become much less disturbing.

Besides imagery rehearsal, there are a number of other strategies you can use to deal with nightmares:

Improve the quality of your sleep

One of the factors that can trigger nightmares is poor sleep. It can be a vicious circle: nightmares interfere with your sleep, making you more susceptible to further nightmares. You'll find tips on how to improve your sleep and cope with disturbed nights in the insomnia entry above.

Deal with external stresses and problems

Nightmares often seem to occur when you're very stressed or anxious or low. They're also a common reaction to traumatic life events. If you can overcome these issues, the chances are your nightmares will disappear. (You'll find lots of information on all these problems elsewhere in this book.)

Certain types of medication can also prompt nightmares – for example, beta blockers (used to treat high blood pressure and heart problems) and the SSRI antidepressant paroxetine. If you think this might be the reason for your nightmares, have a chat with your GP.

Treatment of sleep terrors isn't well developed, but the strategies we suggest to deal with nightmares (with the exception of image rehearsal) are thought to be beneficial for terrors too.

Sleepwalking

Sleepwalking – or somnambulism, to use the technical term – is one of the most remarkable and dramatic forms of sleep problem. Anyone who's watched a partner or family member make their way, zombie-like, around the bedroom and perhaps even down the stairs and out the front door, will know just how bizarre and unsettling sleepwalking can be to witness.

Not that the sleepwalker is aware of it. Sleepwalking – like night terrors – happens during the deep, so-called non-REM sleep. This is why sleepwalkers are so difficult to wake, and why, in the morning, they usually have no memory of their nocturnal wanderings. It also means that when people sleepwalk they're probably not acting out a dream: you dream during relatively lighter REM sleep. (Because children get more deep sleep than adults, it's no surprise that they're much more likely to sleepwalk and suffer night terrors.)

Sleepwalking is generally pretty low-key – perhaps a few minutes' movement and then back into bed. That said, sometimes the episodes last longer and the individual can perform quite complex actions (getting dressed or unlocking the door, for example). Their eyes may be open, they may talk – even responding to questions in some cases. But they are clearly not awake: the sleepwalker's movements are clumsy and slow, their facial expression blank and their speech confused.

If a person is sleepwalking frequently, and it's causing them distress or interfering with their day-to-day life, a doctor might diagnose sleepwalking disorder. But things don't need to reach this stage for sleepwalking to cause problems: moving around while asleep can lead to serious accidents.

How common is sleepwalking?

Lots of children sleepwalk (see pp. 163–4), but relatively few adults do. Only 0.4 per cent of adults sleepwalk at least once a week, though 2–3 per cent may take an occasional midnight stroll. Most of these adults were sleepwalkers as kids.

Sleepwalking seems to run (so to speak) in families. If a first-degree relative sleepwalks, you're 10 times more likely than other people to do the same.

How to Cope with Sleepwalking

There are a number of steps you should take if you or a loved one sleepwalk.

Be safe

Your number-one priority is to ensure that the environment is as safe as possible. That means, for example, moving any objects that might cause

Problems with nightmares: a personal account

For years I went through periods – generally a week or two but occasionally longer – during which I had at least one nightmare a night. They were usually very upsetting: a regular one involved my husband being diagnosed with a terminal illness; in another, I was in a terrible car crash. I'd wake up absolutely grief-stricken; sometimes I'd be sobbing. And the memory stayed with me for hours, as if the experience in the dream was real. But gradually I've realized that these periods coincide exactly with when I'm at my most stressed and most tired. Working that out has made a big difference. Whenever I feel things are getting on top of me, I make a conscious effort to get plenty of sleep and to relax. Then the nightmares either don't materialize or, if they do, they're much less distressing and far less frequent.
Jan, aged 42

the sleepwalker to trip, restricting access to the stairs and closing potentially dangerous windows.

Don't wake a sleepwalker ...

... unless they're about to hurt themselves. Instead, gently guide them back into bed. Rousing a sleepwalker isn't dangerous; but people who wake up while sleepwalking can be groggy, confused and sometimes distressed.

Identify the triggers

Why people sleepwalk isn't well understood by scientists, but a number of common triggers have been identified – for example, stress, alcohol, exhaustion, fever and certain medications (such as Zolpidem, which – ironically – is often prescribed to treat insomnia). If you can work out your own sleepwalking triggers, you can modify your behaviour accordingly.

Get as much good-quality sleep as you can

Lack of sleep is often a factor in sleepwalking, so follow the guidelines we

Dream a little dream

We all dream, don't we? It seems highly likely, but in fact surprisingly little research into the prevalence of dreaming has been carried out.

One honourable exception was a study of 1000 Austrians, aged 14 to 69. Here's what the researchers found:

- Sixty-eight per cent remembered dreaming at least once during the previous month.
- People under 30 recalled more dreams than those over 50. Wealthy people remembered more dreams than poor people.
- Nightmares were reported by 4 per cent of the individuals surveyed. People on low incomes, and those living in communities numbering more than 5000, were especially prone.
- Younger people were more likely to dream in colour; in all, 37 per cent of those surveyed reported doing so.
- Twenty-nine per cent of people had recurring dreams, with women experiencing this more often than men.
- About a quarter of the people questioned said that they were sometimes aware that they were dreaming while dreaming.

set out in the insomnia entry on p. 339. Even if you don't have insomnia, these tips will help to ensure that your sleep is as good as it can be.

OTHER SLEEP PROBLEMS

There are many other types of sleep disorder, which perhaps reflects just how deceptively complex the whole business of sleep is. Most of these problems are pretty rare. That said, there are a few that are sufficiently common to warrant a mention in this book. We say a mention, because they're not really psychological issues. If you think you may be suffering from one of the problems we discuss below, talk to your family doctor. They'll be able to put you in touch with the appropriate specialists.

Breathing-related sleeping disorders

Snoring is caused by the sleeper's airways becoming partially blocked, and it's a very common feature of sleep – especially as you get older or heavier or if you've been drinking or taking sleeping pills.

Snoring isn't necessarily a problem, but in some cases it can disrupt the snorer's slumbers. This is because, without them realizing it, snoring can involve a series of very brief arousals from sleep. The biggest price for heavy snoring, however, is usually paid by the snorer's partner, whose sleep can be severely disrupted.

For some people however, heavy snoring can be a sign of a serious condition known as sleep apnoea, in which breathing actually stops for a short time (usually 10–30 seconds). This makes for very disrupted sleep – with the usual unpleasant consequences the following day. Moreover, untreated sleep apnoea can have dangerous effects on your heart and cardiovascular system. (Happily, there are now extremely effective treatments for the condition.)

Besides heavy snoring and daytime sleepiness, common symptoms of sleep apnoea include snorts, gasps and choking sounds while asleep, morning headaches and a very dry mouth. Older, heavier men tend to be most at risk.

Narcolepsy

The main feature of narcolepsy is daytime sleep attacks – the overwhelming and often irresistible urge to sleep, no matter where you are or what you're doing. As you might imagine, the consequences can range from the inconvenient and embarrassing to the downright dangerous.

But sleep attacks aren't the whole story. People with narcolepsy may also experience the following:

Cataplexy – a sudden loss of muscle strength, lasting a few seconds or several minutes, this can be relatively mild, for example only affecting facial muscles, but sometimes the whole body may be affected. Cataplexy is often triggered by strong emotions – attacks while a person is laughing are typical.

Sleep hallucinations – extremely vivid and often frightening illusions that occur as the person is falling asleep. (The technical term is hypnagogic hallucinations.)

Sleep paralysis – the terrifying sensation when waking up or falling asleep of not being able to move or speak.

Restless legs and periodic limb movement

Doctors have only very recently begun to recognize and understand restless legs syndrome. People suffering from the problem experience a feeling of unbearable discomfort in their legs, which can only be relieved by moving them. While these feelings can strike at any time, they tend to be worse when the person is inactive or at night. As a result, sleep can be severely disrupted.

Periodic limb movement disorder can seem rather similar, but the crucial difference is that in this case the movement of the legs (and other limbs too) is involuntary – it is a product of twitching muscles.

Both problems are more common in older people.

Related problems

You may well find that your sleep is affected if you're having problems with **worry**, **depression**, **pain**, **addictions**, **stress** or **trauma** (nightmares in particular are a typical feature of Post-Traumatic Stress Disorder). **Being overweight** is often a major factor in snoring and sleep-related breathing disorders.

One sleeping problem can lead to others. Insomnia, for example, is sometimes the result of the disruption to sleep caused by snoring and other sleep-related breathing disorders. So it's a good idea to read through all of this entry, rather than just the section that seems especially relevant.

For advice on sleep problems in children, see pages 157–64.

Problems with sleepwalking: a personal account

Jeff, my partner, is a sleepwalker. Three or four times a month, I'll wake up and he's pottering around the room with his eyes open. It's as though he's hunting for something: he opens the wardrobe doors, kneels down to look under the bed, sometimes pulls back the curtains as though he wants to look outside. He's usually mumbling away to himself. If I say anything to him, he normally nods his head vigorously and gives an incomprehensible answer. After a few minutes, he climbs into bed, closes his eyes and settles back down for the night. When we first got together, I found it quite unnerving; now I'm used to it. Apparently he was worse as a child – up every night when he was eight or nine. His dad still sleepwalks and so does his brother, so I guess it's in the genes.

Alison, aged 37

Where to go for more information

Two excellent books on dealing with insomnia are:

Overcoming Insomnia and Sleep Problems (Constable Robinson, 2006) by Colin Espie; *A Woman's Guide to Sleep Disorders* (McGraw-Hill, 2004) by Meir Kryger

For snoring and sleep apnoea, we recommend:

No More Snoring (John Wiley, 1999) by Victor Hoffstein and Shirley Linde; *Snoring from A to ZZZZ* (Spencer, 2003) by Derek Lipman; *Snoring and Sleep Apnea* (Demos, 2008) by Ralph Pascualy – though bear in mind that, despite the title, this focuses almost entirely on sleep apnoea.

If you're suffering from restless legs syndrome or periodic limb movements, try:

Restless Legs Syndrome (Demos, 2006) by Mark Buchfuhrer, Wayne Hening and Clete Kushida; *Restless Legs Syndrome* (Fireside Books, 2006) by Robert Yoakum.

You'll find a wealth of useful information on sleep and sleep problems on the websites of the American Academy of Sleep Medicine (www.aasm-net.org) and the National Sleep Foundation (www.sleepfoundation.org). Also worth checking out are:

ⓘ www.nhlbi.nih.gov/sleep (the website of the US National Center on Sleep Disorders Research)
ⓘ www.talkaboutsleep.com
ⓘ www.sleepquest.com
ⓘ www.sleepapnea.org (run by the American Sleep Apnea Association)

Stress

....

I'm picking and choosing in terms of the stress factor.
If it's not fun, I'm not going to do it.
Anita Baker

We all go through times when life seems a struggle. We might be trying to balance the demands of our job against the responsibilities of family life. We might be worried about our health. Our relationships might be going through a difficult phase or we might be wondering how to make ends meet.

These are obviously tricky situations, but sometimes we're able to ride them out without them causing us too much stress. It's when we think we can't cope though that stress really takes hold. This is because stress is the result not just of difficult situations, but of our reaction to them.

Stress is what we feel when we believe we can't cope with the demands facing us.

Because stress is all about our response to potential problems, our ability to cope often depends on how we're feeling at the time. If we're tired or low, we're more likely to think we can't cope and therefore to be much more stressed. A situation that might make us extremely stressed when we're feeling down might hardly affect us when we're well rested, positive and happy.

Some typical signs of stress are:

- feeling anxious and tense
- feeling unable to cope
- thinking that you've got too much to do
- feeling under pressure from other people
- being irritable and grouchy
- feeling weighed down with responsibilities
- feeling lonely or isolated
- feeling tired

- worrying about the future
- having problems relaxing or sleeping
- having headaches
- finding it hard to concentrate.

Stress is all about agitation and anxiety. This is because your body reacts to stress with something called the fight or flight response. Your blood pressure and heart rate are raised and you become highly alert and ready for action, just like animals facing a predator or some other threat.

This isn't bad for you in the short term. Without the fight or flight response our ancestors wouldn't have outrun the wolves, sabre-toothed tigers and bears they encountered on hunting trips.

But stress is not healthy in the long term. As well as high blood pressure, prolonged stress can cause muscle fatigue and prevent the immune system from working effectively. So when you're stressed you're more likely to get colds, or suffer from problems like eczema or asthma. Highly stressed women find it more difficult to become pregnant because their fertility decreases. And as if all that weren't enough, the chances of you having an accident increase when you're very stressed.

All of which makes stress sound like something to be avoided at all costs – which of course is impossible. Everyone gets stressed occasionally. What you need to avoid is frequent and long-lasting stress, which can damage your health and make life a misery.

Stress and the common cold

Over the last 20 years, the psychologist Sheldon Cohen has been researching the links between stress and the common cold. Volunteers are exposed to cold viruses and then tracked to see who falls ill.

It turns out that volunteers with a lot of stress in their lives are twice as likely to develop a cold than their more relaxed colleagues. And the longer the situation causing the stress has been going on, the more probable it is that the affected person will catch the cold.

Professor Cohen and his team have also shown that flu vaccines are less effective for highly stressed people. All in all, the research is a vivid illustration of the way stress interferes with our immune system, making us more vulnerable to infection.

Happily, the techniques we set out in the section below have been shown to be highly effective at helping people to cope with stress.

If you're having a very extreme reaction to recent stressful circumstances, and if you're finding it hard to cope with everyday life as a result, you may be suffering from what doctors call adjustment disorder. This is a short-term condition: once the problem causing you stress has been resolved, your symptoms should disappear within six months.

There are some life events that are almost bound to trigger extreme stress – such as a violent assault, sexual abuse or a serious car accident. These kinds of incidents can give rise to acute stress disorder and post-traumatic stress disorder (PTSD). We're focusing here on the more common forms of stress, but you can find more information about PTSD on pages 97–106.

How common is stress?

'There are very few certainties that touch us all in this mortal experience,' wrote the ancient Greek poet Philemon, 'but one of the absolutes is that we will experience hardship and stress at some point.'

And indeed stress-related problems are one of the main reasons why people visit their GP – at a cost of 5.3 billion to the UK economy in 2000.

Stress is an inevitable part of life – which makes knowing how to deal with it all the more important.

How to Manage Stress

If you ask what is the single most important key to longevity, I would have to say it is avoiding worry, stress and tension. And if you didn't ask me, I'd still have to say it.
George Burns

Stress is the product of a combination of factors, namely difficult situations and whether or not you feel you can cope with them. To beat stress, you can either try to minimize those difficult situations or understand that you really are equipped to deal with them. The strategy you choose will depend on what's making you stressed. Sometimes you may need to use both.

Minimize stressful situations

Let's start by outlining some techniques to help you minimize potentially stressful situations.

Don't just say 'yes': take control!

One of the major causes of stress is the number of demands that are made on people, often at work but also in family life. It's like a scene from some sci-fi B movie: millions of people under the power of endless to-do lists, rushing frantically from one urgent assignment to the next while, no matter how hard they work, the list just keeps on growing.

You need to take control of the demands made on you, and here's how:

- Make sure you really understand what's being asked of you. Write it down if that helps, and discuss it with the person making the request so that you both agree on what's involved.
- If you have a sense that you won't be able to do it, turn down the request or offer to do something less demanding instead.
- Tell people when you'll be able to get to the task – and set yourself a realistic schedule, perhaps allowing some extra time.
- Often the most stressful requests are those that demand a lot of effort for little reward. So see whether you can reduce the effort required, or make the task more rewarding.
- Manage your time by planning ahead. Make a list of the things you need to get done in the week, prioritize the most important ones, and then schedule them in. Make sure you leave time for regular exercise and for fun – laughter is a great way to de-stress and, according to research, to boost your immune system.

Problem-solve

Instead of letting your problems stress you out, you need to take action to deal with them. Easier said than done, of course, but there are some simple yet very effective steps you can take to help you.

First, identify the situation that's worrying you. Then try to think of all the possible solutions to the problem. Write them down. Weigh up the pros and cons of each solution. Discuss the situation with other people if that helps. Be prepared to take radical action if it's absolutely necessary – you may have to face the fact that you need to change jobs or end a relationship, for instance.

Stress and work

If you want to minimize stress in your life, choose your job carefully. One in five people in the UK says he/she experiences high levels of work-related stress. And a recent study of nearly 1000 young people in the early stages of their careers revealed that 1 in 20 can expect to experience serious depression or anxiety every year as a direct result of work, with those in high-stress jobs twice as likely to be affected as those in low-stress occupations.

Here are the top five jobs for stress junkies and the top five careers for those who crave the quiet life, according to a study carried out at the Institute of Psychiatry:

Most stressful jobs	Least stressful jobs
Head chefs in large restaurants	Postmen and postwomen
Schoolteachers	Librarians
Slaughterers	Hairdressers
Construction workers	Legal/accounts administrators
Top managerial positions	Speech therapists

Believe in your ability to cope

Here are some ways in which you can boost your belief that you really are equipped to cope.

Make time for friends and family

Research shows that people deal with stress much better if they have a good social network – people they can talk to about their problems or simply go out and have a good time with. So make sure you don't let life's hassles stop you from seeing friends and family. And try to think of someone you can share your worries with.

Problems with stress: a personal account

As a teacher, the issue is not whether you're going to be stressed, but how you handle it. When I first started, I was regularly in tears. And I could be really snappy with the students: I felt constantly on edge. I used to have problems sleeping, especially on Sunday nights. It's taken me a few years to get there, but I now have a few key strategies I use to keep myself sane. I try to do at least 20 minutes of yoga every day, and I swim three times a week. These activities help clear out all the hassles of the day from my brain. Plus I never take work home; I prepare all my lessons at school, even if that means getting in really early or staying late. I need to keep a dividing line between work and the rest of my life. And I have a couple of very good friends at school: it's great to be able to swap horror stories!

Jenny, aged 33

Tackle negative thinking

'I can't cope'; 'I'm never going to get this done'; 'I'm going to screw this up'; 'If I don't do this perfectly, I might as well not have bothered.' Stress has a major effect on the way we think, making us very negative and self-critical. Any sense of perspective is lost: everything is terrible; only perfection will do.

The philosopher William James had it right when he said: 'The greatest weapon against stress is our ability to choose one thought over another.' We need to get a grip on our negative thinking and turn it around:

First, identify the negative thoughts you have when you're stressed – keeping a diary is a good way of doing this.

Weigh up your negative thoughts. Ask yourself how accurate they are. What's the evidence for and against them? What would you tell a friend who had these thoughts? How will you look back on them in a week's time, a month's time and a year's time?

Try to challenge and dismiss your negative thoughts when they're actually occurring. See whether you can replace them with more realistic views of the situation. One worthwhile tactic is to reframe the problem as a challenge – and a challenge that you can meet. So, instead of worrying that the report you're writing is going to be terrible, remind yourself that you've written lots of successful reports in the past, set yourself a reasonable time limit and challenge yourself to produce the best you can by that deadline.

Visualize yourself coping

Often when you're stressed your mind is full of images of things going wrong. And these negative images only increase your stress. You need to turn those negative images into positive ones:

- Identify the problem that's causing you stress.
- Note down the parts that worry you most.
- Think how you could deal with these particularly stressful parts.
- Imagine yourself successfully using the coping strategies you've chosen.
- Repeat this 'positive visualization' several times.

Use relaxation techniques

There are lots of ways to relax, and it's worth taking the time to find the ones that suit you best. Yoga, massage, hypnosis and meditation can all be really effective. Some people find it helpful to write down and carry with them words of encouragement or advice to use in moments of stress. You might also like to try this visualization technique:

1. Find a quiet and comfortable place where you won't be disturbed. You can try this exercise with some relaxing music.
2. Close your eyes and imagine your favourite, most relaxing place.
3. Focus on the colours, the scenery, the sounds, and the smells.
4. Do this for five minutes, once or twice a day.

Look after your physical health

There's lots of research to show that taking regular exercise, eating well and getting plenty of sleep help us combat stress. Foods rich in magnesium – such as green vegetables, nuts, seeds, pulses and whole grains – are thought to be calming.

Cut out smoking and keep your caffeine, sugar and alcohol intake within sensible limits. These steps may cause you short-term stress but it'll be worth it in the long run!

Related problems

Almost all of the problems we discuss in this book are made worse by stress. It can play a particularly big part in **insomnia**, **anxiety** and **depression** and is also often a factor in **smoking and drug and alcohol addictions**.

Although **bereavement** is frequently enormously stressful, it's an experience that needs to be dealt with in its own right.

Where to go for more information

How to Deal with Stress (Kogan Page, 2007) by Stephen Palmer and Cary Cooper is especially good on combating stress at work. Richard Carlson's *Don't Sweat the Small Stuff* books are light-hearted and entertaining, but also full of sound advice.

Useful websites worth checking out are:

ⓘ www.stress.org (the website of the American Institute of Stress)
ⓘ www.mindtools.com, which specializes in providing guidance on work-related stress.

Tiredness

We all go through periods of exhaustion when life is particularly busy and demanding, when we're not sleeping well or when we're under great stress. At such times, we're so tired that the smallest chore seems beyond us: both body and mind are drained.

Such fatigue is perfectly normal and usually short-lived: as soon as we're able to recharge our batteries, it lifts. This entry, though, looks at exhaustion that doesn't appear to have an obvious cause.

If you suffer with this kind of tiredness it can cause real problems, making difficult all kinds of activities you used to do easily, whether work or hobbies, childcare or socializing. Not surprisingly, chronic exhaustion can make you feel very down. You can become frustrated and irritable, and prey to all sorts of worries, asking yourself: Why do I feel like this? Am I making things worse somehow? Will I ever get back to normal?

The most severe form of this problem is called chronic fatigue syndrome (CFS). It involves:

- fatigue that has lasted at least six months
- fatigue that isn't the result of activity or a medical condition, and which doesn't disappear once you've rested
- at least four of the following symptoms: muscle pain, joint pain, headaches, tender lymph nodes, sore throat, feelings of poor memory, unrefreshing sleep, feeling exhausted even 24 hours after you've been active.

Problems with chronic tiredness: a personal account

Two years ago my father died, and my partner had a promotion that involved him working away from home a lot. I was left trying to bring up two small kids and hold down a part-time (but stressful) job. Naturally, I got ill. I spent about 10 days in bed with the flu and then tried to get back to my normal routine. But no matter how much I told myself I should be over it, three months later I still felt absolutely drained – in fact, almost on my knees much of the time. My GP told me I was exhausted (which I knew very well), but couldn't find any physical cause. Eventually, I had to give up work and my mother had to uproot herself in her late sixties to come and help with childcare and housework. When my husband said he was resigning his job, I made my doctor refer me to a therapist. Although it's taken many months, and a few ups and downs, I'm now back almost to my best. Still exhausted – but this time from work and kids: the normal stuff!

Rebecca, aged 35

CFS can have a dramatic impact on sufferers' lives; in some severe cases they may be unable to work and even become virtually housebound. Depression and high levels of anxiety are common.

Chronic fatigue syndrome is a relatively new term, but the condition has a long and sometimes controversial history. Nineteenth-century doctors called it neurasthenia; more recently, it's been known as ME (myalgic encephalopathy) and as post-viral fatigue syndrome (PVFS). Many people with the illness prefer the latter names; they argue that there's much more to the condition than fatigue.

The other objection to the term CFS goes to the heart of the controversy surrounding the illness: its cause. ME and PVFS suggest a physical origin, perhaps a fever or a problem in the way the immune system functions. Some experts, however, have argued that CFS is largely psychological and a form of depression.

It's true that stressful life events often precede the onset of chronic

The vicious circle of inactivity

Most of us rest when we're exhausted: it's natural and healthy. So it's hardly surprising that many people try to cope with their chronic fatigue by cutting back on how much they do.

One study in the Netherlands, for example, measured the activity levels over 12 days of 277 people with CFS and 47 physically healthy people. (The participants wore actimeters – motion-detection devices – on their ankles.) Sure enough, the individuals with CFS were less energetic than the healthy group, doing less and taking longer breaks between periods of activity. Around a quarter of the participants with CFS were extremely inactive.

The Dutch researchers found that the less people did, the worse they described their symptoms as being. This is understandable: if you're feeling terrible, you're unlikely to want to tackle household chores, for example. But there's good evidence to suggest that resting doesn't help people with CFS; in fact, it can make the illness worse.

The reason for this is that our bodies are designed to be upright and to be used. It doesn't take a huge amount of inactivity to produce negative changes. For example, one study found that a dramatic alteration in muscle mass occurs within 4–6 weeks of bed rest, together with a significant reduction in muscle strength. Other research shows that three weeks of bed rest reduces VO2 max (the amount of oxygen the body can process during activity and the best measure of physical fitness) by 28 per cent.

So, resting too much can trigger a vicious circle. It reduces our physical fitness, which makes activity even more draining, leading us to rest even more. This is why gradually increasing your activity levels (as described below) is so important in overcoming CFS.

fatigue, but so too do flu-like illnesses. At present, we simply don't know what causes the condition. But if you're suffering from chronic fatigue, regardless of whether your symptoms meet the official criteria for CFS, it's probably better to focus your attention on how you cope in the present than on what may have triggered it originally. And, as we'll see in the coming pages, there is much you can do to overcome chronic fatigue.

How common is chronic tiredness?

Around 15 per cent of people are currently experiencing fatigue that's lasted six months or more, though in most cases their exhaustion is the product of lifestyle factors (perhaps the pressure of work or the demands of bringing up a family). Persistent fatigue is also a feature of some serious illnesses, such as cancer or Parkinson's disease.

CFS is thought to affect somewhere between 0.2 and 2 per cent of the population, with more women affected than men.

Self-assessment

If you're concerned that you may be suffering from chronic fatigue syndrome, have a go at the following questionnaire.

	None or a little of the time	Some of the time	A good part of the time	Most of the time
1. I feel tired for a long time after physical activity.	1	2	3	4
2. My concentration is poor.	1	2	3	4
3. My muscles feel very tired after physical activity.	1	2	3	4
4. I get headaches.	1	2	3	4
5. I need to sleep for long periods.	1	2	3	4
6. I get muscle pain after physical activity.	1	2	3	4
7. I sleep poorly.	1	2	3	4

8. I have problems with my speech.	1	2	3	4
9. My memory is poor.	1	2	3	4
10. I get muscle pain even at rest.	1	2	3	4

© Springer, 2000 Hadzi-Pavlovic, D., Hickie, I. B., Wilson, A. J., Davenport, T. A., Lloyd, A. R., & Wakefield, D. (2000). Screening for prolonged fatigue syndromes. *Social Psychiatry and Psychiatric Epidemiology*, 35, 471–9

You may have chronic fatigue syndrome if you've scored 3 or 4 on at least three questions. Remember though that, like any self-assessment exercise, this one can't provide a definite diagnosis. For that, you need to see a health professional.

How to Overcome Chronic Tiredness

First, a word of clarification. The advice in this section is designed for people suffering from chronic fatigue. In other words, people whose tiredness prevents them from being active, rather than those who are tired because they've been active.

Talk to your doctor
If you're in this situation, where your tiredness is preventing you from being active, your first step should be to talk to your doctor. They'll be able to check whether there's any obvious medical reason for your fatigue.

Break the circle by raising activity levels
Assuming your exhaustion isn't the result of another illness, you need to gradually increase your activity levels. As you'll have read above, CFS tends to lead people to do less. Partly, this is because resting seems a sensible and natural response to fatigue. People may also worry that they're going to make their illness worse. As a result, they can misinterpret normal bodily sensations after activity – for example, aching muscles or breathlessness – as signs that they ought not to push themselves. Moreover depression,

which affects many people with CFS, brings its own feelings of exhaustion, aches and pains and drastically reduced energy levels.

The less you do, unfortunately, the more painful and exhausting it is when you are active. And before you know it, the vicious circle of inactivity has been formed.

To break this circle, you need to build up your muscle strength steadily and systematically, using an approach called 'graded activity': you measure your activity levels; you stabilize them; and then you increase them, as follows:

Keep a diary

Start the process of increasing your activity levels by keeping a diary (this is the measuring phase). For the next week or two, record what you've been doing for every hour of the day. Then work out how many hours during that fortnight you've been active and how many you've spent resting.

Plan your weekly schedule

You can now begin to plan your weekly schedule. Divide your weekly total of activity and rest equally over the seven days, so you have fixed periods of activity alternating with regular rests.

What you're doing here is stabilizing your activity levels, building structure and balance into your week and nipping in the bud any tendency to 'boom and bust' – that's to say, overdoing it when you feel OK, then being unable to get anything done for the next day or two.

Increase your activity levels

Once you're comfortable with this routine, you can start to increase your activity levels – though don't wait until your fatigue has disappeared as that may take a while. Make a list of the things you'd like to be able to do and prioritize two or three of them. Aim for a variety of activities – for example to do with work, household chores, exercise and fun.

Set yourself a few long-term goals and break those down into shorter-term ones. If, for example, your long-term goal is to get back to the hikes in the countryside you used to enjoy so much, your short-term goals might involve gradually increasing the amount of time you spend walking each day, and steadily getting used to differing types of terrain.

Take things gently. Start at a level you're comfortable with and gradually increase the amount you do (this is called 'pacing'). It's better to keep going slowly but steadily, despite your fatigue, rather than have your symptoms dictate how much you do. You're bound to feel some increased discomfort as you get used to your new routine: it's a sign that your body is adapting and growing stronger. Keep a record of your progress and reward yourself when things go well.

Challenge negative thoughts

To help you succeed with your new schedule, practise challenging your negative thoughts. You might find yourself thinking, for example, 'My legs ache. I should take an early break before I do myself some harm.' Or: 'It's not worth bothering: I can't do this like I used to.' Don't let these thoughts throw you off course.

Write down all the evidence you can come up with both for and against your negative thoughts. Imagine what you'd tell a friend in a similar position. What positive ways are there of looking at the situation? (For example, 'It's good that my legs are aching: it means my muscles are getting stronger,' or, 'Perhaps I can't do this as well as I could two years ago, but a few weeks ago I wasn't able to do it at all.')

Test out your thoughts: for example, if you think you're too tired to walk to the shops, have a go. The chances are, not only will you be able to manage it after all, but your confidence will receive a huge boost when you do.

People often spend a lot of time worrying about their chronic fatigue, and they tend to assume the worst (psychologists call this 'catastrophizing') – so have a look at the entry on worry on pp. 106–12. If there are specific issues that are causing you anxiety and stress, adopt a problem-solving approach (again, you'll find details of how to do this in the worry entry).

Get good-quality sleep

Insomnia is a very common feature of CFS. It's hard to sleep well at night if you've not been especially active during the day – and certainly not if you've had a nap. Of course, a lack of good-quality sleep only increases feelings of fatigue – and thus another vicious circle is formed.

If insomnia is a problem for you, have a look at our tips on how to improve your sleep on p. 340. It's particularly important to:

- make sure you get up and go to bed at the same times each day (including weekends)

- not go to bed too early
- try not to nap during the day
- use your bed for sleeping, not resting.

Prepare for setbacks

Overcoming chronic fatigue, like dealing with most problems, is often a lengthy business. Persevere: it isn't going to happen overnight, but you'll get there in the end.

One of the challenges you're likely to face is the occasional setback – that's to say, a period when you're unable to keep to your schedule or when your symptoms seem especially bad. For example, if you're very stressed or down, or if you fall ill, things are bound to be more difficult for a while.

Try not to let things slide. Look back through your schedule and remind yourself how far you've come. If you can't get back on track completely, prioritize the tasks you particularly need or want to do. Then gradually build up to where you were before the setback. Draw up a plan in advance for how you'll handle things if you do find yourself in choppy waters.

If you'd like help in tackling your CFS, do ask your doctor to refer you to a specialist. The best results have come through the use of Cognitive Behaviour Therapy (the approach drawn on in this entry and throughout the book).

Related problems

Chronic fatigue often brings with it feelings of **depression** and **anxiety**, and can cause **sleep problems**.

Where to go for more information

Overcoming Chronic Fatigue (Robinson, 2005) by Mary Burgess and Trudie Chalder is an excellent guide to the topic, written by two of the leading clinical psychologists working in this area. Also worth seeking out is *Chronic Fatigue Syndrome: The Facts* (Oxford, 2008) by Frankie Campling and Michael Sharpe.

Part III

Resources

ASSESSMENT MEASURES

We would like to thank the researchers and their publishers for permission to use the assessment measures in *Know Your Mind*.

Addictions
Alcohol Use Disorders Identification Test
Babor, T. F., Higgins-Biddle, J. C., Saunders, J. B., & Monteiro, M. G. (2001). *AUDIT: Alcohol Use Disorders Identification Test*. Second Edition. Geneva: World Health Organization.
Drug Abuse Screening Test
Skinner, H. A. (1982). The Drug Abuse Screening Test. *Addictive Behaviors*, 7, 363–71.
Canadian Problem Gambling Index
Ferris, J. & Wynne, H. (2001). The Canadian Problem Gambling Index: Final Report. Ottawa: Canadian Centre on Substance Abuse.
Fagerstrom Tolerance Questionnaire
Heatherton, T. F., Kozlowski, L. T., Frecker, R. C., & Fagerstrom, K. O. (1991). The Fagerstrom Test for Nicotine Dependence: a revision of the Fagerstrom Tolerance Questionnaire. *British Journal of Addiction*, 86, 1119–27.

Anger
Clinical Anger Scale
Snell, W. E., Jr, Gum, S., Shuck, R. L., Mosley, J. A., & Hite, T. L. (1995).
The Clinical Anger Scale: Preliminary reliability and validity. *Journal of Clinical Psychology*, 51, 215–26.

Anxiety
Autonomic Nervous System Questionnaire
Stein, M. B., Roy-Byrne, P. P., McQuaid, J. R., Laffaye, C., Russo, J., McCahill, M. E., Katon, W., Craske, M., Bystritsky, A., & Sherbourne, C. D. (1999). Development of a brief diagnostic screen for panic disorder in primary care. *Psychosomatic Medicine*, 61, 359–64.
Obsessive–Compulsive Inventory
Foa, E. B., Huppert, J. D., Leiberg, S., Langer, R., Kichic, R., Hajcak, G., & Salkovskis, P. (2002). The Obsessive–Compulsive Inventory: development and validation of a short version. *Psychological Assessment*, 14, 485–96.

Social Phobia Inventory
Connor, K., Davidson, J., Churchill, L., Sherwood, A., Weisler, R., & Foa, E. (2000). Psychometric properties of the Social Phobia Inventory. *British Journal of Psychiatry*, 176, 379–86.
Impact of Event Scale – Revised
Weiss, D. S., & Marmar, C. R. (1997). The Impact of Event Scale – Revised. In J. Wilson & T. M. Keane (Eds), *Assessing psychological trauma and PTSD* (pp. 399–411). New York: Guilford.
Penn State Worry Questionnaire
Meyer, T. J., Miller, M. L., Metzger, R. L., & Borkovec, T. D. (1990). Development and validation of the Penn State Worry Questionnaire. *Behaviour Research & Therapy*, 28, 487–95.
The Whitely Index
Pilowsky, I. (1967). Dimensions of hypochondriasis. *British Journal of Psychiatry*, 113, 89–93.
Body Dysmorphic Disorder Questionnaire
Phillips K. A. (2005). The Broken Mirror: *Understanding and Treating Body Dysmorphic Disorder*. New York: Oxford University Press.

Bereavement
Inventory of Complicated Grief
Prigerson, H. G., Maciejewski, P. K., Reynolds, C. F. 3rd., Bierhals, A. J., Newsom, J. T., Fasiczka, A., Frank, E., Doman, J. & Miller, M. (1995). Inventory of Complicated Grief: a scale to measure maladaptive symptoms of loss. *Psychiatry Research*, 59, 65–79.

Childhood problems
Screen for Child Anxiety Related Emotional Disorders (SCARED)
Birmaher, B., Brent, D. A., Chiappetta L., Bridge, J., Monga, S., & Baugher, M. (1999). Psychometric properties of the Screen for Child Anxiety Related Emotional Disorders (SCARED): a replication study. *Journal of the American Academy of Child and Adolescent Psychiatry*, 38, 1230–36.
Center for Epidemiological Studies Depression Scale for Children (CES-DC)
Weissman, M. M., Orvaschel, H., & Padian, N. (1980). Children's symptom and social functioning self-report scales. *Journal of Nervous and Mental Disease*, 168, 736–40.
Vanderbilt ADHD Diagnostic Parent Rating Scale
Wolraich, M. L., Lambert, W., Doffing, M. A., Bickman, L., Simmons, T. & Worley, K. (2003). Psychometric properties of the Vanderbilt ADHD Diagnostic Parent Rating Scale in a referred population. *Journal of Pediatric Psychology*, 28, 559–68.

Depression
Zung Self-Rated Depression Scale
Zung, W. W. K. (1965). A self-rating depression scale. *Archives of General Psychiatry*, 12, 63–70.

Eating problems
Eating Attitudes Test
Garner, D. M., Olmsted, M. P., Bohr, Y., and Garfinkel, P. E. (1982). The Eating Attitudes Test: Psychometric features and clinical correlates. *Psychological Medicine*, 12, 871–8.

Hallucinations
Cardiff Anomalous Perceptions Scale
Bell, V., Halligan, P. W., & Ellis, H. D. (2006). The Cardiff Anomalous Perceptions Scale (CAPS). *Schizophrenia Bulletin*, 32, 366–77.

Memory problems
Lapses in Everyday Memory Questionnaire
Sunderland, A., Harris, J. E., & Baddeley, A. D. (1983). Do laboratory tests predict everyday memory? A neuropsychological study. *Journal of Verbal Learning and Verbal Behavior*, 22, 341–57.

Mood swings
Mood Disorder Questionnaire
Hirschfeld, R. M. A., Williams, J. B. W., Spitzer, R. L., Calabrese, J. R., Flynn, L., Keck, P. E. Jr, Lewis, L., McElroy, S. L., Post, R. M., Rapport, D. J., Russell, J. M., Sachs, G. S., & Zajecka, J. (2000). Development and validation of a screening instrument for bipolar spectrum disorder: the Mood Disorder Questionnaire. *American Journal of Psychiatry*, 157, 1873–5.

Pain
The Chronic Pain Grade Questionnaire
Von Korff, M., Ormel, J., Keefe, F. J., & Dworkin, S. F. (1992). Grading the severity of chronic pain, *Pain*, 133–49.

Paranoia
Green et al. Paranoid Thought Scales
Green, C., Freeman, D., Kuipers, E., Bebbington, P., Fowler, D., Dunn, G., & Garety, P. A. (2008). Measuring ideas of persecution and reference: the Green et al. Paranoid Thought Scales (G-PTS). *Psychological Medicine*, 38, 101–11.

Relationship problems
Couples Satisfaction Index
Funk, Janette L., Rogge, Ronald D. (2007). Testing the ruler with item response theory: Increasing precision of measurement for relationship satisfaction with the Couples Satisfaction Index. *Journal of Family Psychology*, 21, 572–83.

Sexual problems
Sexual Function Questionnaire
Quirk, F., Haughie, S., & Symonds, T. (2005). The use of the Sexual Function Questionnaire as a screening tool for women with sexual dysfunction. *Journal of Sexual Medicine*, 2, 469–77.
International Index of Erectile Function
Rosen, R. C., Cappelleri, J. C., Smith, M. D., Lipsky, J., & Peña, B. M. (1999). Development and evaluation of an abridged, 5-item version of the International Index of Erectile Function (IIEF-5) as a diagnostic tool for erectile dysfunction. *International Journal of Impotence Research*, 11, 319–26.
Premature Ejaculation Diagnostic Tool
Symonds, T., Perelman, M. A., Althof, S., Giuliano, F., Martin, M., May, K., Abraham, L., Crossland, A., & Morris, M. (2007). Development and validation of a premature ejaculation diagnostic tool. *European Urology*, 52, 565–73.

Sleep problems
SLEEP-50
Spoormaker, V. I., Verbeek, I., van den Bout, J., & Klip, E. C. (2005). Initial validation of the SLEEP-50 questionnaire. *Behavioural Sleep Medicine*, 3, 227–46.

Tiredness
Schedule of Fatigue and Anergia (SOFA/CFS)
Hadzi-Pavlovic, D., Hickie, I. B., Wilson, A. J., Davenport, T. A., Lloyd, A. R., & Wakefield, D. (2000). Screening for prolonged fatigue syndromes. *Social Psychiatry and Psychiatric Epidemiology*, 35, 471–9.

Useful organizations

British Association for Behavioural and Cognitive Psychotherapies
Victoria Buildings
9–13 Silver Street
Bury
BL9 0EU
Tel: 0161 797 4484
Email: babcp@babcp.com
Website: www.babcp.com

British Psychological Society
St Andrews House
48 Princess Road East
Leicester
LE1 7DR
Tel: 0116 254 9568
Email: enquiries@bps.org.uk
Website: www.bps.org.uk

The European Association for Behavioural and Cognitive Psychotherapies (EABCT) website (www.eabct.com) provides links to national cognitive therapy organizations throughout Europe.

Other useful organizations include:

The Mental Health Foundation
9th Floor
Sea Containers House
20 Upper Ground
London
SE1 9QB
Tel: 020 7803 1100
Email: mhf@mhf.org.uk
Website: www.mentalhealth.org.uk

MIND (National Association for Mental Health)
15–19 Broadway
London
E15 4BQ
Tel: 0845 766 0163
Email: contact@mind.org.uk
Website: www.mind.org.uk

Rethink
89 Albert Embankment
London
SE1 7TP
General enquiries: 0845 456 0455 or info@rethink.org
National advice service: 020 7840 3188 or advice@rethink.org
Website: www.rethink.org

The Royal College of Psychiatrists
17 Belgrave Square
London
SW1X 8PG
Tel: 020 7235 2351
Email: rcpsych@rcpsych.ac.uk
Website: www.rcpsych.ac.uk

SANE
1st Floor
Cityside House
Adler Street
London
E1 1EE
Tel: 020 7375 1002
Helpline: 0845 767 8000
Email: info@sane.org.uk
Email support service: saneline@sane.org.uk
Website: www.sane.org.uk

Index

abstinence, overcoming
addictions 49
activities 22–3
    and chronic fatigue 363–4,
        365–6
    and chronic pain 256–7
    overcoming depression 193–5
    see also exercise
acupuncture, pain management
    259
addictions 26–54
    alcohol 26–32
    drugs 33–8
    gambling 38–43
    how to overcome 48–54
    smoking 43–7
adjustment disorder 355
ageing: erection problems
    321–2
    memory problems 233–5,
        238–9
    sleep requirements 340
aggression: domestic abuse
    275–6
    and men's sexuality 319
    road rage 56
agoraphobia 73, 78
air travel, jet lag 248
alcohol 26–32
    and domestic abuse 275
    and erection problems 324
    and insomnia 341
    and paranoia 265
    and sex 305
    units 21
Alcoholics Anonymous (AA)
    52–3
Alzheimer's disease 234, 242–3
amphetamines 33, 34
anger and irritation 55–64
    and self-injury 294
    tantrums 173–81
anniversaries, after bereave-
    ment 134, 135
anorexia 210, 211–17
anti-anxiety drugs 33
anti-convulsant drugs 258
antidepressants 196
    for anxiety 124
    for bulimia 210

causing nightmares 346
for childhood depression and
    anxiety 152
for insomnia 343
for mood swings 250
pain management 259
for paranoia 267
for self-injury 294
antihistamines 344
anti-inflammatory drugs 259
anti-psychotic drugs 231, 267
anxiety 65–125
    about memory problems
        242
    body image worries 112–19
    childhood sleep problems
        160, 162–3
    in children and young people
        137–53
    fears and phobias 65–72
    health anxiety 119–23
    obsessions and compulsions
        79–88
    panic 72–9
    separation anxiety 138, 141
    and sexual problems 324–5,
        328
    shyness and social anxiety
        88–97
    and stress 354
    trauma and post-traumatic
        stress disorder 97–106
    worry 106–12
apnoea, sleep 336, 338, 350
arguments see conflict
arousal, sexual problems 305–8
assertiveness 16–18
Attention Deficit Hyperactivity
    Disorder (ADHD) 164–73
attention-seeking, tantrums
    175, 176, 178
attitudes to psychological
    health 5

barbiturates, drug abuse 33, 34
Beck, Aaron T 4
bedrooms, overcoming
    insomnia 341, 342
bedtime routines 159
bedwetting 153–7

benzodiazepines 33, 34, 124
bereavement 126–36, 229
beta blockers 346
'binge drinkers' 30
binge eating 199–211, 212
bipolar disorder 246–51
body clock, sleep problems 157,
    159
Body Dysmorphic Disorder
    (BDD) 112–19, 210
body image: anorexia 211
    bulimia 200–1, 208
    worries about 112–19
body mass index (BMI) 218–19
borderline personality disorder
    289–90
boundaries: for children 149
    coping with tantrums 180
brain: alcohol and 30–1
    exercising 239
    pain management 257
break-ups 286
breakfast 21
breathing exercises, panic
    attacks 77
breathing-related sleep
    disorders 349–50
British Association for
    Behavioural and Cognitive
        Psychotherapies 5
British Psychological Society 5
bulimia nervosa 199–211
bullying 148

caffeine, and insomnia 341
calory requirements 222, 223–4
cancer, smoking and 43–4
cannabis 32–3
carbamazepine 250
cars, road rage 56
cataplexy 350
childbirth, postnatal depression
    188, 191–2
children 137–85
    bedwetting 153–7
    child abuse 183–5
    depression, fears and anxiety
        137–53
    eating disorders 216
    grief 134

hyperactivity 164–73
overweight 218
sleep problems 157–64, 347
tantrums 173–81
chronic fatigue syndrome
(CFS) 361–8
chronic pain 252–9
cigarettes 43–7
clitoris, orgasm 307
cocaine 33, 34–5
Cognitive Behaviour Therapy
(CBT) 4–5
for anorexia 215
for anxiety 124
for bulimia 205, 210
for childhood depression and
anxiety 152
for depression 196
for mood swings 250
overcoming jealousy 285
for paranoia 267
for post-traumatic stress
disorder 103–5
for self-injury 294
colds, and stress 354
commemoration, coping with
grief 134
communication: relationship
problems 274–6, 278–81
tantrums as 175–6
with children 149
with teenagers 182
compulsions and obsessions
79–88
concentration, improving
children's 171–2
conduct disorder 175
confidence, children 150
conflict: relationship problems
269–87
with teenagers 182–3
context, memories and 238,
242
control, reducing stress 356
'controlled crying' 161–2
Coolidge, Calvin 89
counselling, relationship
problems 285–6
countries, happiness 10
couple therapy 285
crash diets 220
cravings 51–2, 223
crying, 'controlled' 161–2
cues, improving memory 242
cycling, and erection problems
325
cyclothymic disorder 246

daytime naps 341
death, bereavement and grief
126–36
death rates, and trust 263
dementia 234, 235, 242–3
depression 186–98
anorexia and 212
in children and young people
137–53
and insomnia 343
mood swings 244–51
postnatal 188, 191–2, 196
desensitization, overcoming
fears and phobias 69–70
desire, loss of 303–5
Dialectical Behaviour Therapy
(DBT) 294
diaries: anger 61–2
bedwetting 155
bulimia 206
chronic fatigue 366
food 215
hallucinations 230
memory problems 239
obsessive–compulsive
disorder 85
panic attacks 76
paranoid thoughts 265–6
self-injury 292, 293–4
shyness and social anxiety
93–4
sleep problems 159
tantrums 176
weight-loss 221–2
diazepam 124
diet see food
dieting: anorexia 211
bulimia 200, 207–8
crash diets 220
distraction, coping with
tantrums 177–8
diuretics, bulimia 200,
206–7
divorce 272, 274–6
doctors, referral for psycho
logical therapy 4
domestic abuse 275–6
dreams 349
see also nightmares
drinks: and bedwetting 155
and childhood sleep
problems 160
and insomnia 341
see also alcohol
drugs: addiction 33–8
and paranoia 265
see also medication

dyspareunia 309
Dysthymic Disorder 188

eating problems 199–25
being overweight 217–25
binge eating 199–211
undereating 211–17
Ecstasy 33, 34, 36
ejaculation problems 327–33
emotions: anger and irritation
55–64
and bulimia 201
grief 127–8
mood swings 244–51
empathy, relationship problems
278–9
endorphins, exercise and 23
episodic memory 233
erection problems 306, 320,
321–7
exercise 22–3
and anorexia 212
brain exercises 239
children and young people
149
and chronic pain 257
and depression 193
improving memory 239
for insomnia 340
losing weight 222
overcoming chronic fatigue
366
reducing worries 111
and sleep 24, 161
see also activities
exhaustion 361–8
exposure: body image worries
117
childhood problems 151
health anxiety 123
obsessive–compulsive
disorder 87
overcoming fears and
phobias 69–70
post-traumatic stress
disorder 104
expressive writing 17

faces, remembering 90–1, 240
fainting 71, 76–7
family therapy, for anorexia 215
fantasy, sexual 315, 316
fat, saturated 20
fatigue see tiredness
fears and phobias 65–72
childhood sleep problems
160, 162–3

in children and young people
137–53
illness phobia 120
jealousy 283–4
panic attacks 77
post-traumatic stress
disorder 98
fight or flight response 354
fish, in diet 20
'5 a day' for mental health 7
flashbacks, post-traumatic
stress disorder 98
'flow' 23
fluoxetine 124, 152, 210
food 18–21
and ADHD 169–70
children and young people
148
and depression 193
eating problems 199–25
food diaries 215
losing weight 223–4
and mood swings 249
obsession with 213
and overweight 217–18
stress reduction 359
forgetfulness 232–43
Freud, Sigmund 115
fruit 19

gambling 38–43
Generalized Anxiety Disorder
(GAD) 106–12
goals, improving children's
concentration 171
grief 126–36, 229
guilt, and depression 187

hallucinations 226–31, 350
hallucinogenic drugs 33, 36
happiness: happiest countries
10
mood swings 244–51
Positive Psychology 13–14
and relationships 16
health: health anxiety 119–23
pessimism and 15
hearing voices 226–7
heart disease, anger and 64
heartbeat, Panic Disorder
74
heights, fear of 67–8
herbal remedies: for depression
196
for insomnia 344
heroin 33, 34
Holmes, Kelly 288

Hormone Replacement
Therapy (HRT) 311
hormones, for erection
problems 324
Hughes, Howard 86
hyperactivity 164–73
hyperventilation, panic attacks
77
hypoactive sexual desire
disorder 304
hypochondriasis 119–23
hypomania 244–51

illness phobia 120
imagery rehearsal, for
nightmares 346
immune system, and stress 354
implicit memory 233
impotence 321–7
impulsiveness, children 164–73
insomnia see sleep and sleep
problems
intercourse see sexual problems
Interpersonal Therapy (IPT):
for anorexia 215
for bulimia 210
for depression 196
irritation and anger 55–64

jealousy 282–5
jet lag, and mood swings 248

laxatives: and anorexia 212
bulimia 200, 206–7
legs, restless legs and periodic
limb movement 337, 338,
350–1
life events: end of a relation
ship 286
stress 355
light therapy, for depression
196
listening skills, relationship
problems 279
lithium 250
long-term memory 232–3
LSD 33, 34, 36

mania 246
manic depression 246
MAOIs (monoamine oxidase
inhibitors) 196
marijuana 32–3, 34–6
masturbation 315, 331
mediation, relationship
problems 286
medication: for addictions 53

for ADHD 172
for anxiety 124
for bulimia 210
causing nightmares 346
for chronic pain 258–9
for dementia 242–3
for depression 196
for erection problems 324
for hallucinations 231
for insomnia 342–4
for mood swings 250–1
for paranoia 267
for premature ejaculation 332
for self-injury 294
meditation: for depression 196
see also mindfulness
memory: and context 238
grief and 133
memory problems 232–43
post-traumatic stress disorder
98, 104–5
remembering faces 90–1
menopause, sexual problems
311
mental images, shyness and
social anxiety 94
milk, for insomnia 344
mind-reading, relationship
problems 277
mindfulness 12
and chronic pain 258
for depression 196
overcoming jealousy 284
overcoming paranoia 267
overcoming self-injury 293
mnemonics, memory problems
241
monitoring behaviour,
overcoming addictions 49
mood swings 244–51
motivation, overcoming
addictions 48–9
mourning 126–36
muscles: cataplexy 350
pelvic floor muscles 312, 326,
332
periodic limb movement 351
music, effect on mood 194
myalgic encephalopathy (ME)
362

names, remembering 240
naps, daytime 341
narcolepsy 337, 350
National Institute for Clinical
Excellence (NICE) 4, 152
nations, happiness 10

negative thoughts 9–12
  body image worries 117
  children and young people
    151
  and chronic pain 257–8
  and depression 187, 195
  jealousy 284
  losing weight 220–1
  obsessive–compulsive
    disorder 85–6
  overcoming chronic fatigue
    367
  and self-injury 293
  shyness and social anxiety
    93–4
  stress reduction 358–9
  worrying 110
neuroleptic drugs 231, 267
nicotine 34, 44–5, 47, 341
nicotine replacement therapy
  (NRT) 53
night terrors 157, 158, 163, 345,
  346
nightmares 338, 345–6, 348,
  349
  children 157
  post-traumatic stress
    disorder 98, 103–4

obesity 218, 221
obsessive–compulsive disorder
  (OCD) 79–88
oestrogen, and sexual problems
  311
opioid drugs 33
oppositional-defiant disorder
  (OPD) 174–5
optimism 15
organizational skills, improving
  children's concentration 171–2
orgasm 313
  difficulties 307–8
  masturbation 315
  premature ejaculation 327–33
overweight 217–25

pain: chronic pain 252–9
  during intercourse 309–10,
    317
painkillers 33, 258
panic 72–9
Panic Disorder (PD) 73–6
paralysis, sleep 350
paranoia 36, 260–8
paroxetine 346
passive smoking 43–4
pedometers 222

pelvic floor muscles 312, 326,
  332
penis, erection problems 306,
  320, 321–7
'performance anxiety', sexual
  problems 325, 328
periodic limb movement 337,
  338, 350–1
persecutory delusions 261
pessimism 15
phobias see fears and phobias
physiotherapy, pain manage
  ment 259
Positive Psychology 13–14
positive thoughts 12–14
post-traumatic stress disorder
  (PTSD) 97–106
post-viral fatigue syndrome
  (PVFS) 362
postnatal depression 188, 191–2,
  196
pregnancy, smoking during 44
premature ejaculation 327–33
prescription drug abuse 33
problem solving 11–12
  reducing stress 356
  worry management 110
procedural memory 233
Prozac 124, 152, 210, 332
psychiatrists, childhood
  depression and anxiety 152
psychological therapy, referral
  for 4
psychosis, marijuana and 36

qualifications, therapists 5

relationships 14–18
  children and young people
    152
  expressive writing and 17
  grief and 128
  relationship problems 269–87
  sexual problems 312–13,
    326–7
relaxation 12–13
  and chronic pain 258
  stress reduction 359
rest, and chronic fatigue 363–4
restless legs 337, 338, 350–1
rewards: and childhood sleep
  problems 162
  improving children's
    concentration 171
  for weight loss 224
Ritalin 172
road rage 56

role models, for children 150
routines: and ADHD 172
  bedtime 159
  and bedwetting 155
  children 149
  improving memory 242
  and mood swings 248, 249
  overcoming insomnia 341

safety behaviours: body image
  worries 117–18
  children 151
  fears and phobias 70–1
  panic attacks 76–7
  shyness and social anxiety
    94–6
St John's Wort 196
salt 20–1
saturated fat 20
schizophrenia 227, 260, 261
Seasonal Affective Disorder
  (SAD) 188, 196
self-esteem: anorexia and 211
  and bulimia 200, 209
  children 150–1
  overcoming jealousy 285
  overcoming self-injury 291–2
self-image see body image
self-injury 288–95
Seligman, Martin 13–14, 15
semantic memory 233
sensate focus, for sexual
  problems 313–14, 332
separation anxiety 138, 141
sexual abuse, children 184, 185
sexual problems 296–333
  arousal problems 305–8
  erection problems 306, 320,
    321–7
  loss of sexual desire 303–5
  men's sexual problems 318–33
  orgasm 307–8, 313
  pain during intercourse
    309–10, 317
  premature ejaculation 327–33
  relationship problems 286
  retarded ejaculation 329
  sexual aversion disorder 305
  women's sexual problems
    296–318
short-term memory 232, 233
shyness and social anxiety
  88–97
sleep and sleep problems 23–4,
  334–52
  breathing-related sleep
    disorders 349–50

children and young people 148–9, 157–64
and chronic fatigue 367
and depression 186–7, 193
insomnia 336, 338, 339–44
and mood swings 249
narcolepsy 337, 350
nightmares 338, 345–6, 348, 349
periodic limb movement 337, 338, 350–1
post-traumatic stress disorder 103–4
restless legs 337, 338, 350–1
sleep apnoea 336, 338, 350
sleep deprivation 157
sleep paralysis 350
sleep terrors 157, 158, 163, 345, 346
sleepwalking 157, 158, 163, 338, 346–8, 351
sleeping pills 342–3
smoking 43–7, 53, 341
snacks 24, 341
snoring 349–50
SNRIs (serotonin and noradrenaline reuptake inhibitors) 196
social life: improving memory 239
overcoming addictions 52
social anxiety 88–97
stress reduction 357
spinal cord, pain management 257
SSRIs (selective serotonin reuptake inhibitors): for anxiety 124
for bulimia 210
causing nightmares 346
for depression 196
for paranoia 267
for premature ejaculation 332
star charts 171
starchy foods 19
stimulant drugs 33, 172
stress 353–60
and bulimia 207
and chronic fatigue 362–3
and nightmares 346, 348
panic attacks 76
and paranoia 265
post-traumatic stress disorder 97–106

relationship problems 270
and self-injury 294
sexual problems 312
sugar 20
suicide and suicidal thoughts: body image worries 114
and depression 187, 197
self-injury and 289
support networks: and depression 193
helping the bereaved 134–5
overcoming addictions 52–3
overcoming self-injury 292
stress reduction 357
for weight loss 224

tantrums 173–81
teenagers: bulimia 208
depression, fears and anxiety 137–53
difficult behaviour 181–3
sleep problems 157–64
television, and sleep problems 159, 160, 162–3
TENS machines, pain management 259
therapists, qualifications 5
thoughts 9–14
addictive beliefs 50–1
anger and irritation 62–3
grief 127–8
paranoia 260–8
positive thoughts 12–14
post-traumatic stress disorder 97–8, 103–4
see also negative thoughts
time management 356
time out, coping with tantrums 178
tiredness: and childhood sleep problems 161
chronic tiredness 361–8
coping with stress 353
overcoming insomnia 342
tranquillizers: for anxiety 124
for hallucinations 231
for paranoia 267
trauma and post-traumatic stress disorder 97–106
tricyclic antidepressants 196
triggers: addictions 50
anger 62
mood swings 248, 249
panic 73

self-injury 292–3
shyness and social anxiety 93–4
sleepwalking 348
tantrums 176
trust, and paranoia 262–3, 265
tryptophan, for insomnia 344

undereating 211–17
urine, bedwetting 153–7
urine alarms 156

vaginismus 309, 312, 317
Valium 124
valproate 250
vascular dementia 234
vegetables 19
verbal mnemonics 241
violence, domestic abuse 275–6
visual mnemonics 241
visualization: and childhood sleep problems 163
stress reduction 359
voices, hearing 226–7
vomiting: anorexia 212
bulimia 199–200, 206–7, 208

water, drinking 21
wealth: and a nation's happiness 10
and paranoia 262–3
weight: anorexia 211–17
and bulimia 209
how to lose weight 219–25
Wolf Man (Sergei Pankejeff) 115
women's sexual problems 296–318
work 22
after bereavement 133–4
and stress 357
working memory 232
worry 106–12
body image worries 112–19
childhood sleep problems 162–3
in children and young people 152
depression and 195–6
and insomnia 342
and paranoia 266
wounds, self-injury 288–95
writing, expressive 17